SAGGISTICA 42

SHOW-OFF, UNRELIABLE, ERRATIC
Both Narrator and Protagonist in Petronius's *Satyrica* and *Fellini-Satyricon*

SHOW-OFF, UNRELIABLE, ERRATIC
Both Narrator and Protagonist in Petronius's *Satyrica* and *Fellini-Satyricon*

Andrea Perruccio

BORDIGHERA PRESS

Library of Congress Control Number: 2023948763

Printed in the United States.

Published by
BORDIGHERA PRESS
John D. Calandra Italian American Institute
25 West 43rd Street, 17th Floor
New York, NY 10036

SAGGISTICA 42
ISBN 978-1-59954-209-6

TABLE OF CONTENTS

PREFACE

This study is divided into three chapters. The section-headings inserted into each chapter should help readers who try to find their way within a comparative approach to classics and cinema: an ancient, fragmentary Latin novel is compared to a cinematic adaptation that confronts the challenge of a literary text to be conveyed to the screen. In the last decade, quite a number of scholars have examined Federico Fellini's movie *Fellini-Satyricon* (1969), a daring version of Petronius Arbiter's novel *Satyrica* (probably 66 AD). Regrettably, no specific attention has been paid, as far as I am aware, to the transformation of the indisputable centrality of a first-person homodiegetic narrator in the novel into the fluctuating, semi-central character in Fellini's film, i.e., to the adjustment of Petronius's *Encolpius* to Fellini's *Encolpio*. Among the researchers, who have concerned themselves with an 'inter-semiotic' (Jakobson, 1959) book-to-film translation from the novel to the movie, I would recommend those from whom I have drawn several ideas for my essay: Sullivan, 1991 (revised in 2001); Sütterlin, 1996; Brunet, 2002 (summarised online in 2006); Paul, 2009; De Berti-Gagetti-Slavazzi, 2009 (edited collection of the Milan 2007 Conference Proceedings).

Chapter 1 provides a synoptic table illustrating similarities and divergences between the mere plot of Petronius's *Satyrica* and the audio-visual (i.e., final) screenplay of *Fellini's Satyricon* (Bartesaghi, 2009). Relevant passages and items of the Petronian text are discussed in footnotes, which introduce the reader to a first-level grasp of its more relevant historical and literary topics (sect. 1.1). On this basis, I have underlined both the dream-like quality of Fellini's visual, non-literary narrative (which nurtured the coincident drawings and dreams recorded in *Il libro dei sogni*, [*The Book of Dreams*]), and his talent for graphic and communicative synthesis, that was possibly inspired by some landmarks of American comic art, known to him through Italian magazines for children. In view of some noteworthy Fellini pronouncements on his purely fantastic and imaginative connection to Petronius's world, what stands out the most is the personality of a film director severed from any need for historical knowledge of the ancient past, as well as alien to the *bric-à-brac* of the Roman cinematic tradition, with its spectacular ingredients (sect. 1.2). With the help of his co-writer Bernardino Zapponi, Fellini resorted to a free adaptation from the *Satyrica*: I have indicated where additions, expansions, or radical changes from the Latin novel (Stubbs, 2006) occur at each of the three different stages: treatment-screenplay-movie (sect. 1.3).

Chapter 2 dwells upon Encolpius, a wanderer nudged by chance, a supposedly cultivated *scholasticus*, who forms a homosexual love-triangle with Askyltos and Giton: I aim at describing the most remarkable characteristics of Encolpius *as first-person narrator* in some episodes and aspects of the *Satyrica* (sect. 2.1). In his dialogue with the rhetor-poet Agamemnon (*Sat.* 1.1-5.20), Encolpius appears in full command of words and action, while manipulating his interlocutor – and us readers (sect. 2.2). On the other hand, the Quartilla section (16.1-26.6) shows our hero reduced to silence, unable to perform sexually, and, paradoxically, the victim of an assault by women and catamites (sect. 2.3). Throughout the Feast of Trimalchio (26.7-78.8), I have highlighted the passages where Encolpius (intentionally or accidentally?) loses his way, confronted by a staging of courses disguised as antics (and antics in form of food), and is never quick to get the meaning of Trimalchio's word puns, entangled by the host's tricks and deceptive riddles: in the confusion between the real and the artificial (Rosati, 1999; Freudenburg, 2017), we readers are almost never able to tell when Encolpius is narrating straight or pretending (sect. 2.4). Just as importantly, with regard to the intermingling of erotic infatuation and sexual impotence within Encolpius's recollected (mis)adventures, I have argued that – although within a playful treatment of sex throughout the novel – his sexual episodes often prove disappointing, mainly because of Giton's alleged infidelity (Zeitlin, 1971a; Courtney, 2001; Richlin, 2009); whereas, I have explored incidents (e.g. *Sat.* 81ff.) in which the protagonist is clearly acting a part, by *playing the role* of a forlorn and humiliated lover, with groans that recall celebrated laments in Latin literature, from Catullus to Ovid (Laird, 1999). As for the bugbear of Priapus' wrath, it remains debatable whether the offended patron of fertility caused the impotence of Encolpius, that emerges throughout much of the *Satyrica* (Schmeling, 2011), or is a temporary one (Setaioli, 2018): reasons for the alleged offense are anyhow unknown to us (sect. 2.5-6).

In spite of his apparent quality as a reliable narrator, claiming to offer his first-hand experiences as an eyewitness, Encolpius might be a chronic liar: we readers can only rely on the recollections he volunteers... This assumption has prompted me to review the perspectives on (and implications of) the narrator's role – as divergent from the protagonist's – suggested by Beck, 1973, and diversely developed by Jones, 1987; Laird, 1999; Jensson, 2004; Goldman, 2006 and 2008. Rather than based on a misleading author-narrator overlap view, Encolpius' discrepancies might be induced by more productive distinctions: such as between a young, naïve *actor* and an older, self-critical *narrator*; or between an *agent* narrator (involved in events) and a *transparent* one (inclined to recording); or might even be the result of recollections *performed* by a single Encolpius-actor, impersonating all characters, and himself as a youth. Nevertheless, since emotional interactions often link the narrator to his past *self*, I have collected examples showing when and where we readers aren't capable (Rimell, 2002) of separating statements made by the character from utterances pronounced in hindsight by the narrator (sect. 2.7).

By laying aside Petronius, the empirical, flesh-and-blood author (identified quite simply with Encolpius-narrator by Sullivan, 1968), and underscoring the textual function of an 'implied' author (i.e., a *puppeteer-image* of the author's character constructed by the reader), I have paid attention to the concept of the narrator's 'unreliability' as a function of irony (Booth, 1961; 1974): it occurs whenever implied author and reader – as derived from the restricted account given by actions and poses of the speaking voice – create a secret complicity that *excludes* the narrator. This theoretical approach has set up the scene for innovative Aragosti, 1979 and for Gian Biagio Conte's 1996 influential study on the 'hidden' author in the *Satyrica*: as a homodiegetic first-person narrator, our *mythomaniac* Encolpius, imbued by his declamatory upbringing, tends to foolishly identify with heroic roles among mythical and epic characters (e.g., Achilles, Odysseus, Aeneas), accordingly dramatizing his miserable everyday reality. Irony creates a distance between the hidden author, who does away with Encolpius's protective illusions, and the set of values embodied by the narrator: so much so, that the reader-author collusion methodically pokes fun at Encolpius the narrator. Studying 'unreliability' in more detail, I have shared the view (Olson, 2003) that 'textual signals' can help the reader decide whether the first-person narrator's *short sight* may be caused by external, amendable circumstances or by deep-rooted behavioural traits: in short, between 'fallible' narrators (Huck, in *Huckleberry Finn*; Marlow, in *Lord Jim*) and 'untrustworthy' ones (the speaker of *The Tell-Tale Heart*; Benjy, in *The Sound and the Fury*), our Encolpius's unrepentant character, with his visionary world steeped in literature, has appeared to me as more probably 'untrustworthy' (sect. 2.8).

Because of the dense inter-textual and allusive texture of the *Satyrica*, I have highlighted Encolpius-narrator's fondness for comic distortions and satirical moods (Collignon, 1892; Schmeling, 2011; Goldman, 2012), which cover every known Greek-Roman literary genre (epic-lyric-elegiac poetry, drama, historiography, rhetoric), as well as philosophy, or even 'consumer' literature (Barchiesi, 1996) (sect. 2.9). I have suggested that this 'Encolpio-centrism' can cope quite well with the importance of readers for the construction of Encolpius-narrator, matching their assessment of inter-textuality, allusion, or textual references. I have also spoken out *theoretically* in favour of a flexible author-narrator-reader interaction (Eco, 1979; 1990), in view of its possible application to the *Satyrica*. The notion of the (implied) author – under siege throughout the spread of the death-of-the-author propositions (Barthes, 1967; 1977) – should not be dissolved, but rather *repositioned*. Likewise, I must have appeared quite sceptical about certain efforts of semiotics, reader-response criticism and cognitive sciences, to show that *the reader* does have a *decisive* effect on what textual construct means: I have explained how an eminent reader-oriented interpretation of the *Satyrica* (Slater, 1990) raises grounded motives of uncertainty, e.g. by matching literary interpretation to textual criticism as similar 'forms of reading'. On this issue, I have shared different views. On the one hand, the treatment of unexpected endings, in some sections of the novel, keeps readers off-balance, somehow equating the absence of 'purpose' in the *Satyrica* to the 'aimlessness' of Encolpius (Schmeling, 1991); on the other, distant episodes and passages – echoing each other – can be connected by scholarly readers, who can thus re-analyse their initial readings (Rimell, 2002; 2007). However we *read* the novel through Encolpius's eyes, the result is that the narrator's recollection, less entertaining than troublesome, tends to obscure reality, not to clarify it (sect. 2.10).

Chapter 3 frames the unsteady and controversial *centrality* of Encolpio, a questionable protagonist of *Fellini-Satyricon* (Burke, 1989), as the result of the recurring disappearance of Fellinian characters (once neatly focused in the '50s.), that had started with Guido, in *Otto e mezzo* (1963). Encolpio enters the movie as a voice-over to the left of a tracking shot, in sync with Ihan Mimaroğlu's 1967 electronic *Prelude*; then as a shadow slowly taking shape against a graffiti wall: I have had the abstract perception of aphasia shifting to articulated expression, within what Fellini would call 'a journey from chaos to cosmos' (Grazzini, 1988). As a result, in this 'crumbled memory' of the graffiti (Copioli, 2020), I have pictured some sort of 'hyper-graffiti' idea (inspired by Marcus, 2002): a conceptual matrix, transcending Fellini's individual films, which may be traced back to his semi-unconscious *scribbling* of doodles, both at a biographical and at a cinematic level (sect. 3.1). In the final sequence, Encolpio's words "the wind is fair" are accompanied by the same electronic passage of the opening scene, and a similar back-tracking shot shows a wall, but now fractured into three cracked frescoes, which recall Encolpio and other characters. I have developed the suggestion (Sala, 2009) that a different kind of music would have most likely changed the *ending* of the movie: within this circular return of the film on itself, isn't Encolpio's *fade out* – into the darkness of the opening shot – a kind of journey into an enigmatic 'nothingness'?

As part of ambient sounds, I have featured the multi-faceted presence of wind (Dyer, 2009), throughout *Fellini-Satyricon*, as capable of cooperating – with dialogues and music – in emphasizing framing and camera movements. Fellini's use of these devices in crucial episodes (Eumolpo's first legacy to Encolpio; the Lica-Encolpio wedding on the ship; the nymphomaniac; the labyrinth; the death of Ascilto) produces an operation of science fiction *in reverse* (Zanelli, 1969), focused on a defunct Roman world, with which the director has no real relationship. I have wondered again: is Encolpio undertaking a final voyage of *discovery*? What is the point of our hero's 'evolution' into the immobility of a frescoed form? (sect. 3.2). Trying to explain Fellini's fascination with his 'two daredevils', Encolpio and Ascilto, I have found it eloquent that some Fellinian pronouncements evolve around the suggestion of both the youngsters identifying with acts of an existence left to chance, and to their 'pansexual dreams' (Cancogni, 1968). Fellini's endorsement of the generation uprising, against the *world of the fathers*, appears motivated by his attraction to the sense of freedom inspired by the American hippie movement, as validated by the warm reception of the movie at the New York 1970 premiere (Villa, 2020). Are Fellini's statements reflected by some means in *Fellini-Satyricon*? Within a dynamic editing, the handling of close-up, panoramic, and tracking shots underscores Encolpio's jerky acting; primarily, subjective shots, almost absent in the first half of the film, emphasize particular moments of Encolpio's altered mental status during Enotea's cure. I have shared recent insightful remarks (Burke, 2020), that *apparent* signs of Encolpio's personal or moral transformation turn out to be inconsistent in the second half of the movie: in sequences of allegedly increasing awareness ("Festival of Myrth"; "Garden of Delights"), Encolpio tends to become a parody object, in a process reaching the peak with his *forced adaptation* to heterosexuality, induced by Enotea's pharmacological treatments. I have found evidence of it – by taking into account significant perspectives of 'gender' and 'decolonial' approaches (Waller, 2020; Greene, 2020) – in the absence of a real heterosexual partner in Encolpio's mindset: as a matter of fact, the sexual intercourse with the black slave-girl in the patricians' villa starts as a threesome with Ascilto, but changes into a twosome that *expels* the woman; on the other hand, the initiatic sexual relationship with Enotea, an archetypal earth mother, is merely symbolic: portrayed as a full-figured African woman, she restores the virility of a blue-eyed and blond-haired Encolpio (sect. 3.3).

As regards the entire construction of *Fellini-Satyricon*, I have highlighted the director's inclination to place narrative blocks next to each other in a *fresco* ('several views at the same time': Dyer, 2020), with layered and *round* characters replaced by puppet-like ones (Eumolpo is an exception). What is lost in depth, is achieved in the *spectacular* shape given to a scenic setting, where flat characters are surrounded by disfigured walk-on actors, deformed by heavy make-up. I have argued that this pictorial, two-dimensional representation of 'social portraiture', not far from the (albeit different) *Dolce vita*, emerges from the combination of the horizontality of the CinemaScope format with long focal length effects (Vanelli, 2020), that meet Fellini's demand for a portrait gallery, with perfectly focused characters in a minimal field depth. I have collected examples of sequences (characterising the fragmentary pace of the movie, as to female figures and environments), where scenes confront scenes, within a strong tension between two polarities (sect. 3.4).

While choosing faces to give to Encolpio and friends, and reexamining the past, could Fellini 'overlook being a Christian'? Absence of an after-life perspective in the film doesn't mean absence of dismay in front of spiritual transcendence. In the ancient characters of a movie realised as the documentary of a dream, with actors remaining ambiguous apparitions (Moravia, 1978), the director may have encountered the projection of moods and 'terrors of today's man', deeply rooted in his unconscious. I have pointed out that impressive camera movements occasionally catch faces, tinged with anxiety, who pose, look at the lens, and watch us spectators, as if amazed to glimpse witnesses of their (and ours!) own sinking in the dark. A sharp sense of the transience of life; an existential despair in a tension of death (as the other side of unbridled sexuality); masks possessing the vitality of dying animals, like 'spots of shadows and lights' (Taddei, 2000): these hints may be regarded, I suppose, as glimmers of some kind of *religiosity*, underlying the entire *Fellini-Satyricon*. In all of this, Fellini couldn't evade an inevitably unintentional *moralistic* approach to the pagan world, evident through his recourse to Carcopino's *Daily Life in Ancient Rome* as his main non-Petronian source: its moralising descriptions and comments fostered Fellini's visual textures of some cinematic clear-cut sequences (the roaring multitudes in the *Suburra;* the miserable world of the *insula Felicles;* the homosexual Encolpio-Lica marriage), which fruitfully *contradict* (Brunet, 2002; 2006) the initial choice of filtering Fellini's Christian moral judgments on antiquity, viewed through 'the eyes of that time' (sect. 3.5).

In my general conclusion, with a view to analysing the transition from a literary medium to a visual and aural one (Lothe, 2000), I have emphasized that some similarities between the *Satyrica* and *Fellini-Satyricon* are undeniable: any alleged discrepancy between an *entertaining* Petronius and a *funereal* Fellini is a legacy from the past, bearing witness to some critics' lifetimes (e.g., Segal, 1971). A painful backdrop, an aura of premonition of death, an elegant ability to smile – common to both works – might correspond to some unconscious analogies, grasped by the film director himself and his collaborators, between the conditions of breakdown and redemption in the ambiguities of Petronius's and Fellini's ages (Pace, 2009b). Anyhow, resemblances can't be taken at face value, especially as far as Encolpio's character is involved. I've made it clear that, in erotic matters, Encolpio's successful masculinity in *Fellini-Satyricon,* associated with homosexuality rather than with heterosexuality, very rarely appears jocular or hilarious, as it proves linked to a painful backdrop underlying even its clownish and farcical sequences. A clear counterpoint to it is the extensively playful attitude to sex in the *Satyrica,* where Encolpius's eros is celebrated in all its instinctive features. There's even more. I have tried to argue that in a dreamlike film, where life-death strains permeate sequences with physical deterioration, Encolpio's sexual impotence is the object of gloomy and caustic parody, whereas Encolpius's impotence in the novel is tragicomically treated by the amused irony of the hidden author. *Irony and parody* take the lion's share in the *Satyrica,* through the permanent mockery of a mythomaniac Encolpius, as its indisputable protagonist and wide-ranging narrator. In the film, satire is instead aimed at a disputable 'protagonist' (*absent* from six relevant episodes) and at an ineffective, if not plainly *failed* first-person narrator (sect. 3.6).

My sincere thanks go to Anthony Tamburri for including my work in this prestigious collection under his direction. My unlimited gratitude is reserved for Frank Burke, who has generously furthered and supported my project, and for Marco Vanelli's constructive criticism: I have benefitted from the discussions with them. I am grateful to Franco Bellandi and Luca Soverini for encouraging my study on Petronius's novel. I express my thanks to Rosita Copioli, for her wise advice, and to Ester Brunet and Max Goldman, who made their very valuable papers available to me. For her kind assistance and professional competence, I wish to thank Rosalynd Pio, who has patiently revised and corrected the English draft of my essay. I am indebted to Susan Tintori and Francesco Costantini, who have helped me proofread my work.

ABBREVIATIONS

AJPh	*American Journal of Philology.*
AN	*Ancient Narrative.*
Bartesaghi *aud.*	*Fellini-Satyricon*: audiovisual screenplay (cf. Bartesaghi, 20, 325-533).
BMCR	*Bryn Mawr Classical Review.*
CIL 4	*Corpus Inscriptionum Latinarum*, C. Zangemeister, R. Schoene, and A. Mau, eds. Vol. IV (Berlin 1871-1909).
CR	*Classical Review.*
CW	*Classical World.*
JCS	*Journal of Classical Studies.*
JRS	*Journal of Roman Studies.*
MD	*Materiali e discussioni per l'analisi dei testi classici.*
MH	*Museum Helveticum.*
OLD	*Oxford Latin Dictionary*, ed. P.G.W. Glare (Oxford 1968-1972).
QDIUB	*Quaderni del dottorato di italianistica dell'Università di Bari.*
REL	*Revue des Études Latines.*
RENT	*Routledge Encyclopedia of Narrative Theory*, eds. D. Herman, M. Jahn, and M.L. Ryan (London/New York 2005).
RhM	*Rheinisches Museum.*
RIFL	*Rivista italiana di filosofia del linguaggio.*
TAPhA	*Transactions of the American Philological Association.*
WJA	*Würzburger Jahrbücher für die Altertumswissenschaft.*
Zanelli A	*Fellini-Satyricon*: treatment (cf. Zanelli, 1969, 111-145).
Zanelli B	*Fellini-Satyricon*: published screenplay (cf. Zanelli, 1969, 149-273).

CHAPTER 1
AS IF ONE WERE RECONSTRUCTING AN ANCIENT AMPHORA.[1]

> I have a mass of material at my command. The problem has always been not to find but to choose.
>
> Arthur Conan Doyle (1927)

> Maigret ne put savoir si son interlocuteur persiflait ou s'il parlait sérieusement. Un drôle de bonhomme, vraiment, ni figue ni raisin, ni jeune ni vieux, ni beau ni laid, qui était peut-être vide de pensées, mais peut-être aussi bourré de secrets.
>
> Georges Simenon (1931)

1.1 A SURREALISTIC FRESCO

> Dear Federico, Rome, October 23, 1969
> I take advantage of the end of the postal strike to inform you that I have watched your *Satyricon* and that it impressed and astonished me, kept me awake, and above all delighted me. Nothing is missing. I shall dream of it as often as I can. I know that some of the choices could be discussed, but you achieved the essentials: the constant dramatic nature of the monsters, i.e.: of ourselves. People leaving the movie theatre, and saying 'I didn't like it', seemed to have emerged from the film itself. I think it is right, in the name of our old friendship that separates us, to speak to you like this, and I hope that you too will take it in the right way. A big hug from me and my regards to Bernardino Zapponi, as well. Ennio

With his peculiarly humorous note,[2] five years after the end of his partnership with Federico Fellini, Ennio Flaiano[3] loyally and

---

[1] Unless otherwise credited, translations from Latin and Greek are my own. For Petronius Arbiter's *Satyrica* I will follow Patrick Walsh's translation (Walsh, 1997). I will adopt the Latin spelling for the characters in Petronius, and the Italian one for *Fellini-Satyricon*.

[2] My trans. It is worth noting, beside the sharp comment on "the constant dramatic nature of monsters, that is of ourselves," Flaiano's witticism on their "vecchia amicizia che ci disunisce." About this letter to Fellini, see Perruccio, 1991, 389; Longoni-Rüesch, 1995, 331; 594; Pacchioni, 2014, 56; Ruozzi, 2016, 152.

[3] Ennio Flaiano (1910-1972) produced narrative works and prose writings, including: *Tempo di uccidere* (1947); *Diario Notturno* (1956); *Una e una notte* (1959); *Il gioco e il massacro* (1970). As a screenplayer he co-wrote with Fellini: *Luci del varietà* (1950); *Lo sceicco bianco* (1952); *I vitelloni* (1953); *La strada* (1954); *Il bidone* (1955); *Le notti di Cabiria* (1957); *La dolce vita* (1959); *Le tentazioni del Dottor Antonio* (1962); *Otto e mezzo* (1963); *Giulietta degli spiriti* (1965). On the collaboration Flaiano-Fellini see Pacchioni, 2014, 49-78; Ruozzi, 2016, 145-52; Alonge, 2020, 168-73; Carrera, 2020, 129.

tastefully congratulates Bernardino Zapponi, the screenwriter who replaced him from *Toby Dammit* (1968) onwards,[4] and tries to restore his troubled friendship with the Italian director. What does Flaiano's comment on the film suggest to us, more than fifty years after the very controversial release and reception of *Fellini-Satyricon* (1969)?

"A lush, surrealistic fresco of life in pre-Christian Rome" (Bondanella, 2002, 29). *Fellini-Satyricon* is loosely based upon the fragmentary Roman novel *Satyrica*, attributed to Petronius Arbiter and (not unanimously) dated to the time of the rule of Nero (AD 54-68).[5] The following overview consists of a synoptical table, where similar or identical incidents between the novel and the screenplay of the film, are to be found at the same height in both columns; mismatches result instead in blank spaces in one of the two columns.[6] The most relevant textual losses in Petronius's narrative (*lacunae*) are indicated with <***>; some footnotes will introduce the reader to a first-level, inevitably rough understanding

[4] Bernardino Zapponi (1927-2000) collaborated on six Fellini films: *Toby Dammit* (1968); *Fellini-Satyricon* (1969); *I clowns* (1970); *Roma* (1972); *Il Casanova di Federico Fellini* (1976); *La città delle donne* (1980). On Flaiano's and Zapponi's collaboration with Fellini, see Bondanella, 1992, 341-43; Pacchioni, 2014, 79-95; Alonge, 2020, 169ff.

[5] Ascertained relations between Petronius and other authors (Lucan, Seneca), besides reliable sources, make it likely that the author of the *Satyrica* is the *arbiter elegantiae*, at Nero's court, described by Tacitus *Ann.* 16.17-20: see Connors, 1994, 232 n. 1; Petersmann, 1999, 105 n. 1; Schmeling, 2011, xiv; see *contra* Holzberg 2006, 90-1. Moreover, historical, linguistic, and literary evidence encourage one to situate the novel in the reign of Nero (specifically AD 66): see von Albrecht, 1995, II, 1212-3; Habermehl, 2006, xiii; Prag-Repath, 2009, 7-9; Schmeling, 2011, xiv-xvii. Anyway, Laird, 2007, 164 remarks that "its date has not yet been properly settled," and that the postponement of its deadline into the second century AD shouldn't be excluded. The spelling of the title as *Satyrica* (regularized with titles of ancient works, like Lollianus' *Phoinikika*, Heliodorus' *Aethiopica*, Xenophon's *Ephesiaca*) is generally accepted in the UK, USA, and Germany, whereas in France, Spain, and Italy the spelling *Satyricon* is a genitive plural, transliterated as it was for *Satyrikōn libri* (Schmeling, 2011, xvii).

[6] For the ensuing synoptical tables I am indebted to Gagetti, 2009, 303-18: the Italian names of characters in the movie will replace the Latin ones of Petronius's novel. Encolpius *is turned* into Encolpio... Since the published script (Zanelli, 1969, 149-273) corresponds to a movie-stage very far from the final version, in my investigation I will follow Bartesaghi 2009, 325-533 (*audiovisual-script*: "sceneggiatura desunta": henceforth Bartesaghi *aud.*), i.e., *inferred* from the DVD of the film (p. 320 n. 4: cf. CDE/Videa, Milano-Eagle Pictures 2005-Dolby Digital 5.1, mono 2.0-software used: Windows Media Player). Its rich and thorough scan indicates scenes, timing and number of each shot, description of content, dialogues, music, sound effects. *Vice versa*, for the two extant screenplays, see below, n. 38.

of some major literary topics and key sequences from Petronius's *Satyrica*, some of which will be explored in detail in chapter 2.

The appropriate analysis will lay the groundwork for explaining what directed Fellini towards the Latin novelist Petronius. In particular: where the film episodes relate to Petronius; where they differ from the Latin novel; where Fellini and the screenwriter Zapponi added new material to the "skeleton" (Stubbs 2006, 214). of the surviving sections of the original Latin text, either deriving them from different classical sources or entirely inventing them.

Petroni Arbitri *Satyrica* Chapters 1-141.11 Books 14-17[7]	***Fellini-Satyricon*** Scenes 1-75 Shots 1-1081 (Bartesaghi *aud.*)
<***> (**Chapters 1-5**) In a Greek town around the Bay of Naples (Puteoli?), Encolpius severely criticizes the corruption of eloquence[8] and the hollow school-system based on declamatory education. Agamemnon shifts the blame from teachers to parents. (**6-8**) Encolpius realises that his roommate and friend Ascyltos has disappeared,	(**Scene I. Shots 1-6**) Encolpio rages that Ascilto has "stolen" Gitone, slave and sexual partner of the

[7] Puteoli may be the *Graeca urbs* of *Sat.* 81.3 (Ernout, 1958, xlii; Walsh, 1970, 75-6; von Albrecht, 1995, II, 1214 n. 475). In his *Hypothetical schematic reconstruction* of the novel in 24 books, assumed "for diagnostic purposes," Schmeling, 2011, xxiii-xxiv includes also events (Books 1-14; 17-24) not included in the extant "documented episodes" of Books 14 (1-26.6); 15 (26.7-99); 16 (100-124.2); 17 (124.3-141.11): presumable beginnings of the novel in Massilia; introduction of Encolpius as narrator; sacrilege against Priapus; affairs with Lichas and Tryphaena; interruption of Quartilla's Priapic ritual; theft of a cloak (Books 1-14). After the departure from Croton, in Lampsacus (Priapus's birthplace) the novel is likely to end with Encolpius's initiation into his cult (Books 17-24). Walsh, 1997, xvii views "the notion of a monster *Satyricon*" (24 books) "with some scepticism"; Harrison, 1999, xviii finds a length of some 400.000 words "greatly excessive" (cf. Rimell, 2002, 2 n. 12); Vannini, 2010, 7 conjectures a length approximately double than Apuleius' *Metamorphoses*; for Gianotti, 2012, 565 the extant *Satyrica* corresponds to almost one twentieth of the original.

[8] The stance *de causis corruptae eloquentiae* – a commonplace from the first century AD onwards – is not far from the allegations made by Ps. Longinus' *De Sublimitate* 44.1-2; Seneca's *Epistulae* 114.1-3; *Naturales Quaestiones* 3.18; 7.31; Quintilian's *Institutio oratoria* 1.2.1-8; 6. *pr.* 3-8; 12.1.1ff.; *passim*; Tacitus' *Dialogus de oratoribus* 28-35 (see Laird, 2007, 158; Schmeling, 2011, 2).

leaves Agamemnon, and accidentally finds his missed Ascyltos in a brothel (*lupanar-fornix*).[9]	former, from him. (**2.7-17**) Encolpio finds out that Ascilto sold Gitone to the comic actor Vernacchio. (**3.18-80**) Gitone appears on stage: Vernacchio is challenged and forced to return him to Encolpio. (**4.81-90**) Encolpio and Gitone get lost in the murky streets of the Suburra. (**5.91-106**) They enter a brothel (***see Sat. 7-8***).
<***> (**9-10**) <***> (**11**) Giton claims that Ascyltos attempted to have sex with him:[10] Encolpius and Ascyltos have a heated argument over the ownership of Giton and agree to split at a later date. Encolpius tries to have sex with Giton, but Ascyltos interrupts them and beats Encolpius.	
	(**6.107-8.138**) Encolpio and Gitone arrive at the *Insula Felicles*, a crumbling tenement block where their intercourse is interrupted by Ascilto. (**8.139-163**) After a quarrel, Encolpio and Ascilto divide up their possessions and Gitone leaves with Ascilto. (**8.164-166**) As Encolpio is in despair, a dull rumble heralds a natural disaster.
<***> (**12-15**) At the market Encolpius and Ascyltos are involved in an intricate dispute over a tunic stolen from Encolpius: Ascyltos regains the robe. (**16-26**) They meet Quartilla, devotee of Priapus, who	

[9] We know at least forty-five brothels at Rome in the later empire (seven unearthed at Pompeii): see Kay, 1985, 166-7.

[10] Ascyltos' advance, in Giton's report to Encolpius (*Sat.* 9.5), is a mocking adaptation (*Si Lucretia es, Tarquinium invenisti* "If you are Lucretia, you have met your Tarquin!") from Livy 1.58.2 *tace, Lucretia, Sex. Tarquinius sum; ferrum in manu est* ["shut up, Lucretia, I'm Sex. Tarquinius; my sword is in my hand"]. On metaphors of weaponry for *mentula* ("male organ"), and on 'sword' as 'penis', see Adams, 1982, 19ff.; Schmeling, 2011, 28.

asks them not to divulge the cult's secret.[11] Repeated sexual intercourse takes place with Quartilla, Psyche and her maids over the space of three days.[12] Later at their lodgings, an invitation arrives – on behalf of Agamemnon – to a dinner at the estate of Trimalchio,[13] *lautissimus homo*, after a preliminary stop off at the baths before the meal.	(**9.167-190**) The *Insula* collapses due to an earthquake. (**10.191-204**) In an art gallery, Encolpio, admiring the works, runs into the poet Eumolpo, who is complaining at the greatness of the classics, lamenting the miserable state of society and of modern art (***see Sat. 83-4 and 88***). (**11.205-216**) The two men make their way to Trimalcione's dinner.
(**27-28**) At the baths, Encolpius and Ascyltos watch Trimalchio's gym-	(**12.217-234**) Part of the guests take a bath in an outside pool: Trimalcione joins them.

[11] Son of Dionysus (or Zeus, or Hermes) and Aphrodite, Priapus protected gardens and vineyards. As his worship was transferred to Rome, he became patron of fertility of the earth and breeding; personification of the erect phallus, it was protector of passageway spaces into private and public buildings as 'apotropaic', i.e. effective against the Evil Eye (Aragosti, 1995, 490 n. 400; Clarke, 1998, 174-5; 199-201; Richlin, 2009, 83-4). As a debated leit-motiv of Petronius's novel (cf. p. 53 n. 105), an early offense against Priapus (for reasons unknown to us) was responsible for his hounding of Encolpius, a similar persecution to the one adopted by Poseidon against Odysseus in the *Odyssey* and by Juno against Aeneas in the *Aeneid* (Sullivan, 1991/2001, 261), or by Aphrodite against Hippolytos in Euripides' homonymous tragedy (Aragosti, 1995, 515 n. 441): full discussion in Slater, 1990, chapt. 3; Courtney, 2001, 152 ff.; Rimell, 2002, 17; 98-103; 109-110. For the so-called *Carmina Priapea*, a collection of poems dating later than AD 100, see von Albrecht, 1995, II, 1056-60; Courtney, 2001, 224; Callebat, 2012, *passim*.

[12] The episode ends with a mock wedding. With Quartilla and Psyche assuming the role of *pronubae*, and the seven-year-old Pannychis the one of Giton's bride, the traditional ritual of Roman marriage (*nuptiae*) is subject of parody (*Sat.* 26.1 *incesta veste*: "adorned with the robe designed to rape"). Its inspiration in mime might be corroborated by Laberius' title *Nuptiae* (Walsh, 1997, 162); "the travesty is paramount" (Schmeling, 2011, 79).

[13] In Martial 3.82.32 the *cognomen Malchio* perhaps indicates a very arrogant (and effeminate) parvenu: for the name *Trimalchio* see Aragosti, 1995, 174 n. 61; Courtney, 2001, 52; Schmeling, 2011, 84-5.

nastic activities. (**29-30**) They arrive at Trimalchio's and apprehensively stop in close proximity to the *triclinium.* (**31-34**) Trimalchio joins his guests in the dining room, where the host seriously reflects on the shortness of a human lifespan.[14] (**35-38**) Tawdry and extravagant courses are served.[15] A table companion provides information on Trimalchio's wife, Fortunata and on the social status of other guests. (**39-64**) Ordinary talks about neighbors, weather, hard times, public games, education of children. Further pretentious and grotesque courses impress the bystanders, at the same time as Trimalchio defines the vastness of his holdings and splurges his non-existent erudition.[16] Entertainments and declamations against incompetent doctors, lack of religion, softness of contemporary youth. Homeric episodes played by actors are ex-	(**13.235-372**) In the *triclinium,* the guests take their places according to their social status. Game of glances between Encolpio and the beautiful Trifena (***see Sat. 100 ff.***). Trimalcione flaunts his wealth and prides himself on his ability to be a poet (***see Sat. 59***). Eumolpo starts a poetry recital on the fall of Troy (***see Sat. 89***), but is abused by the diners. Arrival of Abinna and his wife. Trimalcione argues with his wife Fortunata (***see Sat. 74***) and reflects on the shortness of a human lifespan (***see Sat. 34***). When he recits some verses, Eumolpo accuses him of counterfeiting the epic poet Lucretius: (**14.373-379**) Trimalcione's slaves are ordered to throw Eumolpo in the furnace, and a fight follows in the kitchens.

[14] A slave serves an articulated *larva argentea* (*Sat.* 34.8 "a skeleton of silver"): ancient Egyptians (Herodotus 2.78) would send around a wooden skeleton in a coffin among the table companions, as a warning about mortal life. For skeletons (*larvae* used in magic, meaning "the evil spirits of the deceased": Schmeling, 2011, 124), see Apuleius *Apol.* 63.1. About the "theatrical" character of the presentation of the *larva,* see Rosati, 1999, 88 n. 7.

[15] Some of the dishes are not of Petronius's own invention (Ernout, 1958, 32 n. 2). The *Cena* has Plato's and Xenophon's *Symposiums* as major Greek literary antecedents (Bodel, 1999, 38 ff.), as well as a symposiac poetic tradition dating back to the Phaeacian banquet, in Homer *Od.* 8 ff. (Sullivan, 1968, 125ff.; von Albrecht, 1995, II, 1220; Schmeling, 2011, 81; 222). For direct Latin referents (Aragosti,1995, 44 n. 45), cf. Ennius' *Hdyphagetica;* Lucilius' *Cena* in Book XX; Varro's *Peri Edesmaton;* Horace's *Cena Nasidieni* (*Serm.* 2.8). The prodigality of the "gargantuan dinner" reflects Trimalchio's vulgarity: see Walsh, 1970, 29; 38-40; 115.

[16] Evidence of this may be the preposterous juxtaposition (*Sat.* 55.5-6) of Cicero and Publilius Syrus (first century BC): the instance has probably been inserted to mock Seneca, who was fond of citing the mimographer to underline his moral teaching (Sullivan, 1968, 191ff.; Walsh, 1997, 174; Panayotakis, 2009, 60-1). For Senecan parody in Petronius see Freudenburg, 2017, 5; Schmeling, 2011, 617 s.v. *Seneca. Vice versa,* about Seneca's possible attacks against the *arbiter elegantiae* (cf. *Dial.* 10.12.5; *Ep.* 122.18), see Habermehl, 2006, xii n. 7.

plained by Trimalchio with coarse mistakes. (65-70) The marble-carver Habinnas and his wife Scintilla come on stage.	
(71) Trimalchio describes his own funerary monument at length, the achievement of which is entrusted to Habinnas. (72-77) Trimalchio, caught by Fortunata while enjoying a homosexual, attacks her regarding her filthy previous life. (78) The bystanders act out Trimalchio's funeral: "Imagine you've been invited to my wake."[17] Encolpius and Ascyltos run away: "we took to our heels as rapidly as if there really were a fire."	(15.380-387) Trimalcione takes his guests to the tomb where he will be buried. (16.388-403) Trimalcione demands that they simulate his funeral. (16.404-27.421) During the funeral a tale is told: a beautiful woman in Ephesus, a recent widow, decides to let herself die of starvation beside her husband's corpse in his tomb. The guardian of the bodies of executed prisoners hears her moaning, comforts her and eventually lies with her; when one of the corpses is stolen and the soldier expects punishment, the woman hangs up the body of her husband in the place of the criminal, so that the soldier's life is saved (*see Sat. 111-112*).
(79-82) Ascyltos seduces Giton causing Encolpius's wrath; they quarrel with each other and decide	(28.422-428) Eumolpo entertains Encolpio with a poetic praise of the wonders of the universe.

[17] The Roman *parentalia* (13-21 February: cf. Ovid *Fast.* 2.533-570) used to come to an end with a funeral banquet; on the festivity, see Lübker, 1989, 489 s.v. *Feralia*.

to live in separate lodgings, with Gitoni unexpectedly following Ascyltos.[18] (**83-89**) In a picture gallery (rich in works by Zeusis, Protogenes, Apelles on homosexual subjects) Encolpius bumps into the old poet Eumolpus, who talks about the decay of art and illustrates a picture of the defeat of Troy by means of verses adjusted from Virgil's *Aeneid*, book II.[19] (**90-99**) The bystanders drive Eumolpus out with stones. <***> Encolpius invites him to dinner. Intertwining of jealousies and *advances* among Encolpius, Eumolpus and Giton. They finally board a ship.	
(**100-112**) Encolpius realises that the captain of the ship is Lichas, who is leading his woman Tryphaena to Tarentum: they are both old enemies by whom Encolpius and Giton don't want to be discovered. They attempt to disguise themselves as Eumolpus's slaves, but are eventually identified. After Eumolpus's speech in their defence, peace is agreed thanks to	(**29.429-36.488**) Encolpio wakes up on a beach and sees Ascilto and Gitone chained hands and feet. Encolpio, in turn, is bundled on to the ship of Lica, a treasure seeker who takes precious things and people to the young Cesare, the emperor exiled on an island.

[18] The very effective epic parody (from Virgil's *Aen*. 2.664ff.) of *Sat*. 81.2-6, after Encolpius's painful separation from Ascyltos, is anticipated in *Fellini-Satyricon* sc. 1.1-6, at the very beginning of the movie.

[19] The *Troiae Halosis* (*Sat*. 89 "*The Capture of Troy*") is composed by Eumolpus after the manner of Seneca (with echoes of Virgil's account in *Aeneid* 2: Sullivan, 1968, 187-8; Walsh, 1970, 46; 1997, 185); an analogous poem (*Halosis Ilii*) was recited by Nero watching Rome burn in AD 64 (Suetonius *Ner*. 38.2). But a negative parody of Nero's work in Eumolpus's poem may be inappropriate: see Rimell, 2002, 17; 60-76; Schmeling, 2011, 369ff.

Tryphaena, and Eumolpus tells the story of the widow of Ephesus.[20]	(**37.489-512**) Lica falls in love with Encolpio and "marries" him on deck, with Trifena as wedding officiant. (**37.513-39.521**) Lica sings for Encolpio; at dawn a whale is caught by the crew. (**40.522-42.561**) The young albino Cesare is overthrown and compelled to kill himself: the assailants take possession of the ship and behead Lica. On the mainland, the army of the new Cesare carries huge spoils of victory in triumph.
(**113-115**) The tale arouses hilarity, but a sudden storm drags Lichas into the sea. Our three heroes are saved by local fishermen; Lichas is burned on a funeral pyre. (**116-124**) Encolpius, Giton and Eumolpus approach Croton: in need of elevated content in contemporary poems,[21] Eumolpus gives a demonstration of epic poetry on the civil war that opposed Caesar, Pompey and Crassus.[22] Since the Crotonian population consists of rich inhabit-	

[20] The tale (*Sat.* 111-112) belongs to the genre of the *Fabulae Milesiae*. Short folktales of an erotic nature, named *Milesiaka*, were composed by Aristides from Miletus (around 100 BC), then rearranged and introduced in Rome by Cornelius Sisenna († 67 BC), according to Ovid *Trist.* 2.443-4 (Aragosti, 1995, 25 n. 31; Jensson, 2004, 259ff.). This literary genre will regain strength with Boccaccio's *Decameron* and Poggio Bracciolini's *Facetiae* (von Albrecht, 1995, II, 1218; 1996, III, 1473). On the Milesian tale of the *Matrona Ephesi* (then adapted by La Fontaine: Ernout, 1958, 121 n. 1), see Slater, 1990, 108-11; Laird, 1999, 239-46; Rimell, 2002, 123-39; Vannini, 2010, 23ff. (with bibliography).

[21] *Sat.* 118.1 *multos, iuvenes, carmen decepit* ("Poetry, my young friends, has beguiled many into believing that they have set foot on Mount Helicon") recalls Horace (*Ars* 24), as made explicit by the subsequent *odi profanum vulgus et arceo* (*Sat.* 118.4 "I hate the common mob, and keep it at arm's length"; cf. Horace *Carm.* 3.1.1, resuming Callimachus *Hymn.* 2.2: Aragosti, 1995, 435 n. 335).

[22] *Sat.* 119-124 includes the *Bellum civile*, "The Civil War," recited by Eumolpus *ingenti volubilitate verborum* (124.2 "his monstruous deluge of words"). Lucan's *Pharsalia* book I (in turn following Livy's outline of the course of the war) is recalled in the Petronian 295-line epyllion (Connors, 1994, 227ff.): on alleged polemics between Petronius and Lucan, see Courtney, 2001, 183ff.; below, p. 61 n. 130.

ants without heirs and legacy-hunters, Eumolpus will pose as a childless wealthy man, the others as his slaves.	
	(**43.562-49.675**) In the tablinum of a patrician villa, a noble couple frees the slaves, says goodbye to the children and commits suicide. Encolpio and Ascilto enter the deserted mansion, watched over by the *imagines maiorum*. With a very young slave-girl (*la schiavetta*), sole survivor in the slave dormitory, they start playful affairs. (**50.676-57.784**) In a desert landscape, while Ascilto satisfies the sexual desires of a nymphomaniac, her slave explaines to Encolpio that in a Ceres temple the demigod Ermafrofrodito operates miraculous healings. A marauder, Encolpio and Ascilto kill the guardians of the sanctuary and steal the Ermafrodito, with the purpose of making a profit from it, but the very delicate child, a sickly albino, dies under the burning sun in a parched desert. The man blames Ascilto, but is killed in the ensuing fight. (**58.785-903**) Probably as a result of the theft, Encolpio is captured and thrown into a labyrinth, where he has to face an antagonist disguised as Minotauro at the "Festival of Mirth," held each year in the local theatre and consisting of mocking hoaxes and malicious jokes perpetrated on a stranger. When he joins his deserved and voluptuous Ari-

(**125- <***> 133**) Eumolpus's plan seems to be successful. The mistress Circe from Croton asks Encolpius for sex, but he is struck by impotence; after failing again to make love with her,[23] in spite of magical cures, he prays to Priapus for healing.	anna on the bed, in front of a watching crowd, he realises he has 'lost his sword' and is pushed off by the woman. Eumolpo shows up and informs Encolpio that his impotence is due to the god Priapus.
(**134-139**) Encolpius visits the priestess-sorceress Oenothea, who claims she can provide the cure desired by him: but after foretelling Encolpius's future, her ointments and poultices don't achieve any outcome. Encolpius flees in dispair, and is caught up by Circe's slave, in love with him <***> (**140**). A legacy-huntress from Croton places her son and daughter with Eumolpus, in order to seize his non-existent inheritance: Encolpius lies down with her child,	(**59.904-60.975**) Eumolpo, now a rich trader whose ship will be soon sailing to Africa, suggests Encolpio visit the "Garden of Delights," an outdoor brothel. Encolpio fails to be cured, whereas Ascilto succeeds with some very young hookers. Eumolpo sets up a meeting with Encolpio for the next day on the sailing ship (***see Sat. 99***). (**60.976-62.996**) The owner of the Garden directs Encolpio to see Enotea, a sorceress who was once cursed by a wizard for teasing him sexually: as a punishment, the fire banished from the city was to be found by the citizens between her thighs. (**62.997-70.1033**) Encolpio and Ascilto decide to make their way, carrying gold with them as payment to Enotea. While Ascilto is fatally wounded by the ferryman (*il traghettatore*) in an argument for the gold, Encolpio begs for help, is cured by the sorceress and thanks

[23] *Sat.* 132.8-16 is an irreverent Petronius's apostrophe to his own penis, modelled after Odysseus' monologue to his heart (Homer *Od.* 20.13-22; cf. *Sat.* 132.13 *non et Ulixes cum corde litigat suo, et quidam tragici oculos tanquam audientes castigant?* "didn't Ulysses have words with his heart, didn't figures of tragedy rebuke their eyes as if they had ears?).

discovering himself impotent again. But he eventually reveals that he has somehow been cured of his impotence by the intervention of *Dii maiores* and Mercurius.	the god Mercury for healing him (***see Sat. 140***).
(**141**) <***> As the ship from Africa with Eumolpus's alleged load doesn't arrive, making the legacy-hunters suspicious, Eumolpus orders that his friends will come into possession of his wealth, provided they are ready to cannibalize his corpse <***>.	
	(**71.1034-73.1072**) Encolpio and Ascilto hurry to the ship, but Ascilto dies from wounds. Encolpio arrives at the ship, but Eumolpo lies dead on a bier on the beach. He has left a will that grants all his assets to those who will eat his body: some agree to and get going on it.
	(**73.1073-75.1081**) Encolpio embarks with a group of youths: his voice-over starts telling further adventures, as fulfillment of new dreams, but he and most of the characters of the plot gradually turn into figures on a fresco in Pompeian colors, ruined remnants in the backdrop of the sea.

1.2 THE UNDECIPHERABLE CLARITY OF DREAMS.

Faced with the "battered torso" (Sullivan 1991/2001, 259). of Petronius's ancient novel, and after showing his sophisticated attitude towards literary adaptation with the thoroughgoing transformation of Poe's *Never Bet The Devil Your Head* in *Toby Dammit*

(1968),[24] Fellini apparently chose the Petronian text "*because* of its incomplete survival,"[25] taking up a difficult challenge, both with himself and with his audience. Whereas Renaissance Humanists would project on Antiquity their own pre-established ideas, Fellini was not inspired by any such preconceptions:

> For me the ancient world is a lost world and my ignorance of it leaves me with no connection to it other than a fantastic, imaginative one, nurtured by hypotheses and impressions severed from facts and historical knowledge.[26]

He actually aimed at searching a non literary, but absolutely visual narrative, of dream-like quality. In this respect, *Little Nemo in Slumberland*, the American beautiful strip animated by the cartoonist Winsor McCay (about a child who experiences fantastic dreams), may have inspired both the visual style of *Fellini-Satyricon* and the coincident drawings we find in *Il libro dei sogni* ("The Book of Dreams"), the dream notebooks he had begun after *La dolce vita* (1959), under the influence of the Jungian psychologist Ernst Bernhard.[27]

---

[24] See Bondanella, 1992, 237. *Toby Dammit* marks a transition toward the artificial cinema of *Fellini-Satyricon*: both movies were almost entirely shot at Cinecittà Studio, through the special effects of an original "synthetic staginess" (Sharrett, 2002, 122: its peak will be reached with the plastic sea of *Il Casanova di Federico Fellini*, 1976, which marked an epoch).

[25] Paul, 2009, 206. On Fellini's previous readings of the novel (cf. Fellini, 1980/2015, 159), see Zanelli, 1969, 16-18; Bondanella, 1992, 239; Sütterlin, 1996, 176-8; Taddei, 2000, 298; Stubbs, 2006, 213; Copioli, 2020, 139.

[26] Fellini, 1980/2015, 160 (trans. Christopher B. White): see also Zanelli, 1969, 68.

[27] The comics played an important role in the development of Fellini's imagery (see Bondanella, 1992, 3-29): he was familiar with McCay's 1905-1927 *Little Nemo* (see also Bondanella, 2002, 10); Frederick Burr Opper's series *Happy Hooligan*; and liked Lee Falk's *Mandrake*, as well as Alex Raymond's *Flash Gordon*: through magazines for children such as "Il Corriere dei Piccoli" and "L'Avventuroso" (whose readers became acquainted with some milestones of American comic art), Fellini assimilated strategies of "graphic and communicative synthesis" (Bellano, 2020, 62): preparatory sketches for *Fellini-Satyricon* are finely introduced and commented by Betti, 1970. "The Book of Dreams" (*Il libro dei sogni*: cf. Toffetti, 2020) — a compilation of journals in which Fellini recorded dreams, nightmares, and visions "through drawings and notes" (Villa, 2020, 485) — reproduces in facsimile size: volume 1 (1960-1968); volume 2 (1973-1990); loose pages, and pages given as gift (see Pacchioni, 2020, 98ff.; Suderburg, 2020, 82ff.). About Ernst Bernhard (Berlin 1896-Rome 1965) and his influence on Fellini, see Kezich, 2002, 215-21; Carrera, 2020, 132.

> Perhaps the ancient world never existed, but there's no doubt that we dreamed it. *Satyricon* should possess the enigmatic transparency, the undecipherable clarity of dreams.[28]

Fellini's overwhelming ingenuity, expanded to gestures, incidents, and locations, eventually needs to be rationally *objectified* in filmmaking: dreams, inherently elusive, unintelligible, and "alien," do possess contents deeply belonging to each of us; but "in broad daylight our unique cognitive relationship to them has to be intellectual and conceptual."[29] Thus:

> I was like an archaeologist piecing together fragments of ancient vases, trying to guess what the missing parts looked like. Rome itself is an ancient broken vase, constantly being mended to hold it together, but retaining hints of its original secrets. (Chandler 1995, 171-2.)

The film does resemble a kind of discovery of an unknown breed. Fellini's adaptation, paying no attention to the traditional cinematic approach to the Roman world ('re-creation'; 'authentic' costumes and sets, and so on), is neither related to what we have learned from school-books, nor to the kind of "costume drama filled with togas, bulging biceps, chariot races, and gladiator contests" (Bondanella 1992, 243). To put it into Fellinian terms, nothing to do with the impressions given by "torches and braziers, and the bric-à-brac of the Roman cinematic tradition."[30]

Some further pronouncements reveal the passion with which Fellini vividly illustrates his ideas on this problematic film:

> The ruins? The Appian Way? Or better yet the photos of ruins and the Appian Way you see in history books or on postcards? Watered-down ghosts, lifeless features, cemetery perspectives soaked in funeral sadness for smug photographers' exhibitions.[31]

---

[28] Fellini, 1980/2015, 164 (trans. Christopher B. White).

[29] Federico Fellini to Alberto Moravia, in Zanelli, 1969, 69 (my trans.).

[30] Federico Fellini, in Zanelli, 1969, 61(my trans.); about the compulsory and ritual ingredients of cinematic tradition, see Grazzini, 1977, 298.

[31] Fellini, 1980/2015, 160 (trans. Christopher B. White).

The co-writer Zapponi remarked on the scarcely related episodes of the film, reflecting the extensive textual losses/gaps in the Petronian manuscript: "Petronius's book, like Shakespeare, switches from buffoonery to torment, from tragedy to dirty farce ... then, sudden silence, sentences pronounced by whom we don't know, people jumping out of nowhere and enunciating their motto, like wretched men from hell.... *We had to expand the gaps in Petronius's book, not bridge them.* The movements of the characters became more puppet-like, rarefied ... elusiveness was to drag on in anxiety."[32] As a matter of fact, even though Encolpio supposedly links the episodes of the film, at least for as long as the motivation for action is provided by "the competition for Gitone's affection," abrupt cuts tend to shake the most indulgent viewer.[33] But the peculiar climate, a dream-like, or rather a *nightmarish* one, reverberates in some of Fellini's twinkling director's notes:

> [...] Dust – Darkness (Evocation) [...] Black tails – Hoarse voices gurgling words that become muddier and muddier. Drowned people trying to speak [...] The horrible fixity of the bas-reliefs. Empty eyes. With no pupils. Bronze eyes [...] Lots of homes under construction. Bridges. Collapse. (Earthquake at the *Insula Felix*, the terrifying palace-skyscraper, immense, dark, swarming like Breughel's Tower of Babel). A film about the Martians. It should have the same allure made up of alarm and tension as the first Japanese films had for us. You never knew if those characters were laughing or crying [...] Arrhythmic – faint – Indirect – Unpredictable. Exasperating slowness, the speed of microbes. Acted poorly, with extremely long periods of silence, faltering language. Broken, hesitant; an impersonal dubbing, detached like the voices for news on the radio [...] A great, suggestive, and mysterious fable. A film made up of fixed, immobile frames, without dollies or other movements of the camera. A film to contemplate, similar to dreams: and it leaves you hypnotized [...][34]

---

32 Bernardino Zapponi, in Zanelli, 1969, 84 (italics mine); on this issue, see Sütterlin, 1996, 208 n. 708.

33 See Paul, 2009, 205; cf. pp. 202-3 for a synopsis of *Fellini-Satyricon* as an illustration of its narrative fragmentation.

34 Fellini, 1980/2015, 165-7 (trans. Christopher B. White). The ineffability of our ancient past produces a Fellinian cinematic device of its own: the out-of-sync effect. In addition to a va-

It is no coincidence that, by giving up and dismissing adjectives usually connoting Petronius's novel in proven literary exegesis ('picaresque', 'allusive', 'derisive', 'modern', 'theatrical', a.s.o.), the director and the screenwriter regarded the book as a start for an unreal voyage, such as *Gordon Pym*, or even as a kind of sea journey of adventure, like the ones created by Conrad and Verne.[35] Fellini was seeking to bring back to life characters so far away from contemporary life, and to catch them by surprise, in order to invent a Roman world

> as if evoked by a supernatural ectoplasmic operation. I like to imagine that the movie, like an archaeologist who uses pottery shards to attempt to reconstruct a fragmentary, incomplete, and mutilated form […], should indicate the boundaries, the realities of a vanished world […]. Historical accuracy, bookish documentation, and self-satisfyingly erudite anecdotes have no place in a story that aims to revive characters so distant from us, to capture them as if by surprise in the same freedom with which they move, scuffle, tear each other to pieces, are born and die, like beasts in the dense wilderness when they don't know they're being watched. (Fellini 1980/2015, 162-3)

Consequently, some sort of detachment was indeed necessary:

> The film should offer a glimpse of an excavated universe, suggest images obscured by the earth, a movie broken with its uneven structure; it should have long, well-organized episodes, others more distant, out of focus, that cannot be rebuilt because of their fragmentary nature. Not a historical film, but a science fiction movie. It should be Ascilto, Encolpio, and Trimalchio's Rome,

---

riety of discordant sounds and musical styles, the dialogue throughout the movie "is made strange by deliberately out-of-sync dubbing" (Paul, 2009, 212): within Fellini's fondness for a "babbling jungle of vocal histrionics," during the postsynchronization process of *Fellini-Satyricon* dubbing voices "float freely around the characters and the screen" (Sisto, 2020, 254-5). Let's consider that *just eleven* Italian actors dub *all major and minor* characters of the film: cf. below, *Principal Credits*.

[35] Bernardino Zapponi, in Zanelli 1969, 83-4.

more remote and fantastic than the planets in Flash Gordon. (Fellini, 1980/2015, 163) [36]

For the first time in Fellini's career, the demanding effort to contend with a "science fiction," at least at an awareness level, would rule out any autobiographic component: it had to cope and integrate with Fellini's imaginative working over so fascinating a text: therefore he resorted to philological consultants, such as Ettore Paratore and his former assistant Luca Canali, in order to add items from literary and historical works to the fragmentary Petronian narrative. Some important 'external' (non-Petronian) works were actually kept in mind and carefully studied: Tacitus' *Annales*, Suetonius' *De vita Caesarum*, Apuleius' *Metamorphoseon Libri* (*Asinus aureus*), Comparetti's *Virgilio nel Medio Evo*, Carcopino's *La vie quotidienne à Rome à l'apogée de l'empire*.[37] The extensive use of these books helps us understand why, and to what extent, new material was employed by Fellini and Zapponi, and embedded in the Petronian basic plot, in the transition from story treatment to screenplay, and from screenplay to movie.[38]

1.3 A SUPERNATURAL ECTOPLASMIC OPERATION

At the *treatment* stage, beside incidents retained by Fellini and Zapponi from the Latin source (Encolpius's seeking of Giton; Trimalchio's feast; the basic plot of Lichas's ship; Encolpius's impotence), *four* radical changes occur from Petronius:[39] 1. the two

---

[36] In few words, a "science-fiction exploring the past" (Peter Nichols, in Zanelli, 1969, 62). Christopher Sharrett regards both *Toby Dammit* and *Fellini-Satyricon* as somehow associated with postmodernism "in their admission that there is no history outside of representation": in interviews given during the production of the latter, Fellini expressed his skepticism over "art's ability to represent history" (Sharrett, 2002, 123).

[37] See respectively: Comparetti, 1941; Carcopino, 1967.

[38] Of the two surviving scripts, the first one is kept in duplicate in Rimini (at "Fondazione Fellini"), and consists of a typewritten copy, with handwritten additions, corrections, and revisions (see Bartesaghi, 2009, 321); the second (published by Zanelli, 1969, 149-273; treatment on pp. 111-45) is a tentative script adopted during the film's shooting, and came out at the same time as Fellini's movie (henceforth: Zanelli A = treatment; Zanelli B = screenplay): it differs significantly from Bartesaghi *aud.*, the screenplay inferred from the movie (see above, n. 6).

[39] Stubbs, 2006, 214ff.; Copioli, 2020, 142-4.

mentors/poets, Agamemnon (*Sat.* 3ff.) and Eumolpus (*Sat.* 83ff.), are merged into one, Eumolpo (Zanelli A, 19); 2. Neither of the epic poems recited by Eumolpus in the Petronian novel (*Troiae Halosis* at *Sat.* 89; *Bellum civile* at 119-124) appears in the film; 3. tracks from *Fabulae Milesiae* (*Sat.* 85-87; 140.1-11) are erased, except the amusing *Matrona Ephesi* (*Sat.* 111-112 = Zanelli A, 128-9);[40] 4. in Petronius's narrative, Ascyltos disappears after the quarrel with Encolpius about Giton, before they board Lichas's ship with Eumolpus (*Sat.* 80): in the treatment, Ascylto continues to play an important role almost until the end (his death in Zanelli A, 144).

Five blocks were added by Fellini: 1. the area of the bay of Naples in the opening sequence of the novel (*Sat.* 1-11) has been changed into a Roman one (Zanelli A, 111ff.);[41] 2. a young albino Cesare[42] is murdered (Zanelli A, 131-2); 3. a patrician couple commit suicide in their villa (Zanelli A, 133-4);[43] 4. a sickly demigod Ermafrodito is stolen by Encolpio and Ascilto, but dies in the desert (Zanelli A, 135-8); 5. (not invented but borrowed) the witch Enotea (cf. Oenothea at *Sat.* 134-138), once cursed by a wizard for teasing him sexually, was condemned to provide the fire, that had been banished from the city, from a source between her thighs (Zanelli A, 139-43).[44]

At the *screenplay* stage, we can track down *seven* interventions (revisions or/and expansions of the treatment) by Fellini and

---

[40] For the *Fabulae Milesiae* see above, n. 20.

[41] About the collapse of the *Insula Felicles* in Fellini's film (sc. 9.167-190), Sullivan, 1991/2001, 261 suggests that the state of Roman tenements is probably drawn from Juvenal *Sat.* 3.193-196.

[42] Perhaps a conflation of emperors Caligula (AD 37-41), Nero (54-68), and Eliogabalus (204-222): see Stubbs, 2006, 215.

[43] The sequence might be based on the deaths of Thrasea Paetus (Stoic opponent to Nero: Sullivan, 1991/2001, 262 n. 9) and his wife: cf. Tacitus *Ann.* 16.33-35 (regarding the suicide of Caecina Paetus and his wife at the time of Claudius, cf. Martial 1.13; Plinius the Younger *Ep.* 3.16.6). For a possible – but debatable – reference to Tacitus' account of Petronius's own suicide, cf. Tacitus *Ann.* 16.18-19.

[44] On the expansion of Enotea's role, see Bondanella, 1992, 242. Fellini and Zapponi adapted a medieval story (since around 1220), fancifully attributed to the epic poet Virgil, whose clumsy advances had been refused by the daughter of a Roman emperor: see Comparetti, 1941, II, 106-24. On the Apuleian parallel (*Met.* 10.29-35) to Encolpio's attempt at lovemaking with Enotea in Fellini (neglected by Sütterlin, 1996), see Winkler, 1997, 9. For possible "indecent" influences from the portrait of *Vetustilla* in Martial 3.93, see Sullivan, 1991/2001, 261.

Zapponi: 1. in the opening scene (Zanelli B, 1.1-9), Encolpio appears against a blank wall; 2. in the conclusion (Zanelli B, 67.1249-1253), first Encolpio alone, then the main characters are located on three fissured fragments,[45] like figures "in a freeze-framed faded fresco of Pompeian colors";[46] 3. Eumolpo is introduced much earlier (Zanelli B, 11.240) than Eumolpus in Petronius (*Sat.* 83: almost halfway through the novel); 4. the new emperor, after having his predecessor killed, triumphally marches towards Rome (Zanelli B, 43.767-789);[47] 5. a nymphomaniac is transported across the desert (Zanelli B, 44.790-46.815); 6. at the 'Festival of Mirth', Encolpio faces Minotauro and is discovered impotent with Arianna (Zanelli B, 51.901-1001);[48] 7. in the 'Garden of Delights', Encolpio fails to be cured from impotence (Zanelli B, 53.1012-1062).

At the *movie* stage, it is noteworthy to examine how basic a change the Petronian sequence on board Lichas's ship has been wrought, starting from the 'slapstick comedy' perspective in Petronius's *Sat.* 100.3-115.5, where Encolpius and Giton try to avoid being discovered by Lichas and Tryphaena, but unsuccessfully. Quartilla, priestess of Priapus, is the protagonist of the orgy in the treatment and tells the story of the *Matrona Ephesi* (Zanelli A, 128-9),[49] whereas Eumolpus does it in the Latin version, after bringing about the reconciliation between Encolpius/Giton and Lichas/Tryphaena (*Sat.* 110.6-8); in the screenplay, Fellini and Zapponi place the homosexual marriage between Lica and Encolpio on board Lica's ship (Zanelli B, 33.627-643);[50] thirdly, at the final movie stage (Bartesaghi *aud.* 36.472-488), Fellini adds a wrestling scene between Lica and Encolpio, in which Lica is the winner: suffice it to notice that the

[45] See Zanelli, 1969, 149; Bondanella, 1992, 248; Bartesaghi, 2009, 325-6.

[46] Sullivan, 1991/2001, 260 (see below, chapter 3.1).

[47] The sequence recalls Emperor Galba's march to Rome to replace Nero: Suetonius *Galb.* 10ff.

[48] See Apuleius *Met.* 2.31; 3.11; 10.34.

[49] About the *Fabulae Milesiae* see above, n. 40.

[50] Zanelli 1969, 210-2; Bartesaghi, 2009, 413-18. Possible allusions to Emperor Nero's mock marriages (Tacitus *Ann.* 15.37; Suetonius *Ner.* 28-29), and to the transvestite emperor Eliogabalus, who reigned from AD 218 to 222 (Cassius Dio. 79.33): Sullivan 1991/2001, 263 nn. 12-13.

narrative of Lica's tyrant-role is preponderant both in the treatment and in the movie itself (See Stubbs 2006, 217-8).[51]

What kind of specific liberties does Fellini allow himself, in as much as any literary dimension is "impossible to convey on the screen" (Sullivan 1991/2001, 263)? As a start, let's take a look at some narrative aspects of Petronius's *Satyrica,* particularly relevant as a basic precondition of our analysis of Fellini's 'intersemiotic' book-to-film translation.[52]

---

[51] Burke 2020, 158ff. specifies that throughout the first half of *Fellini-Satyricon* (a film to be regarded as "more an analysis of a changing social order than of a changing protagonist"), Encolpio's "marginality" proves to be an example of "assimilation-as-subjection" to the old order (p. 159), which is the condition of three leading characters: militarily (Lica), politically (Cesare), socially (the patricians); so it is not surprising that all of them end up dead. Power is here equated with violence, because in a society founded on self-interest there is "no importance given to individual development," and personal change means change in fortune. On the other hand, with the "death of the old order," in the second half of the film the evolution of the social order culminates in the final scene, with no "imbalance in either power or wealth," showing a threesome of young peers ready to sail for Africa (p. 160). More on that below, ch. 3.1-3.

[52] The idea of 'intersemiotic translation' was conceived by Jakobson 1959, 261 as "an interpretation of verbal signs by means of signs of nonverbal sign systems" (equivalent to "transmutation").

Chapter 2
ENCOLPIUS NARRATOR.
ILLUSIONISM AS THE OTHER FACE OF REALISM

> The text itself has many meanings; to suggest that only one view is the right one is itself to distort that text.
>
> John Patrick Sullivan (1991)

2.1 A NOVEL WHICH WILL NOT STAY STILL

As a fitting response to Wimsatt-Beardsley's New Critical essay *The Affective Fallacy*, which valued the work itself as a formal object and rejected the idea that readers' reactions have any place in the interpretation of a literary text,[1] Stanley Fish remarked that the merit of Kinetic Art is that it "does not lend itself to a static interpretation, because it refuses to stay still," and consequently doesn't even let the *observer* stay still either: this operation makes "the actualizing role of the observer inescapable" (Fish, 1980, 43).[2] But, apart from Fish's clever move, for us mere mortals, a literary creation commonly assumes a neat physical form: the confortable opacity of a book. Available in shelves and library catalogues, either in paper or kindle format, feverishly or wearily browsed, carefully bound, or left to mould in a basement..., a book encourages a reader to believe it to be *stationary*. But it is difficult for a 'reader-oriented' critic like Fish to regard a text as a documentary record of something that exists or has existed beforehand. Convinced, as he is, that a book is a *changing* object, Fish even wonders if it is an "object" at all, arguing that its fluidity matches the "mobility" of the meaning experience, directing us to the "active

[1] On Wimsatt-Beardsley, 1949, based on theories perceived by reader-oriented critics as overly text-centred ones, see Selden-Widdowson-Brooker, 1997, 19-20; Rabinowitz, 2005, 29; Schneider, 2005, 484.

[2] A reader, attending to the sequence of words as they succeed one another in time and create a state of suspension, should be prevented from setting up a stable image in her/his mind (pp. 22ff.; 68ff.; 97ff.). But some Fish's assumptions (such as readers' expectation of meaning as repeatedly adjusted, thus almost never fulfilled) have been strongly debated, especially as regards his failing to theorise which conventions readers should follow when they read: see Selden-Widdowson-Brooker, 1997, 59. About the major representatives of Kinetic (and Early Cybernetic Art) – visual artists such as Yaacov Agam, Nicholas Schöffer, Gordon Pask, Roy Ascott, and Edward Ihnatowicz – see Preziosi, 2009, 471-4.

and activating" consciousness of the reader.[3] Anyhow, if taken as an effective pun, Fish's *boutade* can help us to read the *Satyrica* more attentively and try to enjoy a text which has "the power to move, upset or change its readers," removing the temptation to "erase difficulties and contradictions by dubbing them as entertainment" (Rimell, 2002, 5). Going then along with the joke of the American scholar, in the following sections I aim to carry out an analysis of relevant episodes of the Petronian novel, in order to take into account the possibility of reading its text as a somewhat ... *kinetic* artefact (a text that, in its own way, *refuses to stay still*), and of building up any possible reaction, to be expected both by the original and by the contemporary *observers*.

In spite of the difficult reconstruction of the length and content of the *Satyrica*,[4] the extant portions of Petronius's work underline the relationship that links a homosexual couple (Encolpius and Giton), forming with Ascyltos "at certain points a threesome" (Laird, 2007, 152),[5] a perfect love-triangle euphemistically described by the word *fratres* (brothers, boyfriends).[6] But, apart from

---

[3] See Fish, 1980, 44ff. Cf. p. 25: "it is no longer an object, a thing-in-itself, but an *event*, something that *happens* to, and with the participation of, the reader." To his analysis of the *Satyrica*, Slater, 1990 (cf. below, nn. 431-9) will apply contributions from both Fish and Wolfgang Iser (e.g. Iser, 1978), the exponent of the 'Constance School' (see Schneider, 2005, 485).

[4] About the surviving sections see Schmeling, 2011, xxiiff. (cf. above, n. 9). The *Satyrica*, an *open* work consisting of scarcely related episodes, is further *opened* "by the massive textual losses in the manuscript tradition": Sullivan, 1991/2001, 260.

[5] The sexual predator Eumolpus will replace Ascyltos as the second triangle's vertex, particularly from *Sat.* 100 on: Aragosti, 1995, 326-7.

[6] Courtney, 2001, 49. For *frater* as a euphemism for homosexual lover (Habermehl, 2006, 11; Schmeling, 2011, 28; 34), cf. Martial 2.4.3 (*frater* and *soror* like *nomina nequiora*, "ambiguous terms"); 10.65.14 (cf. *OLD* s.v. 731.3b). Literary Roman texts from Catullus to Martial (around 50 BC-AD 100), as results of a traditionally "male and active" narrative voice (Schmeling, 2011, 62), portray the adult male as 'penetrator' of women and slave teenage boys (on this "Priapic model" see Williams, 2010, 18; on Juvenal 9.22-26; 128 see Bellandi, 2021, 42 nn. 148-9), whereas a post-adolescent male attracted to an adult one is disdained as *mollis/cinaedus/pathicus* ("lascivious, catamite, submitting to anal sex"). Beyond their sexual relationship (yet obscured by the problem of determining their single social status: Vannini, 2010, 5 considers indisputable their *ingenuitas*, "free birth"), each of the characters tries to have sex with other males and females, but Encolpius's love for Giton absorbs all his attention, leading to his progressing towards the normative man/boy pair. So, when Encolpius and Ascyltos accuse each other of having been penetrated (*Sat.* 9-11; 81.3-6: Schmeling, 1994-95, 211ff.), their slanging match is very likely to suggest "unexpectedly fluid roles for the *fratres*" (Courtney, 2001, 49; cf. Richlin, 2009, 85). About Giton' performances of

the sexual overtones of their names (a jocular *nomen-omen* effect),[7] Encolpius towers over major and minor characters as first-person narrator and, in most cases, as the protagonist. Claiming to be cultivated, but (intentionally or accidentally?) light-headed and childlike, thrust fortuitously rather than by safeguarding certainty, our protagonist moves about aimlessly from place to place, with no apparently planned route. Absence of purposes and goals in the novel, as well as the aimlessness of Encolpius, apparently result "from a lack of interest in the ending as a purpose" (Schmeling, 1991, 359ff.).[8]

As Edward Courtney has pointed out, among recurring Petronian symbols and narrative patterns, a reader is impressed by incidents where "characters repeatedly lose their way" and move in circles (Courtney, 2001, 227-8): at *Sat.* 6.3-4 Encolpius is lost and returns to his starting-point: "I had failed to take careful note of the route, and did not know the way to our lodging. So whichever direction I took brought me back to the same place" (*nec viam diligenter tenebam nec quo loco stabulum esset sciebam. Itaque quocumque ieram, eodem revertebar*). When he, "exhausted by the chase," asks a little old lady (*anicula*) for directions (6.4-7.1), a surreal connotation is given by his hunch that the woman may be some goddess in disguise, rescuing a lost hero (7.1-2):[9] "She then got up and began to lead the way. I thought she had second sight (*divinam ego putabam*) and followed her." Sadly, for Encolpius, he ends up be-

---

slave-roles, and his sexual "objectification" by many characters, see Lee Clark, 2019, 25ff.; 63ff.; 99ff. Lambert, 2004, 440 argues that "age-differential" models of male same-sex relationships, and active-passive polarity, date back to the Lyric poet Theognis 1.65 (sixth century BC): Greeks differentiated *paides* (boys) from *neoi* (youngsters) and *andres* (men).

[7] *Encolpius* (*egkolpios*) = "Bosom companion"; *Giton* (*geitōn*) = "Neighbour"; *Ascyltos* (*askyltos*) = "Indefatigable/Untroubled/Unwearied" (cf. Maass, 1925, 447; Aragosti, 1995, 18 n. 21). The name *Eumolpus* (*eumolpos* = "Bon chanteur/Great-Sweet singer") sounds less sexually prejudicial: but *Sat.* 85-87 shows the pederastic initiation of the Pergamene Youth carried out by Eumolpus as a charming trickster and *fabulator*, a "storyteller" (Labate, 2020, 141ff.). About the above "descriptive names," see Vannini, 2010, 5; for the hidden meaning of Petronian names, see Solin, 2017, 318-25; as to "puns on names" in Juvenal, see Bellandi, 2021, 21 n. 75; 30 n. 107.

[8] Cf. Barchiesi, 1996, 194 n. 7.

[9] Slater, 1990, 33 compares Venus rescuing Aeneas in Virgil *Aen.* 1.305 ff; but the image stems from Athena protecting Odysseus, in Homer *Od.*13.190 ff.

ing lead to a *fornix*, a brothel, with the woman proving to be a procuress... In further episodes the first-person narration reflects on Encolpius-protagonist and his *fratres* going round in circles and returning where they began:[10] which seems to suggest their metaphorical making little (or no) progress towards any goal, and frames a symbolic image of Encolpius as incapable of understanding "his situation in life" (Schmeling, 2011, 23). Furthermore, Victoria Rimell has shown that readers somehow settle into this fictional world thanks to "the brilliant prank of extended first-person narration (Rimell, 2007, 132): multiple and open readings of narrative sequences, "in which nothing is taken seriously and no man's motives are what they seem" (Walsh, 1970, 27), are indeed made possible by the difficult challenge set by Petronius, both for his audience and for today's readers (Panayotakis, 2009, 57).

Intrigued by these issues, I would like to provide a description of some characteristics of Encolpius *as first-person narrator* about the novel (distinguishing him from Petronius as empirical author)[11], with a special focus on a number of prominent frameworks: the dialogue between Encolpius and Agamemnon (*Sat.* 1.1-5.20); the Quartilla section (16.1-26.6); the Feast of Trimalchio (26.7-78.8); Encolpius's love affairs. More or less convincing evidence thus collected should hopefully make possible a comment on (and a comparison with) Fellini's adaptation of Petronius's novel, through the most relevant cinematic abilities of the Italian director, some of which highlighted by Martin Winkler: Fellini's Encolpius in *voice-over*; uncommon "theatrical quality" of the film.[12]

---

[10] At *Sat.* 8.2 Ascyltos loses his way; at 79.1-4, after our heroes escape from Trimalchio's dinner, Giton devises 'the 'Ariadne's thread' (Courtney, 2001, 228), and finds his way home.

[11] On this issue see below, ch. 2.8.

[12] See Winkler, 1997, 9. A *voice-over* commonly refers to a narration that comes from an *unseen*, off-screen voice, which can be heard by the audience, but not by the film characters themselves; it may be often the voice of a *visible* character who expresses unspoken thoughts: about this 'variant' in *Toby Dammit* (1968), cf. below, pp. 109-10.

2.2 FLATTERERS ON THE STAGE

Within the debate on education and rhetorical training (Agamemnon teaches rhetoric at Puteoli), we are abruptly confronted with "key ideas and images" (Rimell, 2002, 18) about such relationships as orator/audience, author/narrator, narrator/reader. Encolpius, eager to "deliver a declamation in the colonnade" (*Sat.* 3.1 *declamare in porticu*), conveys the impression of declaiming excitedly against the decay of oratory, as an alleged defective result of rhetorical education in the Roman school system.[13] But, regardless of this decay being considered as moral rather than political,[14] the reader will be informed through Ascyltos – a few chapters later – that Encolpius's invective *was not to be taken seriously*, because it aimed at impressing Agamemnon, in the hopes of cadging a dinner (10.2 "For God's sake, you're a damned sight worse than I am, praising that poet just to cadge an invitation to dinner"): a charge not denied by Encolpius. After all, if we consider – among other reasons – the irrelevance and predictability of Encolpius's appeal to clichéd Greek models of eloquence, such as Pindar/Sophocles/Euripides or Thucydides/Plato/Demosthenes/ Hyperides (2.7-8), we find it hard to take a proclamation "so riddled with the vices it denounces" (Slater, 1990, 30) seriously. Moreover, the reader doesn't escape the feeling that all these hackneyed views on rhetorical training – and on the correlative "moral degeneration" (Walsh, 1970, 84) of the Roman community – look like being quoted by Encolpius as a parody of satirized current opinions, delivered as "parody on parody":[15] thus even further deprived of any inherent value.

---

[13] *Sat.* 1.1-2 "this, surely, is the same band of Furies goading our teachers of rhetoric (*declamatores*) when they cry: 'These wounds have I sustained for our country's liberty, this eye have I forfeited in your service (*pro vobis impendi*). Give me a helping hand to escort me (*ducem qui me ducat*) to my children, for my legs are hamstrung and cannot support my body's weight.' Utterances even as bad as this we could stomach (*tolerabilia essent*) if they advanced students on the path to eloquence."

[14] Full discussion in Schmeling, 2011, 2.

[15] Schmeling, 2011, 1. Connors, 2008, 176 argues that Encolpius's criticism, against orators who play the role of a citizen showing off the wounds "sustained for our country's liberty" (*Sat.* 1.1), is strongly contrasted "with the extravagant oratorical fictions enthusiastically perpetrated during the empire" (cf. 2.1ff.): but this may be also a pose. Encolpius here op-

At this stage, is Encolpius's indictment *shared* by the rhetor-poet Agamemnon? Far from being offended by Encolpius's remark against teachers (*Sat.* 2.2 "forgive me for saying so, but you teachers of rhetoric, more than any others, have been the death of eloquence": *pace vestra liceat dixisse, primi omnium eloquentiam perdidistis*), he praises the latter's "no ordinary taste" and "good sense" (3.1 *sermonem habes non publici saporis [...] amas bonam mentem*); then shifts the denunciation from teachers to pupils and to their rapacious parents at 4.1-5, finally expressing his educational model (in verses) at 5.1-20. If on the one hand a reader might suspect that Agamemnon hopes "for a sexual encounter" with a young man "of pure taste" (Kennedy, 1978, 176), on the other Encolpius's ability to fall into step with Agamemnon's theories is a deceitful improvisation, constructed to win the admiration of the rhetorician with a shrewd manipulation of the same Agamemnon and the audience. In short, *the pupil* amuses and gratifies *the teacher*, whereas the latter bores the former, who is in search of Ascyltos – his scary competitor for the affections of Giton (6.2) – and is therefore annoyed by Agamemnon's "tide of words" (6.1 *in hoc dictorum aestu*).

In Encolpius's hands, rhetoric is thus a maneuvering tool, the polar opposite of a "lofty and what one may call chaste eloquence," deceptively and boastfully called for by the same young *scholasticus* at *Sat.* 2.6 (*grandis et, ut ita dicam, pudica oratio*): it's here noteworthy how Encolpius's pose deeply contrasts with Agamemnon's severe commitment to rhetoric, in which he "has the misfortune to believe" (Slater, 1990, 31). How else could a reader understand Agamemnon's defense of his role, equal to the parasites from comedy and mime[16] (the "flatterers on the stage" seduc-

poses – as unrealistic in education – the use of those "scenarios," typical of Greek novels, which will end up characterising the narrator's very experiences: on irony at *Sat.* 1.2-3 see Laird, 2007, 159.

[16] Cf. Terence *Eun.* 247-53 (Schmeling, 2011, 12). D. Laberius (106-43 BC) gave a literary form to the 'mime' drama, a kind of farce made up of improvisatory scenes poking fun at real people and events (Fantham, 1989; von Albrecht, 1995, I, 102-3; Conte, 1997, 112-3). On Publilius Syrus see above, p. 6 n. 16. At the time of Caligula (AD 37-41), "sexual scenes

ing rich men for a free dinner: 3.3 *ficti adulatores*), or to a fisherman baiting his hook to attract the attention of his pupils, standing "idle on the rock with no hope of a catch" (3.4 *sine spe praedae morabitur in scopulo*)? On closer inspection, baiting one's audience with food, in order to eat *in turn*, suggests regarding culture as "a currency that might be exchanged for a dinner": as such, it seems to be triggering – but at the same time *upsetting* – a metaphorical literary process which originated very far in time, when in Plato's *Symposium* literature was designed for the dining room, even as a substitute of food itself (Rimell, 2002, 22). Encolpius's narration would therefore result in a bad blow to the traditional hierarchy *orator/audience*, a hierarchy coming here into play under the guise of an increasingly faltering and inconstant *teacher/student* relationship. This perception of role-indistinctions, at the hands of the first-person narrative, will never be overstated in the novel.

2.3 Reduced to Silence

The Quartilla episode (*Sat.* 16-26) does sound like a challenge to common sense. After quite cryptic charges of offense to Priapus against Encolpius, Ascyltos, and Giton (16-17.7; and proposed remedies: 17.8-19.3), an orgiastic assault on our heroes is made by Quartilla, her maids, and (twice!) by a *cinaedus*, a "passive homosexual"[17] (19.4-24); in the end, a mock marriage between Giton and the seven-year-old Pannychis results in a deflowering ritual watched by Encolpius and Quartilla (gaily frolicking) through a chink (25-26.5). But as the story goes, the reader gets gradually convinced that almost nothing can be taken at face value, and senses that something intriguing is at issue, far beyond her/his being involved in the simplistic *reversal* of a predictable Priapic aggression (which would be enactable by males in the service of

---

were presented with the utmost licence" (Walsh, 1970, 26), and some peculiar stage effects of the mimographer Catullus would impress the audience (Conte, 1997, 339 n. 1).

[17] On gr. *cinaidos* (cf. Plato *Gorg.* 494[e]), lit. "one who moves the genitals," see Sullivan, 1968, 49 n. 2. Effeminate *cinaedi* "publicly parade their enjoyment of passivity in such a way that it undermines the prevailing code of masculine values": Lambert, 2004, 441; on *cinaedus* (= *vir mollis/pathicus*) see Bellandi, 2021, 126-7.

the god, certainly neither by women nor catamites, "all very un-Priapic figures" [Slater, 1990, 42]).[18] The narrator's voice tends to seem shaky and fading, dripping with fear, almost exhausted by his incapacity to grasp the meaning of narrated incidents – *soundless*, I would argue: *Sat*. 16.2 "the bolt gave way of its own accord"; 17.1 "We were still reduced to silence, saying neither yea nor nay, when the lady herself entered"; 17.2 "Even then we didn't proffer a word"; 19.1 "We were wholly at a loss about the meaning of this sudden change. We stared blankly now at each other, and now at the women..."; 19.3 "When Quartilla said this, Ascyltos was momentarily struck dumb; I felt colder than a Gallic winter and could not utter a word"; 19.6 "At that moment of bewilderment, our entire resolve melted away. Certain death began to shroud our unhappy eyes"; 21.1 "We would have cried out in our wretched state, but there was no one at hand to assist us."[19]

What impresses most is the interaction between Encolpius's distrust of making any sense out of narrated events and the preponderance of stage effects and role-playing in the Quartilla 'scenes.' The bolt giving way "of its own accord" (*Sat*. 16.2), and introducing the epiphany of a deity (17.1 *intravit ipsa*), is a parody of a literary topos from Callimachus to Apuleius;[20] when Quartilla keeps weeping for a long time, Encolpius waits for an explanation of "this tearful demonstration of grief" (17.2 *lacrimas ad ostentationem doloris paratas*); her charge of sacrilege against our heroes leads with an even metaliterary 'display-idea': "Where did you learn to outdo the story-books in your thieving?," whereby their wickedness even *surpasses fiction* (17.4 *fabulas*[21] *etiam antecessura*

---

[18] On this peculiar "attacco erotico" see A. Aragosti, in Aragosti-Cosci-Cotrozzi, 1988, 110.

[19] Cf. *Sat*. 16.2 *sera sua sponte delapsa cecidit*;17.1 *Tacentibus adhuc nobis et ad neutram partem adsentationem flectentibus intravit ipsa*; 17.2 *Ac ne tunc quidem nos ullum adiecimus verbum*; 19.1 *Cum interim nos quae tamen repentina esset mutatio animorum facta ignoraremus*; 19.3 *[...] Ego autem frigidior hieme Gallica factus nullum potui verbum emittere*; 19.6 *[...] Mors non dubia miserorum oculos coepit obducere*; 21.1 *Volebamus miseri exclamare, sed nec in auxilio erat quisquam*.

[20] Schmeling, 2011, 46. Quartilla's arrival emphasizes astonishment and uncertainty: see P. Cosci, in Aragosti-Cosci-Cotrozzi, 1988, 51.

[21] If *fabulae* refers to Greek "novels" (but Schmeling, 2011, 49 can't exclude "theatre"), Encolpius and his friends are here appointed for the roles of robbers and pirates of Greek romances. The five surviving complete novels (by Chariton, Achilles Tatius, Longus, Xeno-

latrocinia). At 18.2, as the woman sinks "her entire face and breast" into Encolpius's bed, our narrator portrays himself as "shaken simultaneously by pity and fear" (*et misericordia turbatus et metu*), not unlike viewers/readers watching/reading a Greek tragedy, according to Aristotle's assertions in his *Poetics*.[22] After Quartilla's declaration of truce, the entire place resounds with the laughter of mime (19.1 *mimico risu*),[23] whereas our narrating "I" gives up understanding what's really happening.[24] Later, the two Syrians intending to strip the place, aware of being caught in the act, collapse by a couch as if by a prearranged stratagem, and begin to snore (22.5). It is correct to admit that the topos of pretending to sleep, in order to deceive "or to avoid taking notice," is very old (Schmeling, 2011, 67): but what here matters again is that, in tune with the above examples, the ingenious *coup de théâtre* of feigned sleep plays no small part in *blurring the distinction* between reality and fiction.

A further key to the reading of the episode may be provided by the 'final frame' of the mock marriage between Giton and Pannychis. Through a "shamelessly opened" chink (26.4 *per rimam*

---

phon of Ephesus, Heliodorus: from mid-1st to third century AD) conform to a narrative framework consisting of regular shipwrecks, pirate abductions, intrigues of Tyche, intervention of a deity, fulfilled heterosexual desire of a virtuous young couple (Laird, 2007, 153 n. 7; Panayotakis, 2009, 58-9; Freudenburg, 2017, 2). On the controversial thesis advanced by Heinze, 1899 (the *Satyrica* as a parodic reversal of the standard story of a heterosexual couple), see von Albrecht, 1995, II, 1218-9; Conte, 1996, 32-4; Barchiesi, 1999, 126ff.; 140-1; Habermehl, 2006, xxix; Laird, 2007, 153ff.; Schmeling, 2011, xxx-xxxviii; Setaioli, 2011, 2ff.; 369-77.

[22] Cf. Aristotle *Poet.* 53b "It is possible for the evocation of fear and pity to result from the piece [...] anyone who hears the events which occur, shudders and feels pity at what happens" (Heath, 1996, 22).

[23] Ernout, 1970, 15: "ce rire théâtral"; Walsh, 1997, 14: "the laughter of the low stage."

[24] Peri, 2007, 49; 64ff., developing Laird, 1999, 217ff., argues that the reported speech is usually attributed by the narrator to characters showing inferiority or subalternity: here Encolpius has Quartilla address our heroes vehemently with the direct speech (*Sat.* 17.4-9 "Why have you behaved so recklessly? ... "), but he resorts to the reported speech as capable of expressing psychological subjection (18.3 "Shaken simultaneously by pity and fear, I urged her to be of good heart [...] none of us would divulge the rites"): with a resulting contrast between Encolpius's "denied word" ("parola negata") and the sound of laughter, tears, applause, and Quartilla's voice. Mentions of sounds and handclapping (18.7; 20.6; 23.2; 24.2) corroborate the theatrical quality of the episode: see A. Cotrozzi, in Aragosti-Cosci-Cotrozzi, 1988, 69; Panayotakis, 1995, 39.

improbe diductam), Quartilla "viewed (*speculabatur*) their youthful sport (*lusum puerilem*) with prurient attention (*libidinosa diligentia*)." "Then with caressing hand (26.5 *lenta manu*) she drew me to watch the spectacle as well (*ad idem spectaculum*)" (Sullivan, 1968, 239).[25] By contrast with Quartilla's very few sexual contacts during events (quite transient, indeed: with Giton at 24.5-7; with Encolpius at 26.5), her voyeurism/scopophilia (cf. above: *speculabatur/spectaculum*) stands out as a significant feature: from her vantage point, as director/spectator rather than participant in the plot, Quartilla becomes ringleader of the performance. In Slater's appropriate words, she is the "final arbiter of meaning and reality" (Slater, 1990, 45): when Encolpius, asking for an *embasicoetas* (24.1 "a tumbler to have in bed"), receives a *cinaedus* (who assaults him) from Quartilla, because "a catamite is also called a tumbler" (24.3), her humorous word pun exposes Quartilla's ability to determine the reactions of *her* audience, as other characters do with their roles.

As opposed to *Sat.* 1-5, where Encolpius shows full mastery of manipulating his audience (*in primis* the hapless Agamemnon) through the persuasiveness of words and action, at 16-26, with an audience now turning aggressive, our hero can't any longer get hold either of the meaning of *words* or of his freedom of *action*. Hand in hand with Encolpius (who first controls the plot at 1-5, but then blunders and – non metaphorically – *loses the plot* at 16-26), the reader is inevitably expected to identify and catch clues, in order to pay attention to every single piece of the uncanny Agamemnon section and of the Quartilla puzzle, managing to see how all the narrative elements fit consistently together. The reader's role of observer is thus actualized, I think, *both* by staring at the manipulation of Agamemnon at the hands of a freeloader Encolpius, *and* by echoing (empathizing with) the theatrical sudden jumps of Quartilla's audience from tears into laughter (18.4 *ex lacrimis in risum*). In other words, in both sequences the reader will

[25] This is "the first patent example of scopophilia in the work" (for a similar episode, cf. *Sat.* 140.4-11).

accommodate the 'centrifugal' – so to speak – thrust of suggestions and textual challenges spread all over such episodes, and resist the urge to hold onto a 'centripetal' all-encompassing *interpretation* of apparently disconnected scenes ... In the particular case of the Quartilla section, we have seen how Encolpius's very act of telling the tale, dotted with allusive role-playing, does not simply consist of 'theatrical' hints at mime (or comedy or Senecan tragedy), but is strongly affected by the disturbing feeling that *appearances can be deceiving*.[26] It is no accident that such a humorous 'hermeneutic' chaos – a fictional breakdown of Encolpius's confidence in his own act of narrating? – ends up strengthening the link between narrator and actor, and at the same time builds up our perception that the Petronian novel is *a changing object* which, like Stanley Fish's kinetic artefact, is here eventually *refusing to stay still*.[27]

2.4 LOST IN AMAZEMENT

Should this instability of sensory perception (from both sides: narrator and reader) be identified in the *Cena Trimalchionis* as well? In an artificially extended night (*Sat.* 73.6-74.1"'So let's have a ball and go on eating until daylight'. As he was saying this, a cock crew. This worried Trimalchio"), Trimalchio's dinner "is really a repetition of Quartilla's nocturnal celebrations" (Rimell, 2002, 36).[28] The "Campanian millionaire" (Walsh, 1970, 38)[29] and tasteless host Trimalchio, almost continuously on stage from *Sat.* 27.5 to 78.5,[30] is the lord of the feast, "a man of supreme refine-

---

[26] Just look at the images of impotence/failure and death/torture, instead of "prodigious sexual successes" (Slater, 1990, 40: with Encolpius and Ascyltos unable to perform sexually), in an assault-sequence where some women and a *cinaedus* become the 'unnatural' aggressors. Petronian language "evokes" the theatre: see Rosati, 1999, 94.

[27] See above, p. 21 nn. 2-3.

[28] Darkness is a frequent metaphor "for deception or veiling" throughout the novel: cf. *Sat.* 101.11; 103.2; 112.5.

[29] For the analogous portrait of Calvisius Sabinus in Seneca *Ep.* 27.5-8, see Habermehl, 2006, xxx n. 65.

[30] In the sequence 41.9-47.1 Trimalchio's stomach has to respond to nature's call, which encourages the company to gossip freely (41.9 *Nos libertatem sine tyranno nacti coepimus invitare convivarum sermones*).

ment" (26.9 *lautissimus homo*), who dominates the action of the *Cena*-drama, whereas – in the words of Edward Courtney – Encolpius "withdraws from the centre to the periphery as a mere spectator" (Courtney, 2001, 73 n. 4; 75). But what kind of visual capacity does Encolpius actually show as *spectator*? Things are not what they seem for the entire length of the dinner party, as appearances are unfocused, misleading, and unpredictable by definition: the *Cena* can infact be regarded as a series of performances, where the staging of courses and frolics – courses *disguised as* frolics, tricks *in form of* food – must gratify both eye and palate, following a well-established strategy which tends to ignore both the narrator's command and the reader's expectations.

'Novelty' amazes everyone: more accurately, it amazes every reader through our dazed *spectator*'s eyes. "We noticed some other unusual features" (*Sat.* 27.3 *Notavimus etiam res novas*); "unusual enough to rivet the eyes of all of us" (35.1 *novitas tamen omnium convertit oculos*); "waiting to see what new surprise heaven was about to reveal" (60.2 *expectantes quid novide caelo nuntiaretur*); "I am ashamed to recount the unprecedented performance that followed" (70.8 *Pudet referre quae secuntur: inaudito enim more...*); "It was enough to make you spew. Trimalchio, so earnest in his repulsive drunkenness, ordered trumpeters to be summoned to the dining-room as a new form of entertainment" (78.5 *Ibat res ad summam nauseam, cum Trimalchio ebrietate turpissima gravis novum acroama, cornicines, in triclinium iussit adduci*). Is this spectator simply "poor and naïve" (Rosati, 1999, 87)? Probably nowhere in the *Satyrica* is Encolpius's constricted vision better demonstrated than in the *Cena*: let's view further passages, in order to explore some creative processes at work in the novel, and eventually to ask ourselves – with Victoria Rimell – whether, and to what extent, "Encolpius the myopic fool is also our eyes and ears in this fiction" (Rimell, 2002, 44).

The narrating voice concentrates on two ancient eunuchs facing Trimalchio, ushering in some divertissement on *lautus* and derivatives: "As we were admiring these refinements" (27.4 *Cum has ergo miraremur lautitias*). A "most elegant hors d'oeuvre" impresses the audience (31.8 *gustatio valde lauta*): "a donkey ... bearing a double pannier ... two dishes, on the rims of which were engraved Trimalchio's name and their weight in silver ... We were enjoying this refined fare" (32.1 *In his eramus lautitiis*). "That genious of a cook then matched this exhibition of refinement" (70.7 *Has lautitias aequavit ingeniosus cocus*), by bringing in snails on a silver gridiron. In these passages, is Encolpius "serious or poking fun" (Schmeling, 2011, 89.)[31] at the earlier description (cf. 26.9) of Trimalchio as *lautissimus homo*? We cannot be certain.[32] Anyway, "reporting all the details would be tedious" (28.1 *longum erat singula excipere*): Trimalchio, doused with fragrant oil, is being rubbed down "with bath-towels of softest wool"; meanwhile three masseurs are "drinking Falernian before his eyes," and the man is "installed in a litter, wrapped in a scarlet dressing-gown" (28.2-4).

Significantly enough, even before dinner starts Encolpius's amazement is already described as food satiety: "Quite wonderstruck we walked behind" (28.6 *Sequimur nos admiratione iam saturi*), like his later comment on the exhibits at the entrance of the *triclinium*: "Sated with these delights" (30.5 *His repleti voluptatibus*). Whereas the astonishing entrance leaves our hero "lost in amazement at all this" (29.1 *ego dum omnia stupeo*), the dinner looks like a sort of funeral afterlife protected by "a massive dog" painted in colour on the dining room wall (*canis ingens, catena vinctus*): Encolpius gets scared as if in front of a real dog.[33] Then he gathers "his wits" (29.2 *collecto spiritu*) and proceeds to examine the entire wall,[34] which portrays details of Trimalchio's career, since he had learnt accountancy until he was lifted by Mercury on to a high platform (29.3-5). Confused as he is, our spectator observes "a

[31] A similar doubt may be aroused by the passage "we got started on the wine, taking the greatest pains to express our wonder at all the elegance" (34.8 *Potantibus ergo nobis et accuratissime lautitias mirantibus*), after Trimalchio serves "Falernian wine of Opimian vintage" (34.6); but cf. also the "congenial gossip" at 39.1 (*dulces fabulas*).

[32] Courtney, 2001, 85 sounds too confident about it: "*lautitiae*, a word which Encolpius used without sarcasm in 32.1."

[33] A vicious dog will reappear at *Sat.* 64.7, perhaps the same as the one on a chain at 72.7.

[34] It is "a visual echo" (Schmeling, 2011, 95) of Aeneas admiring the work of Daedalus in the temple of Apollo at Cumae, before entering the *Avernus* (Virgil *Aen.* 6.20-33).

team of runners practising under their trainer," also in the colonnade (*in porticu*) (29.7), where *in porticu* may mean either *on* the colonnade walls, or *within* them (Rimell, 2002, 38): are we sure that Encolpius is *not* overshadowing the difference between what is happening in real life and what belongs to the two-dimensional painted freize?

The suspicion is reinforced by the narrator's listing in bulk of what the wall (apparently) portrays at 29.8 (amongst other items, household gods in silver, a marble statue of Venus, a golden container with Trimalchio's beard...); then, after questioning the porter, Encolpius finds out (29.9) that *Iliad* and *Odyssey* are subjects of other pictures on display in the *atrium*, as well: is there a need for a commentary below such a popular narrative (cf. *vice versa* the necessary captions at 29.3 for the details of Trimalchio's career)? Why does Encolpius seem unable to decode the Homeric pictures? Apart from problems caused by gaps in the text at 30.1,[35] rather than explaining Encolpius's inability to interpret what he sees as an alleged "distortion" of the Homeric pictures by Trimalchio,[36] I would support a more flexible approach: "is it an indication of our narrator's (contrived?) ignorance, of the doorman's ignorance or desire to impress, or of Trimalchio's hype?" (Rimell, 2002, 45 n. 21).

Once the company enters the *triclinium*, a dumb Encolpius notices how 'theatrical' the banquet is: "You would have thought it was a dancer's supporting group" (31.7 *pantomimi chorum ... crederes*). Further on, he is stunned by a couple of tricks devised by Trimalchio (33.8: a wooden hen from which pea-hens' eggs were extracted, containing plump little fig-peckers "coated in pepper yolk of egg"; 35.1-6: a circular plate having "the twelve signs of the Zodiac in sequence round it," with appropriate food matching each of the subjects, in form of a rebus), Encolpius is not even able

[35] Very little is gained from the corrupted *non licebat † multaciam † considerare* ("we were unable [...] to examine [...]"), which makes the sentence "awkward" in any case: Schmeling, 2011, 102.

[36] Schmeling, 2011, 101 agrees with Courtney, 2001, 79.

to understand the facetious word pun at 36.2-8.[37] As Trimalchio calls out '*Carpe*', a carver comes forward cutting up some meat; but since the host keeps repeating 'Carpe, carpe', our narrator, suspecting a sophisticated joke, *for the second time* asks his neighbour for explanations: the carver's name being *Carpus*, whenever Trimalchio cries '*Carpe*' (vocative identical with the imperative of *carpere*=to carve), in one shot he is calling on him and giving instructions.[38]

Encolpius is now so worn out that he can hardly tolerate Trimalchio or "swallow another mouthful" (37.1 *non potui amplius quicquam gustare*), but he still has the strength of enquiring (*third time!*) about Fortunata, Trimalchio's wife. Frustration (or a pose superbly contrived by the narrator?) proves to make Encolpius desire "to learn as much as possible" (*ut quam plurima exciperem*), diverting his attention from the pervasive impression of unreality and causing him to "elicit all the gossip" (*accersere fabulas*). A little further on, in front of a massive boar on a tray "wearing the cup of freedom" (40.3 *aper ... pilleatus*), Encolpius exhausts "every fatuous explanation" (41.2 *postquam itaque omnis bacalausias consumpsi*). Once again, faced with the upteenth food-test to solve, he asks for the solution from his "interpreter" Hermeros, who mercilessly stresses on its being "no riddle" (41.3 *non enim aenigma est*):[39] since the day before the boar has been "set scot-free,"[40] he is a freedman today (*libertus revertitur*), thus entitled to wear a *pilleus*. Trimalchio wisely switches between riddles and tricks in capturing his guests. The mislead narrator has no choice but to curse his own "stupidi-

---

[37] Peri, 2007, 84 ff. notes that Encolpius's word "stooges for someone else's" ("*fa da spalla* a quella altrui"): surprised and concerned at the incidents of the *Cena*, his interventions – in reported speech – are always followed by answers given in direct speech, i.e. neat, high-profile, and bright ones.

[38] On this "verbal wit," see Sullivan, 1968, 225ff.

[39] At 41.2 *duravi interrogare illum interpretem meum quid me torqueret* ("I steeled myself to seek the solution to my nagging problem from that informant of mine"), Petersmann, 1999, 117 argues for not changing *quid* (*codex Traguriensis*) to *quod* (easy conjecture by nearly all editors): traits of "vulgar speech" (cf. the use of interrogative instead of relative pronoun in vulgar Latin) may intrude in Encolpius's sophisticated prose, because of the narrator's "intention to create a realistic portrait of the colloquial speech."

[40] 41.4 *dimissus* means here "sent back by sated guests": Schmeling, 2011, 160.

ty" (41.5 *damnavi ego stuporem meum*), and to avoid asking for anything more, in order not to give the impression of never "having dined in respectable company."[41]

Encolpius's sense of loss of control is steadily enhanced by the indecipherable 'codes' of trickery and deceit which entangle him. After Trimalchio has come back from the lavatory, the display of three pigs wearing halters and bells makes the narrator – as well as us readers/spectators! – foresee a circus act, with the pigs "going to perform some tricks" (47.9 *portenta aliqua facturos*): but as Trimalchio dispells any doubt, having the oldest pig slaughtered by the cook, Encolpius seems affected by an increasing sense of heavy saturation. It's an important turning point in the *Cena*, I think. When the pig reappears on a dish, perfectly cooked at amazing speed, and Trimalchio bursts out astounded "Has this pig not been gutted?" threatening to torture the absent-minded cook, our hard-hearted narrator (49.7 *crudelissimae severitatis*) can't contain himself. At this stage, no longer conditioned to look for tricks, while the guests intercede in favour of the cook, Encolpius even goes so far as to erase any sense of sympathy and mercy:[42] "he must obviously be the most slovenly of slaves. Could anyone forget to gut a pig?" (*plane ... hic debet servus esse nequissimus: aliquis oblivisceretur porcum exinterare?*). But a trick occurs this time too: Trimalchio's face softens to a smile, the forgiven cook eviscerates the pig and the slit belly lets sausages and black puddings – *disguised* as liver, lungs, and intestines – come tumbling out (49.10).[43]

When at 54.3 a slave tumbles down (accidentally?) on top of Trimalchio, Encolpius appears now to feel considerably troubled, expecting that when the boy pleads to be forgiven, "some trick was

[41] Codoñer, 1995, 701ff. argues that Encolpius, basically objective as narrator of the *Cena*, shifts from an initial astonishment to the withdrawal state of his *stupor* at 41.5, inasmuch as freedmen at the table would possess the key to the understanding of events. About Trimalchio's resourceful gimmick see Labate, 2020, 85-7.

[42] Sullivan, 1968, 153; Courtney, 2001, 98.

[43] Rosati, 1999, 96-99 remarks that Trimalchio, attracted by "the human ability to control and manipulate nature," aims to show his guests "the entire process of cooking": via an illusionistic trick, reality is imitated with an *automatum* (50.1) and the pig's belly supplies "perfectly processed entrails" in form of sausages and black pudding.

being engineered by comic means" (*per ridiculum aliquid catastropha*[44] *quaereretur*), especially since he has not yet forgotten the uncomfortable precedent (49.1-10) of "the cook who had omitted to cut the pig" (*cocus ille, qui oblitus fuerat porcum exinterare*). Is the narrator 'correct' in his suspicion of some further *automatum*, a theatrical trick created by Trimalchio, or shall we believe – with Aldo Setaioli – that this one is the only "unplanned entertainment" (Setaioli, 2004, 63) of the entire *Cena*? In a similar episode, at 52.3-6, a slave had been finally pardoned after dropping a cup, thanks to the guests intercessions: both incidents make a reader suppose that Trimalchio's feigned anger usually allows his guests to "plead with him to forgive the slave."[45] Moreover, Encolpius's very comment on Trimalchio's issue of the decree declaring the slave free ("my suspicions were not far off the mark": 54.5 *nec longe aberravit suspicio mea*) does merely account for the outcome of the ruse, but can't properly answer a reader's question 'upstream': does Trimalchio's formulaic opening statement, "none of my arrangements is without a purpose" (39.14 *nihil sine ratione facio*), meaning that, if anything unplanned happens, our circumspect and keen host knows how to take advantage of the accident, making 'fortuity' an effective *coup de théâtre*? The question still stands.[46]

Encolpius's sense of oppression is however increasing. During a performance in Greek verses enacted by some *Homeristae* (mock-heroic Homeric actors), where an 'Ajax' plays the madman[47] and

---

[44] The Greek technical term for the end of a play (Collignon, 1892, 276) reveals Encolpius's familiarity with the *ludi* (Rosati, 1999, 93): cf. 31.7 "dancers' group" (*pantomimi chorum*: see above); 36.6 "to the music of a water-organist" (*hydraule cantante*); 47.9; 60.2 "acrobats" (*petauristarios/us*).

[45] Schmeling, 2011, 215 (cf. *Sat.* 30.11-31.1; 49.6).

[46] Freudenburg, 2017, 110ff. detects a number of "accidents and chance intrusions that are not part of his carefully designed script"; yet, as far as the slave's fall is concerned (*Sat.* 54.3), he finds it impossible to know if Trimalchio planned it or "merely made the most of a 'real' accident by playing it up as part of his show. Encolpius cannot tell, and neither can we."

[47] Strong fighter in the Trojan war (also after Achilles' death), Ajax got angry at Odysseus being awarded Achilles' armour, and was struck by Athena with madness: finding himself in the middle of a crowd of shapes, he slaughtered many of them, thinking them fellow fighters. After coming to his senses, he felt so humiliated that he decided to kill himself. Ajax in mythology: Graves, 1979, 81e; 137i; 163-5 *passim*; Kirk, 1984, 214. About the Roman traditional 'acrobatic dance' of Ajax on his sword, see Aragosti, 1995, 259 n. 175.

finishes off a huge, boiled calf (59.2-7), "suddenly the ceiling panels began to rumble, and the entire dining-room shook" (60.1). The startled narrator jumps from his seat, once again scared that "some acrobat might come down through the roof" (60.2 *consternatus ego exsurrexi, et timui ne per tectum petauristaurius aliquis descenderet*), and gets in expectation of a strange augury announced from heaven (*quid novi de caelo nuntiaretur*).[48] A hoop is let down, with jars of perfume to be taken as departing-presents; but when cakes and fruit begin to squirt out saffron, "the juice shot disconcertingly" (60.6 *molestus umor*) even into the faces of our heroes. A reader might wonder whether the liquid proves so "unpleasant" *also* because Encolpius's tensions and suspicions are permanently inflamed. Which perhaps can also explain why our narrator appears definitely *inadequate* – and, for her/his part, a reader becomes *hesitant* – to interpret Trimalchio's riddles unambiguously.

At 69.8, for instance, at the climax of a dessert made up of *food imitating other food,* what appears to be a fat goose surrounded by fish and birds is announced by Trimalchio as "made out of a single body," an utterance which Encolpius blatantly explains as an allusive reference to "clay" (or "wax"), because it reminds him of "counterfeit dinners of this kind served up at Rome during the Saturnalia" (69.9 *facta sunt ... certe de luto. Vidi Romae Saturnalibus eiusmodi cenarum imaginem fieri*).[49] But he fails again. Trimalchio seizes the opportunity to remark that the dish is all made of pork, because his outstanding cook – a former slave suitably called Daedalus[50] – can *convert* any kind of food into any other (70.2): he is a talented sort of chef-demiurge, who can manipulate and en-

[48] Schmeling, 2011, 248 suggests a hint at the technical language of augury, with Encolpius taking the auspices "from the movable ceiling," like a Roman magistrate interpreting *omina* from the sky.

[49] Varro *Lat.* 5.64 informs that "waxlights are presented to patrons at the Saturnalia" (Kent, 1958, 61).

[50] Well-known as a miracle-worker and architect, Daedalus built the Minotaur's Labyrinth at Knossos (Crete), and gave Ariadne, Minos' daughter, a thread which helped Theseus escape the Labyrinth after killing the Minotaur. Daedalus in mythology: Kerényi, 1962, 98; Lübker, 1989, 342.

liven the nature of animals, *metamorphosing* them before everybody's astonished eyes.[51]

With *Sat.* 72 a 'shrewd' reader, presumably ceasing to adopt a 'watchful waiting' attitude, should eventually feel capable of identifying and connecting incidents that are far away from each other all over the *Cena*, within an idea of Petronian "self-referentiality."[52] After Trimalchio's reading out of his will, instructions concerning his tomb, and dictation of its inscription (71.1-12), everyone begins to weep copiously, Encolpius included (72.2 "even I had begun to blub": *coeperam etiam ego plorare*). As the host invites the crowd to a *balneum*, his private bath, our heroes can't pass up a prime opportunity to escape the *Cena*, but at the gate a dog on a chain (*canis catenarius*) "greeted us with such a din that Ascyltos actually fell into the pond (*in piscinam*)." The narrator, equally drunk (*nec non ego quoque ebrius*), earlier scared "at the sight even of a painted dog" at 29.1 (*qui etiam pictum timueram canem*), tries to help his friend, but is pulled *in eundem gurgitem*, "into the same pool" (72.5ff.). Meanwhile Giton throws in front of the barking dog all the morsels left over from the dinner, thus distracting and quietening down the beast (72.9). But the doorman doesn't let them out of the gate, because

---

[51] Rimell, 2002, 54-5 emphasizes how such a narrative incident, worth reading as a "theatrical text" like most of Encolpius's adventures during the *Cena*, somehow recalls the imaginative power of "Ovidian metamorphosis," and consistently demands "the reader's rapidly shifting perspective." Further suggestions are incorporated in the wide-ranging view of Rimell's "innovative and daring scholarly approach to Petronius" (Panayotakis, 2004, 155). The zodiac dish at 35.1-6 introduces metaphors dominating the *Cena* (Labate, 2020, 82-5). By associating "people and personalities with food to be eaten," the dish might suggest that "we are what we eat," and that "the guests are about to eat themselves" (pp. 52-3: e.g. "Ram=chick-peas shaped like a ram's head; Bull=a portion of beef; Twins=testicles and kidneys; Crab=crown; Lion=an African fig"): so the "eater/eaten hierarchy," pin of a "civilised society" implying rejection of cannibalism, proves consequently violated. Rimell argues that in the *Cena* the "tension between inside and outside bodies" (i.e., a kind of breakdown of the "integral self") emerges indirectly at *Sat.* 56.1-3, where Trimalchio regards the professions of doctors and money-lenders as the most difficult after writing: like the writer, a doctor knows what we have *beneath* the skin, and a money-lender discerns the copper lurking *beneath* the silver (pp. 9ff.). *Interiors* can be threatening, like the belly of the Trojan horse in the *Troiae Halosis* (pp. 60-76 on *Sat.* 89), whereas *exteriors* can be misleading, just like the dishes served by Trimalchio during the entire *Cena*. Similarly, Slater, 1990, 144 (on the same *Sat.* 56.1-3): "there are two levels to the literary work, an accessible surface and a hidden interior." *Who* then (and *how*) should (re-)establish the relationship between the two?

[52] Panayotakis, 2004, 153; 2009, 61-2.

nobody can leave by the same entrance: "they come in one way, and go out another" (72.10 *alia intrant, alia exeunt*). At this time, "what were we poor wretches to do, hemmed in as we were in this new kind of labyrinth?" (73.1 *quid faciamus homines miserrimi et novi generis labyrintho inclusi [...]?*).[53]

The passage is a quite transparent catalyst of the peculiar Petronian symbolism. The appearance of the "supreme trickster Daedalus"[54] at 70.2 paves the way for a multi-layered poetic association of the labyrinth with Aeneas' descent into the Virgilian *Avernus*. It suggests the troubles of the hero finally emerging by a different exit,[55] and shows off the epic term *gurges* (72.7: the river Acheron guarded by Charon in the *Aeneid* [Virgil *Aen.* 6.295ff]) as a too imposing word for the water of the Petronian pool/fish-pond, but a particularly suitable one for our unheroic Encolpius.The intertextual grid of the Virgilian hints skilfully covers the entire incident: the dog is offered food by Giton for appeasement (72.9), just like the Virgilian Sibyl silences Cerberus with some narcotic bread,[56] within the keenly constructed parallelism between the *painted* dog at 29.1, that discourages entries, and the *real* dog at 72.7, that discourages exits (Schmeling, 2011, 304). Not much further on, the Giton/Sibyl match will pass the baton to the Giton/Ariadne one. As our heroes succeed in escaping from the *Cena*, taking to their heels "as rapidly as if there really were a fire" (78.8), they will realise they have no torch to show them the way in their wandering (79.1). Giton will then play Ariadne, showing

[53] Trimalchio's house is a sort of underworld labyrinth (Bodel, 1999, 43), where the image of entering and exiting by different doors has some common grounds with Apuleius *Met.* 1.15 (Schmeling, 2011, 306). If the *Cena* can be interpreted *sub specie labyrinthi*, the metaphor is fruitful elsewhere also: cf. the brothel at 7.4; Lichas's ship at 101.7ff. (Fedeli, 1981, 109-13).

[54] Courtney, 2001, 112 recalls Daedalus's previous occurrence at 52.2 (portrayed on a silver bowl, "Daedalus is enclosing Niobe in the Trojan horse"), in Trimalchio's "marvellous" confused amalgamation of three different myths: Schmeling, 2011, 214.

[55] The golden temple of Apollo at Cumae was established by Daedalus (Virgil *Aen.* 6.14ff.): on its doors Aeneas admires the portrait of Daedalus's labyrinth (*Aen.* 6.29-30), before entering the Underworld helped by the Cumaean Sibyl. After overcoming difficulties (*Aen.* 6.125-31), Aeneas will definitely emerge by the ivory door at 6.897-9.

[56] Virgil *Aen.* 6.417-23. Cerberus, the three-headed hound, guards the gates of the Underworld: cf. Virgil *Aen.* 6.395ff. Cerberus in mythology: Kerényi, 1962, 53; 85; 204; Graves, 1979, 103c; 108,7; 139c; Burkert, 1991, 151; 154.

the way through the labyrinth, after wisely marking every post and pillar with chalk signs (79.4), so as to pierce "the impenetrable darkness" (*spississimam noctem*) with their conspicuous whiteness.

2.5 A SECOND ACHILLES, A SECOND AENEAS

If the reader believes (s)he is beholding the world of Agamemnon, Quartilla, and Trimalchio through Encolpius's eyes, how trustworthy can this first-person narrative be? Niall Slater has inquired into the idea of an "expectation of unity" (Slater, 1990, 137), which – in spite of the fragmentary nature of Petronius's text – is raised in our minds, as readers, by Encolpius's first-person voice. Moreover, Gian Biagio Conte has recognised its "inherent quality of verisimilitude," because its claim to offer "firsthand experiences" apparently fosters a convincing ability to grant an "eye-witness testimony" (Conte, 1996, 23). What has emerged so far from the passages scrutinized above, is that the world of the Petronian text is being experienced, through an astounding and hermetic Encolpius, by a reader coming across scenes displayed by the multi-faceted personality of a homodiegetic first-person narrator.[57]

In the dialogue with Agamemnon, a smart and manipulative student tries to cadge an invitation to dinner off a teacher of rhetoric (*Sat.* 1.1-6.1; cf. 10.1-3). Beginning to hare after Ascyltos, he wanders around in circles, losing his way (6.2-7.4). Assailed by Quartilla, her maids (19.4 *tres mulierculae*), and a catamite, he turns out to be incapable of keeping control over events and freedom of action, restricting himself to voyeuristic detachment (16.1-26.6). The *Cena Trimalchionis* demands a more flexible understanding from a reader. Before entering Trimalchio's *triclinium,* Encolpius proves unable to distinguish reality from painted images, even to decode some Homeric pictures (28.6-30.1). Bewildered by Trimalchio's devised tricks and deceptive riddles all over the *Cena,* Encolpius proves to be slow on the uptake of word puns (31.7-49.10): Roger Beck has reckoned 14 (!) misinterpretations of Trimalchio's

[57] Genette, 1980, 244-5 uses "homodiegetic" for a narrative where "the narrator is present as a character in the story he tells" ("heterodiegetic" when the narrator is "absent" from it).

ruses on the part of Encolpius, within ever-increasing harsh assessment of the host's behaviour, up to the peak: 78.5 *ibat res ad summam nauseam*.[58] So, progressively startled by inflaming tensions and suspicions (54.1-70.3),[59] he ends up blind drunk; rescued from the fish-pond, he finds himself helplessly imprisoned with his *fratres* in the "novel labyrinth" (72.5-73.1 *novi generis labyrinth inclusi*). Needless to say, most of these sequences appear strongly permeated by what Victoria Rimell has called "the constant collision and confusion between the real and the artificial": can we ever tell when, or where, Encolpius is narrating "straight or pretending"? (Rimell, 2007, 114 n. 25; 116).

Shrewd narrative techniques make the narrator display his artistic genius. After the *Cena*, as Askyltos removes Giton from Encolpius's side, transferring him to his own bed (79.9), the narrator blames both Ascyltos, as a slave freed for sexual favours, and Giton, for putting on a woman's dress on the day he assumed the *toga virilis* (81.4 ff.): Encolpius depicts himself as an *exul* abandoned by Giton, who jeers with Ascyltos at his loneliness (*derident solitudinem meam*). What follows in the plot is the object of Gian Biagio Conte's scrutiny on a basic aspect of Encolpius's character: his "mythomaniac" infatuation with literary myth (Conte, 1996, 1-35; *passim)*.

According to this line of interpretation, the narrator's mind would tend to get exhausted on identifying with heroic roles among mythical *dramatis personae*, images that belong to Encolpius's sophisticated subsequent literary experiences in Greek and Latin culture. A contemporary reader – consistent with her/his store of knowledge and personal sensitiveness – may add to Conte's examples some further ones, where Encolpius, intoxicated by Greek and Roman elegy, epic, drama, or even judicial oratory, portrays himself as prone to self-glorifying: what will emerge is

[58] Applying important results of Beck, 1973, focused on the distinction beween Encolpius narrator and Encolpius protagonist ("narrating I" vs. "experiencing I"), Beck, 1975, 270 ff. investigates on Encolpius's evaluative language in his report of the *Cena*. Full discussion in Vannini, 2007, 236-7.

[59] In Encolpius's negative views on the *Cena*, Jones, 1987, 810ff. recognises some cases where a deep difference between the narrating voice and the protagonist should not be detected.

the dramatization of the miserable reality of the character's everyday, and the exploitation of high poetic language, in the illustration of mean themes, which will result in a structured and intriguing farce, fruit of a "misconceived tragicizing of experience."[60] In this respect, Encolpius's recalling of his expropriation by Ascyltos (who has just taken away his beloved Giton) sounds like a reiteration of Achilles' conversation with his mother Thetis, after being deprived of Briseis by Agamemnon.[61] Ready to avenge his wrongs, he buckles on his sword: "Then I hurtled out of doors, and stalked like a madman round all the colonnades" (82.1 *mox in publicum prosilio furentisque more omnes circumeo porticus*), not differently from Aeneas, desperately searching for his wife Creusa along the burning streets of Troy.[62] A second Achilles wounded in his pride, a second Aeneas hunting the enemy, Encolpius is an antihero comically self-portrayed, not rarely with erotic connotations, as in turn one of the two epic wanderers by definition: Odysseus and Aeneas (Walsh, 1970, 28; 37). Incidentally, their accounts of venturesome traveling are in the crucial first-person narrative, respectively, of *Odyssey* Books 9-12 and *Aeneid* 2-3: just as the Homeric Poseidon persecuted Odysseus, and Juno tormented Aeneas in the *Aeneid*, Encolpius's enigmatic offense against Priapus causes the god to persecute him.

2.6 HAEC FABULA INTER AMANTES

On the subject of erotic infatuation and physical impotence, how should a reader of the present-day act in the face of the first-person narrative illustrating/recollecting Encolpius's approach to

---

[60] On the "Longing for the Sublime," see Conte, 1996, 37-72; about the agreement between the "hidden author" and the ideal reader, see below, pp. 47-8. Laird, 1998, 199 maintains that, if the "kind of mythomaniac" Encolpius is, depends "on which myths we think he has a mania about," other examples – equally convincing – might replace (or be placed next to) Conte's "selection of models": on Encolpius's soliloquy at 81, recalling also Catullus, Virgil or Ovid, see below, p. 79 nn. 186-7.

[61] Cf. Homer *Il.* 1.348ff. The comparison to Achilles was first investigated by Walsh, 1970, 36ff.; see Labate, 2020, 120.

[62] Cf. Virgil *Aen.* 2.749ff. At *Sat.* 82.1 in *haec locutus* ("having thus spoken") we recognise the Homeric formula *ōs eipōn* (*Il.* 1.68; *Od.* 1.125: Habermehl, 2006, 46); the syntagm *gladio latus cingor* ("I buckle on my sword") – where the prosaic *gladius* replaces the epic *ensis* or *ferrum* (Schmeling, 2011, 346) – adopts the vocabulary of Virgil *Aen.* 2.671 *hic ferro accingor rursus* (Conte, 1996, 9-10).

love and sex, a slippery issue by definition? Let's proceed step by step. At Croton the narrator, scared of presumed investigations that might betray Eumolpus's imposture,[63] will outline himself and his "impoverished and opportunistic fellow-travellers" (Bitel, 2006, 1) as living outside the law (125.4 "how grim it is for outlaws": *quam male est extra legem viventibus*): shall a reader assume *tout court* that in the extant *Satyrica* Encolpius and friends tend to draw inspiration from some looseness of sexual morals? And if so, how serious, pretended, or self-ironic would the treatment of this 'looseness' be? I think caution is required in taking account of this "unrestrained life full of escapades and love affairs" (Petersmann, 1999, 106).[64] What a reader can take away so far since the Quartilla episode, is that sexual excess is shattered by the overwhelming 'theatricality' of action: the reader has been finding out how interchangeable sexual roles go (active-passive; aggressor-aggressed) as far as overbearing both 'diegesis' and 'mimesis',[65] in the spirit of things not being what they seem.[66] This blurring of distinctions, between the real and the artificial, will involve the narrator's attitude towards sex in the other surviving sections of the *Satyrica*, where sex performances are not as 'concentrated' as in Quartilla's home.

Before verifying it in detail, it shouldn't go unnoticed that the Greek-Roman history of 'obscene' literature has a long-established tradition, inherent in the "frank acceptance of the physical side of life" (Sullivan, 1968, 232): which would explain why, in our novel,

---

[63] Eumolpus poses as a childless affluent man, in order to exploit the greed of legacy hunters (*Sat.* 117.4ff.), who at 124.3-4 compete to win Eumolpus's favour: Sullivan, 1968, 67. On Croton as a "poetic environment," see Rimell, 2002, 159 (chapt. 9-10 *passim*); on Juvenal 9.88-90 see Bellandi, 2021, 202-5. On the topos of *captatio* ("legacy-hunting") in Rome, a literary motif looking back to Horace *Serm.* 2.5.23ff., see Bodel, 2003; Schmeling, 2011, 443ff.

[64] About Encolpius's living *extra legem*, "sotto l'imperio della Fortuna," see Barchiesi, 1996, 194.

[65] *Diegesis*, as 'pure narrative', occurs when a poet speaks in his own person (Homer introducing the *Iliad*, vv. 1.1-16: 'indirect presentation'); but when he speaks as if he were one of his characters (Homer in the voice of Chryses: *Il.* 1.17-21: 'dramatic imitation'), that is *mimesis*: cf. Plato *Rep.* 3.392[d] 5ff. (Murray, 1996, 4; 70-1; 171); Aristotle *Poet.* 48[a] 22-24; 49b 11. For an introduction on this subject, see Porter Abbott, 2002, *passim*; Shen, 2005, 107; on the divergences between Plato and Aristotle, see Schaeffer-Vultur, 2005, 309.

[66] Whether or not it is to be regarded as a reversal (Slater, 1990, 42ff.) or a parody of Priapic ritual (Schmeling, 2011, xxvi), the Quartilla section incorporates more sex scenes than the remaining episodes of the extant *Satyrica*.

sex is treated from a viewpoint usually considered abnormal (voyeurism/scopophilia, heterosexual sodomy, performance of active and passive roles in homosexual intercourse, handling of genitals, incest motifs, seduction of children); but, at the same time, it lacks other forms, hinted at (or clear-cut) in satirical literature: lesbianism, oral sex, masturbation.[67] More specifically, within a general playful attitude to sex throughout the *Satyrica*, sexual intercourse very often proves unpleasant and disappointing, with Encolpius, however odd it may appear, being (or pretending to be) very rarely successful "in bed."[68] Anyway, Encolpius's failing engagement in heterosexual relations is not to be overestimated: owing to accidents of survival of the *Satyrica*, in a missing section of the novel his relationship with the high-class prostitute Tryphaena must have been rewarding, as clearly shown by references to it.[69] Moreover, Lichas's wife Hedyle seems to have been seduced by Encolpius in the past (106.2; 113.3).[70]

After planning to split up the love-triangle, at *Sat.* 10.7 Encolpius admits that "it was the sexual itch that motivated this quite sudden parting" (*hanc tam praecipitem divisionem libido faciebat*), but what follows leaves an indelible (self-ironic?) mark on his love affair with Giton: Encolpius's attachment to the boy is indeed "the unifying theme"[71] of the *Satyrica*. But while folding the boy in the closest embrace, Encolpius can't reach the climax, because Ascyltos comes creeping up to the door (11.1-2): from now

[67] See Zeitlin, 1971a, 655 n. 59; Courtney, 2001, 223.

[68] Richlin, 2009, 88. Greek novels offer a diverse landscape. Aragosti, 1995, 35 n. 38 argues that Achilles Tatius' *Leucippe and Clitophon*, departing from the usually idealized erotic-sentimental connotations for more realistic and humanized traits, tends to show a satisfied eroticism. Idem, 470 n. 378 reminds us that in Longus' *Daphnis and Chloe* the protagonist's *défaillance* (3.14.5) is a result of inexperience, rather than impotence.

[69] At *Sat.* 113.6-8, on board Lichas's ship, Encolpius, depressed and upset (*maestus et impatiens*) in front of Tryphaena "sitting in Giton's lap," is both angry with the boy, for robbing him of his earlier girlfriend (*quod amicam [...] auferret*), and with her, for seducing the boy (*quod puerum corrumperet*); resentment and anguish get enhanced by her not addressing him as "her favourite lover" (*gratum sibi amatorem*).

[70] We may add the unknown Albucia (see Schmeling, 2011, 595) and Doris (126.18) to the series of women then "wholly abjured through the hero's passion for Giton" (Walsh, 1970, 77); about Encolpius's relationship with Doris see Setaioli, 2018, 198.

[71] Walsh, 1970, 77.

on, the narrator will (feign to) live in permanent fear of being interrupted in his intercourse with Giton by 'a third wheel', not rarely settled in the position of a (fictional?) jealous husband, forced to confront Giton's infidelity.

Within the dispute over the possession of Giton (79.9-80.9), it has been perceptively noted that Encolpius's elated subjectivity is reflected in a different language from Ascyltos'.[72] The narrator emphasizes 'sublime' aspects of the relationship between Ascyltos and Giton: *iniuria* ("iniquity"), occurs twice; *fides* ("loyalty, trust") 3 times; *amicitia* ("friendship") twice; *sanguinis pignus* ("bond of blood") once; whereas Ascyltos considers Giton as *praeda* ("spoils"), or *partem meam*("my share"), referring to him as military booty. Additionally, Ascyltos describes the quarrel as a mere *discordia* ("disagreement"), while Encolpius believes to be taking part in a noble dispute (*parricidiali manu*, "with murderous intent"; *composui ad proeliandum gradum*, "I poised myself ready for the conflict"), even excusing Giton for his betrayal. Nonetheless, Giton's eventual choice for Ascyltos to be his *frater* (80.6) shows how hopelessly unrealistic Encolpius proves to be.

Astonished (*fulminatus*) by Giton's choice for Ascyltos, Encolpius reflects on being forlorn and humiliated, and groans from the depth of his heart (81.2 *redeunte in animum solitudine atque contemptu, ... inter tot altissimos gemitus*[73] *... proclamabam*). But the ornate rhetorical quality of his monologue, whose narrative texture is not alien to Greek novelists,[74] warns us that Encolpius is here *playing the role* of a deserted lover, as highlighted by his stylistic versatility. Just note: the emphatic *incipit* of the lament with *ergo*; the adjective tastefully spaced from the noun, like in major Roman poetry

[72] Gonoji, 1998, 181-3 explores the multifaceted aspects of Encolpius's "unreliability" as narrator, with regard to love and sex matters, observing attractive similarities between *Sat.* 79.9-80 and the contrast protagonist vs. interlocutor in Circe's episode (127.3ff.); on Gonoji's assumption, see Vannini, 2007, 240. About the fight between Encolpius and Ascyltos at 80.1-4, see Labate, 2020, 113ff.

[73] For a similar utterance cf. Virgil *Aen.* 11.95 (Habermehl, 2006, 33).

[74] In Greek novels we find evocations of recent hostile events, in which the protagonist begs the gods to release him from his present misfortune: cf. Chariton 3.6.6; Achilles Tatius 3.10.6 (Habermehl, 2006, 34; Schmeling, 2011, 342).

(81.3 *non iratum etiam innocentibus mare*: "by the sea that vents its rage even on the innocent");[75] the array of the ascending tricolon *effugi iudicium, harenae imposui, hospitem occidi* ("Did I evade justice, cheat the arena, murder my host").[76] It is here important to clarify that, besides evoking soliloquies common in ancient Roman comedy,[77] or of a hodgepodge of Homeric and Virgilian images (or even a parody of Sophocles and of the playwright Seneca),[78] a more nuanced reading would show how Encolpius's monologue might equally recall well-known laments in Latin literature: Catullus' and Ovid's Ariadne, Virgil's Dido, Ovid's Scylla and Medea.[79] In this specific regard, Catullus' Ariadne would appear particularly appropriate. When Encolpius visits the *pinakotheca*, faced with pictures of mythological *sine aemulo lovers* ("unrivalled": cf. Zeus/Ganymede; Hercules/Hylas; Apollo/Hyacinthus), he portrays himself as the only tragic lover incapable of embracing his loved one without the interference of a rival (83.1-6) (See Jensson, 2004, 160.): this incident may elegantly evoke, in the words of Andrew Laird, "the spectacular context of Ariadne's lament in Catullus' ekphrasis"; and the very arrival of Eumolpus on the scene to the aid of En-

---

[75] Cf. e.g. Lucretius 5.32 *aureaque Hesperidum servans fulgentia mala* ("and the guardian of the gleaming golden apples of the Hesperides"); Virgil *Aen.* 8.26 *nox erat et terras animalia fessa per omnis* ("It was nighttime, and over all lands [a deep slumber restrained] the weary beings"); Horace *Carm.* 3.14.5 *unico gaudens mulier marito* ("Spouse proud of her incomparable husband").

[76] The hyperbolic context, immediately preceding *mendicus, exul* ("a beggar and an exile"), "might be taken for a metaphor": Bitel, 2006. *Exul* occurs at 100.4, with the same connotation of "wanderer, vagrant" ("girovago": Vannini, 2010, 105). Encolpius is playing the role of the jilted lover, but each offense to which he confesses "has a small basis in reality," taking place in his imagination: see Schmeling, 1994-95, 218-9; 2011, xxxv-xxxvi; 343. For the "pointlessness of his past salvation in the light of his continued misfortune" (cf. Achilles Tatius 3.10.6), see Jensson, 2004, 148-9.

[77] Cf. the monologue of Phronesium in Plautus *Truc.* 449-64 (Panayotakis, 1995, 116), or Palaestra's speech in *Rud.* 185-201 (Laird, 1999, 223).

[78] See Collignon, 1892, 121; Slater, 1990, 90; Conte, 1996, 10-1: the *hypotext* (cf. below, p. 83 n. 198) for subsequent 'variations on a theme' is notoriously Homer *Il.* 1.348-50, where Achilles laments alone on the seashore after Briseis' abduction at the hands of Agamemnon.

[79] For Ariadne cf. Catullus 64.132-201; Ovid *Her.* 10; Ars 1.525ff.; Met. 8.172ff.; *Fast.* 3.459ff.; for Dido: Virgil *Aen.* 4.305ff. (also 365ff.; 534ff.; 590ff.); for Scylla (daughter of king Nisus): Ovid *Met.* 8.104ff. Habermehl, 2006, 32 recalls Medea in Ovid *Her.* 12 (on Medea's *epistula* to Jason, see Bessone, 1997).

colpius (83.7), might correspond to Bacchus's as rescuer of Ariadne in Catullus (64.251 ff.).[80]

It's true that Giton regularly betrays Encolpius: but the latter "remains devoted" (Slater, 1990, 248). The narrator can't withstand the blackmail of Giton's tears of repentance (91.6): "though you deserted me, I still love you (*amo te quamvis relictus*), and though the wound (*vulnus*) was deep, no scar (*cicatrix*) remains on my heart [...] did I merit this injustice (*dignus hac iniuria fui*)?"[81] Later on, Eumolpus's reaction to Giton's charm arouses an act of jealousy from Encolpius (94.6): "You must realise that the two emotions [Encolpius's rage and Eumolpus's lust] are incompatible. Imagine that I have gone off my head, give way before my madness, and get out!" (*vide, quam non conveniat his moribus. Puta igitur me furiosum esse, cede insaniae, id est, ocius foras exi*). The narrator's stage-acting, here revealed by the second imperative (*puta*: out of four imperatives in a row!), will then expand on the double semi-tragic attempt at suicide (*mimica mors*), both by Encolpius and Giton (94.8-15), humorously summed up as a *fabula* by Encolpius at 95.1: "while this farce between lovers was being enacted" (*dum haec fabula inter amantes luditur*).[82] Stage-acting or not, readers should not neglect some "romantic elements" (Sullivan, 1968, 234) of his physical relationship with Giton. On board Lichas's ship the *fratres* are about to run into a storm: "if you ever loved Encolpius truly, kiss me while you can, and snatch this joy from the impatient Fates" (114.9 *si vere Encolpion dilexisti, da oscula, dum licet, <et> ultimum hoc gaudium fatis properantibus cape*).

---

[80] Laird, 1999, 221-8 notes also that the current comparison of Encolpius's soliloquy to Achilles' speech is not properly "near the mark," as it is more concerned about his loss of honour than about Briseis herself. On "Catullus's own experiment" of *Carm.* 64, see Fordyce, 1961, 272-5; Fernandelli, 2016, *passim*.

[81] At 79.8 Encolpius may have been unsuccessful with Giton. Cf. his statement: "for my self-congratulation proved unfounded" (*sine causa gratulor mihi*), continuing in prose an erotic-elegiac utterance (cf. 79.8 vv. 1-5, in Phalaecean metre: see Aragosti, 1995, 468 n. 377). If he had been successful, why should Encolpius have then been deserted by Giton, who straight away went on to choose Ascyltos (80.6)? See Schmeling, 2011, 331; 504.

[82] See Slater, 1990, 102-3; for Codoñer, 1995, 711 an ironic narrator distances himself from the narrated events; on the imperative *puta*, see Schmeling, 2011, 386. For the "Doppelsuizid" (Habermehl, 2006, 252) in the Greek novel, cf. Achilles Tatius 3.16.2; Xenophon 2.3.1.

Plain *fabula*? Mere recollections of lovers/friends from a Greek novel, not to be parted by a shipwreck?[83] At Croton, with mistress Circe, our Encolpius falls short of sexual fulfillment twice (cf. 126.12-128.4 and 131.8-132.5). After the narrator's ecstatic description of Circe's appeal at their first meeting in a laurel grove (126.13-18),[84] they lie down together on the grass (127.10).[85] We first infer the heavy disappointment of the aristocratic woman at 128.1, expressed in such a way[86] that a reader can't distinguish if it's due to wounded pride or as a rhetorical pose: "So what is the problem? Does my kissing grate on you (*numquid te osculum meum offendit*)? Am I lacking in vigour for want of food? ... if it is none of these, does fear of Giton haunt you (*numquid Gitona times*)?." Does the 'Polyaenus' Encolpius really intend to seduce Circe?[87] In point of fact, it seems as if here, in spite of his boasted literary knowledge, the *scholasticus* Encolpius – disguised as 'Polyaenus Odysseus' and afraid to be bewitched – had ... forgotten "his antidote to Circean magic," causing the inevitable failure of his sexual performance (Rimell, 2007, 114).[88] At 129.1 Encolpius openly admits to Giton: "My brother, you must believe me. I have no awareness or feeling that I am a man (*non intellego me virum esse*). The part of my body which once made me an Achilles has been laid to rest" (*funerata est illa pars corporis, qua quondam Achilles*

[83] Cf. Achilles Tatius 3.5.4; Xenophon 3.2.12-13; Heliodorus 5.24 (in Schmeling, 2011, 438).
[84] Which seems to be drawing on some Ovidian "fetishistic scopophilia" (Hardie, 2002, 46ff.; 186ff.). For interesting Ovidian passages (*Am.* 1.5.9-10; 17-26; *Met.* 1.497-502; 10.247-58; 281-2), against the background of Encolpius's erotic account at 126.13-15, see Antoniadis, 2013, 185ff. For the description of Circe's beauty, Labate, 2020, 171ff. recalls Latin elegiac sources, such as Propertius 2.3.9-12; Ovid *Am.* 1.5.17-24.
[85] Petersmann, 1999, 114 remarks on the contrast between the "poetically coloured style" and the "the everyday style."
[86] Circe's reaction recalls Corinna's in Ovid *Am.* 3.7.77: Sullivan, 1968, 216-7; Rimell, 2002, 151.
[87] At *Sat.* 127.7 *polyaenus*, "much praised," is a Homeric epithet used by the Sirens for Odysseus at *Od.* 12.184 (Ernout, 1958, 152 n. 2): the pseudonym is here "useful for the deceit agreed upon with Eumolpus at Croton" (Conte, 1996, 91). But Slater, 1990, 247, excluding any intent to seduce Circe, thinks that "to be Polyaenus" means "to give up an old role as lover" (cf. 126.18 "so now for the very first time my erstwhile love-partner Doris sank low in my estimation": *itaque tunc primum Dorida vetus amator contempsi*).
[88] After all, the Crotonian woman is perfectly aware of the Homeric Circe, about whom she jokes at 127.6 (see Panayotakis, 2009, 56). The impotence-motif may also be a parody of the burning desire typical of lovers in Greek novels: see Aragosti, 1995, 470 n. 378.

eram).[89] Even so, all this doesn't mean that our self-examining narrator is incapable of speaking "in almost platonic terms" (Schmeling, 2011, 497-8) about his soul desiring to fly freely away from the body (130.5): "perhaps my body was dilatory, and my desire outstripped it (*forsitan animus antecessit corporis moram*). Perhaps my longing for complete fulfillment (*dum omnia concupisco*) caused me to wait too long, and so exhausted the pleasure (*voluptatem tempore consumpsi*)."[90]

Within such a theatrical pose, it has been keenly pointed out (Courtney, 2001, 224) that Encolpius tends not rarely to perceive reality, and the life of his own body, in terms of recurrent symbolic identities: sex-life, impotence-death. If at 129.1 impotence corresponds to the *funus* of his penis, at 20.2 a hyperbolic image of *mors* is at stake ("She addressed herself to my parts, already cold through suffering a thousand deaths": *inguina ... mille iam mortibus frigida*); whereas at 129.6 ("you are as good as dead": *medius iam peristi*) *medius* suggests facetiously the "genital area." It's not to be excluded that the word *mors,* in the 'theatrical' confession of 130.1 ("never before this day has my wrongdoing incurred death": *numquam tamen ante hunc diem usque ad mortem deliqui*), might hint at the context of the metaphorical 'death'of the *pars corporis* at 129.1.

On the second occasion, after a promising foreplay (132.1 "our lips joined noisily in kiss after kiss ... and our bodies closely joined to each other effected also the union of souls": *iam pluribus osculis labra crepitabant [...] iam alligata mutuo ambitu corpora animarum quoque mixturam fecerant*),[91] Encolpius's frustrated love-affair and sexual flop emerge again due to the reaction of the revengeful

[89] On *pars* referring to sexual organ (cf. *Sat.* 132.12; 138.7; *Priapea* 1.7; 9.1; 30.1; 37.8f.), see Adams, 1982, 45. On *partes* as *genitalia* in Juvenal 9.32-33 see Bellandi, 2021, 115.

[90] Encolpius's mental process might be explained with his temporary incapability to fulfill the teaching of the Ovidian *magister amoris* at *Ars* 2.703-712; 725-728: see Labate, 2020, 175.

[91] In spite of the erotic connotations of the *dignus amore locus* in the 131.8 poem ("a place apt for love": consider the Ovidian style since vv. 1-2 "the waving plane tree spread its summer shade/Daphne was wreathed with berries, cypresses swayed"), the evocation of the nightingale and Procne at vv. 7-8 sheds "a parodic light" on the idyllic description, as Procne and Philomela were turned into birds after their tragic erotic destiny: an ominous foreboding for the love-story between Encolpius and Circe? See Setaioli, 2011, 232ff.

woman (132.2): "the lady was wounded by such blatant affronts, and finally resorted to revenge" (*manifestis matrona contumeliis verberata tandem ad ultionem decurrit*). Which is why at 132.6 ff. Encolpius's rage against his "unresponsive flaccid penis" (Goldman, 2012, 37) leads to a "mock-epic description of his attempt at self-castration" (Sullivan, 1968, 70), by performing a masterful use of *prosimetrum*, alternating segments of prose and verse.[92]

The narrative switch from 'low' prose to 'high' verse (written in Sotadeans, a verse form associated with obscene poetry), with the surrealistic anaphora of "thrice" (lat. *ter*), calls up Aeneas' triple vain attempt to embrace Creusa in Troy and Anchises in the *Avernus*, the Afterlife (132.8 *ter corripui terribilem manu bipennem, / ter languidior coliculi repente thyrso / ferrum timui, quod trepido male dabat usum*): "though thrice my hand took up the fearsome, two-edged steel, / Thrice did my body sudden enervation feel. / With less strength than a cabbage-stalk,[93] I feebly banned / The weapon cruelly servicing my trembling hand [...]."[94]

At 132.9-10 (a resentful speech against his disobedient member) we are tempted to regard Encolpius and his phallus "as two opponents in a rhetorical school" (Panayotakis, 2009, 57), according to a judicial proceeding which the ancient Greeks would call *apodeixis* ("proof"). This supposition may be validated by the ingenious embodiment of Encolpius's penis at 132.9 ("I assailed my wanton parts with a speech on these lines": *hac fere oratione contumacem vexavi*). The term *contumax*, significantly occurring in the Roman forensic lexicon as 'reluctant to legal prosecution,'[95] is a

---

[92] The combination of prose and verse dates back to Varro's *Menippean Satires*, continuing with Seneca's *Apocolocyntosis* (cf. Quintilian 10.1.95): Walsh, 1970, 21; von Albrecht, 1995, I, 594; II, 1164-5; 1221.

[93] On plants or vegetables providing metaphors of the penis, for characteristics that may resemble the *membrum*, see Adams, 1982, 26.

[94] The same two-verse formula with *ter* in anaphora (*ter conatus ibi collo dare bracchia circum; / ter frustra comprensa manus effugit imago*) occurs in Virgil *Aen*. 2.791-3 and 6.700-1: "thrice I tried to embrace her; / thrice her image ran away from my hand, vainly grabbing her." About *Sat*. 132.8, 1-3 see Connors, 1998, 31.

[95] For occurrencies of *contumax* as figuratively "proud and unyielding, stubborn, defiant" (*OLD* s.v. 437.1) see Cicero *Ver*. 2.192; Seneca *Ep*. 73.1; Tacitus *Ann*. 5.3. For this passage Ulpian *Dig*. 11.I.11.4 (*qui omnino non respondit, contumax est*: "who is disobedient to a magistrate, is contumax") is worthy of particular attention: cf. also *Dig*. 3.I.1.3; 4.IV.8; 10.IV.3.2.

masterstroke fitting in very well with the context.[96] Moreover, at 132.11, the familiarity of past and present readers with Virgil's epic is strained by a narrative acme, as the narrator, discrediting his penis, gives shape to a three-verse poem, made up of recognizable quotations drawn from various writings (lat. *cento*) by Virgil, where Dido's indifferent and disdainful silence – in front of Aeneas in the Afterlife – is paradoxically attributed to the *mentula* (See Labate, 2020, 169-70): "She looked away, and kept her eys fixed on the ground. / Her face was no more softened by these opening words / than pliant willow, or poppy with its drooping head" (*Illa solo fixos oculos aversa tenebat, / nec magis incepto vultum sermone movetur/ quam lentae salices lassove papavera collo*).[97] This irreverent discrepancy (Dido's indignant posture and Euryalus' heroic act vs. Encolpius's petty situation) makes us literally "go from pathos to pun" (Schmeling, 2011, 508).

A little further on (132.12), when finally addressing his penis as "that part of the body which men of more austere stamp do not even acknowledge" (*ea parte corporis [...], quam ne ad cognitionem quidem admittere severioris notae homines solerent*), Encolpius refers with grotesque irony first to Odysseus encouraging his own heart to tolerate overwhelming odds, and then to characters of Greek drama addressing their eyes (132.13): "and didn't Ulisses have words with his heart,[98] didn't figures of tragedy rebuke their eyes as if they had ears?"(*non et Ulixes cum corde litigat suo, et quidam*

[96] There are interesting trial-scenes in the novel. Among all: at *Sat.* 70.5, Trimalchio plays a fictional magistrate pronouncing judgement on two slaves quarreling with each other without accepting his decision; at 106-109.7, in the courtroom sequence on board Lichas's ship, the 'defense attorney' Eumolpus tries to deceive the 'plaintiff' Lichas by patronizing Encolpius and Giton, disguised as branded slaves in order not to be discovered.

[97] The obscene *cento* anticipates Ausonius' *Cento nuptialis* (fourth century AD: see Aragosti, 1995, 484 n. 394). Here Encolpius combines: 1. two verses from Dido's reaction to Aeneas' pleading in the Afterlife at *Aen.* 6.469-70 (*illa solo fixos oculos aversa tenebat, / nec magis incepto vultum sermone movetur*); 2. a variation on a syntagm occurring at *Ecl.* 3.83 and 5.16 (*lenta salix >quam lentae salices*); 3. a quotation from the *ante diem* death in Latium of the young Trojan Euryalus – the boy beloved by Nisus – at *Aen.* 9.436 (*lassove papavera collo*: cf. Catullus 11.21-24); both Catullus and Virgil shape their similes "in awareness of Homer *Il.* 8.306-7" (Connors, 1998, 32-4). Note that the personal pronoun "she" (the queen Dido) refers facetiously to the implied feminine *mentula* ("male organ"), a term regularly hinted at, but never used, in the *Satyrica* (see below, pp58 nn. 122-3; 59 25-7).

[98] Cf. Homer *Od.* 20. 18 "endure, my heart; even more dreadful odds did you endure."

tragici oculos suos tanquam audientes castigant?).[99] As a matter of fact, the narrator controversy against his male organ does elaborate an ancient folk-tradition of personification of the penis,[100] developed in Greek and Roman poetry:[101] not infrequent is the literary topos of the angry reproach to the *mentula* in cases of failure to perform.[102] This subject may have affected even an elegiac Roman poet of the 6th century like Maximianus, who has a Greek girl (*Graia puella*) reproach his lover's lack of manhood, and sing the praises of the cosmic power of penis (*laus mentulae*).[103] No wonder the unusual contention seems to reverberate, through Horace, Ovid and the *Carmina Priapea*, from Petronius to modern fiction.[104]

It's hardly surprising that Encolpius, after getting this far, prays "the hostile deity" Priapus (*numen aversum*) for help to remedy his impotence (133.2-3):[105] the seventeen verses of dactylic

---

[99] Collignon, 1892, 320 was the first to suggest that the fateful self-blinding of Oedipus, king of Thebes, is here probably meant: cf. Sophocles *OT*. 1271-2: "and shouting that his eyes shouldn't see / the evil deeds he had endured and committed."

[100] Documented e.g. by a Pompeian inscription: *CIL* 4.1938 *m[en]tula tua iubet*("gives orders"), *amatur*: see Citroni, 1975, 194. On the personification of *mentula* in Greek and Latin literature, see Adams, 1982, 30.

[101] Schmeling, 2011, 506 mentions the Greek Philip's *Garland* (1st century AD: cf. Automedon's epigram in *AP* 11.29); Horace *Serm*. 1.2; Ovid *Am*. 3.7; *Priapea* 83 (but Juvenal 10.204ff. is missing). Citroni, 1975, 194 acknowledges Mart. 3.76.3; 7.55.8; 9.32.5-6; 37.9-10; 11.78.2: in particular, in 9.2.2; 11.19.2; 58.11-2 a speaking *mentula* is to be intended. The comparison between *Sat*. 126ff. and Ovid *Am*. 3.7 (intertextually evoking Catullus 32) suggests a Petronian parody of literary conventions of Latin love elegy: Hallett, 2012, 212ff.; 220; 222.

[102] Among the above passages, in Horace *Serm*. 1.2.69-71; Ovid *Am*. 3.7.69-72 and *Priapea* 83.19ff. the description of the enervated penis is expanded in a debate between the narrator and his phallus.

[103] See *El*. 5.117-15 (a tip I owe to the Latinist, Franco Bellandi). On the poet Maximian, see von Albrecht, 1996, III, 1321; 1334; Conte, 1997, 600; D'Amanti, 2020; Gasti, 2020, 216-7. For his fifth elegy, see Franzoi, 2014, 212-5.

[104] To Eve Ensler's episodic play, staging women speaking with their vaginas (cf. E. Ensler, *The vagina monologues*, New York 2001, mentioned *ad hoc*, by Schmeling, 2011, 509), I would add Alberto Moravia's *Io e lui*, where a self-centered and over-ambitious intellectual stands by helplessy, with his penis as an *alter ego*, deciding for him, and assumptively imposing itself (cf. Moravia, 1971).

[105] *Sat*. 139.2 offers eight verses of dactylic hexameters focused on examples of deities pursuing mortals, with Priapus in the end hounding our hero (v. 8). For Schmeling, 2011, xlix (cf. 544) Encolpius's impotence is "a motif which plays out throughout much of the *Satyrica*"; *vice versa*, Setaioli, 2018, 198ff. (cf. Vannini 2010, 152-3) argues that his impotence is limited (Panayotakis, 2009, 48: "occasionally impotent") to the section of *Sat*. 128.1-140.12: the passage *dii maiores sunt, qui me restituerunt in integrum* ("there are gods with greater power who have restored me to full health") is very likely to show a final and permanent recovery. About the

hexameters are being recited (133.4 "keeping a careful eye on my offering": *cura sollerti deposito meo caveo,* i.e. on the 'dear departed'...), when the "old hag" (*anus*) Proselenos suddenly enters the shrine and leads him out of the porch, into the room of the witch Oenothea, priestess of Priapus (134.1-6), whose reception in a dirty and messed up house (135.3 ff.) humorously recalls and discredits the Greek-Latin commonplace of 'humble hospitality' given to a hero.[106]

Since Encolpius, born under an evil star, "can sell his goods (*bona sua*)[107] to neither boy nor girl," Oenothea will have his dysfunction cured with a specific treatment (134.10 ff.), starting with the anal penetration with a *fascinum* (138.1 "leather phallus"): it remains questionable whether the sodomization is to be seen as an attempt to revive Encolpius's virility, or as an act of punishment for disturbing the rites of Priapus, mentioned in the Quartilla episode.[108] Nothing has survived regarding the possible success of the therapy, owing to the fragmentarily unintelligible context of 138.2-6. But there is still room for Encolpius's last sexual failure.

The legacy-huntress Philomela[109] in earlier years, had extorted (*extorserat*) a lot of legacies at Croton (*Sat.* 140.1): she is now acting

---

gravis ira Priapi ("the heavy wrath of Priapus": *Sat.* 139.2 v. 8) as a questionable "driving force" in the novel, see Schmeling, 1994-95, 210 n. 10 (cf. Idem, 2011, 538); Connors, 1998, 27 n. 25; Jensson, 2004, 167; Labate, 2020, 27. On Encolpius's prayer (*deprecatio*) as a parody of ritual worship, see von Albrecht, 1995, II, 1220.

[106] Consider the similar portrait of the *Dipsas anus* in Ovid *Am.* 1.8.1ff.: Ernout, 1958, 165 n. 1; Walsh, 1997, 198. Schmeling, 2011, 518-9; 523 mentions the traditional descriptions of hospitality, from Eumaeus host of Odysseus (Homer *Od.* 14.55ff.) to Callimachus' Hecale (on which Connors, 1998, 47) welcoming Theseus; from Evander receiving Aeneas in Virgil *Aen.* 8.97ff. to the Philemon/Baucis greeting to Jupiter/Mercury (Ovid *Met.* 8.631ff.); for the unmasking of the "insincerity of so much of the so-called 'serious' literature," see Setaioli, 2011, 316.

[107] Euphemism for "genitals": cf. 140.2 *bonitatique*; 7 *bonitatem.* For *bonitas* ("a degree of goodness or excellence") cf. *OLD* s.v. 237 2b; as soil fertility: Lucretius 5.1247; Caesar *Gall.* 1.28.4; figuratively, as sexual capacity: Columella 8.5.24 *mariti bonitas.* On *bonitas* in Latin language, see Traina, 1973, xx.

[108] See Schmeling, 2011, 535 on *Sat.* 16.3.

[109] The *matrona*'s Greek mythological *alter ego* served her sister's son Itys to her wicked brother-in-law Tereus for supper: the Petronian Philomela 'serves' her children's fresh bodies to barren old men. Philomela in mythology: Graves, 1979, 46 *passim*; 94,1; Lübker, 1989, 927; on tragic sources of literary traditions in Ovid *Met.* 6.587ff. (concerning the myth of Procne and Philomela), see Ciappi, 1998.

as a permissive matchmaker for her daughter and son, willing to foist them on childless old men. She approaches Eumolpus, entrusting her children "to his sage counsel," and leaves the children in his residence (140.2-4). While the "chaste" (*frugi*) con-man invites the girl to "some sacral sodomy" (*ad pygesiaca sacra*),[110] Encolpius makes his approach to her brother "to see if he would submit to my advances" (*temptaturus an pateretur iniuriam*): "the boy was well schooled, and did not demur, but on this occasion too that hostile deity searched me out" (140.11 *nec se reiciebat a blanditiis doctissimus puer, sed me numen inimicum ibi quoque invenit*).[111]

As empathizing readers, we look forward to seeing our rogue hero healed from his disease... The *incipit* of *Sat.* 140.12, after the mishap with Philomela's son, sounds somehow pleasing and propitious: "there are gods with greater power who have restored me to full health" (*dii maiores sunt, qui me restituerunt in integrum*). Thanks to Mercury,[112] he feels "more favoured than Protesilaos or any other of the ancients" (*me gratiosiorem esse quam Protesilaum aut quemquam alium antiquorum*): according to the myth, the Greek Hermes had transported Protesilaos – the first hero to land at Troy and first to fall – from Hades, as the gods allowed his bride, Laodameia, to return from the dead for three hours.[113] But on closer inspection, we

---

[110] On heterosexual anal intercourse cf. Martial 9.67.3-4; 11.104.17-20. Kay, 1985, 281 argues that anal intercourse between male and female, normally a contraceptive measure (or practiced when a male didn't want to be confronted by the female parts: Schmeling, 2011, 541), is in Martial indicative of sexual liberation. About this kind of Photis' "generosity" (*liberalitas*) towards Lucius, cf. Apuleius *Met.* 3.20.4.

[111] For Schmeling, 2011, 543 the description of the boy, as both *ephebus* (140.4) and *puer* (140.11), causes some troubles in the correct reading of Encolpius's *iniuria*: but in the episode of the Pergamene Youth (85.1-87.5) interchangeable occurrences of *ephebus* (5) and *puer* (6) are to be found as well. Juvenal 10.295 ff. shows how easily an attractive *puer* can make his parents anxious: beauty (*forma*) and modesty (*pudicitia*) very rarely get along, particularly when the lavish perversion of debauchers (*prodiga corruptoris improbitas*) tries to tempt parents with money (vv. 304-5).

[112] Mercury, god of thieves, Odysseus' protector as the Greek Hermes, against Circe (Homer *Od.* 10.275-308: Sullivan, 1968, 75) performs the same function as Aphrodite in Chariton's novel; Pan in Longus'; Isis in Xenophon's (Walsh, 1970, 79).

[113] Protesilaos in mythology: Graves, 1979, 74a; 162 *passim*; 163i; 169n. If his precocious death at Troy (*Il.* 2.695ff.) was a punishment due to Laodameia's rush to have intercourse with her husband (which delayed the fulfillment of wedding rites and offerings to gods), an idea of lechery related to this myth might explain Ovid *Her.* 13.81-4 (Aragosti, 1995, 520 n. 445). For

realise that the narrator's sexual capability might be just temporarily recovered. True, Encolpius identifies Mercurius with a 'rescuer', playing the role of reviving his penis from the dead; but at the same time, he lets the reader suspect that a restoration *longer than three hours* ... may not mean a permanent recovery (See Schmeling, 2011, 544). Again: is all that reality or pose?

Filtered through the narrator, the treatment of sexuality in the *Satyrica* appears to consist of a double-faced setting: an integration of indecent episodes, suited to an "erotic-themed fiction,"[114] with a plain style (*sermo urbanus*) as its narrative instrument: obscene actions regularly coexisting with clean vocabulary.[115] A peculiar humour originates from artfully chosen words,[116] either concealed or (more often) accurately replaced by metaphors resulting in *erotic*, rather than merely 'sexual', connotations. In the passages we have detected, surrealistic intertextual juxtapositions and word puns create theatrical effects: *inguina ... mille iam mortibus frigida* (20.2); *funerata ... pars corporis, qua quondam Achilles eram* (129.1); *medius iam peristi* (129.6); *vides, quod aliis leporem excitavi?* (131.7); *Illa metu ... confugerat in viscera* (132.8 vv. 5-6); *illa solo fixos oculos aversa tenebat* (132.11 v. 1); *contumacem vexavi* (132.9); *non et Ulixes cum corde litigat suo ...?* (132.13); *nisi illud tam rigidum reddidero quam cornu* (134.11); *Eumolpus ... tam frugi ... non distulit puellam invitare ad pygesiaca sacra* (140.5).

Niall Slater describes some scenes of the Quartilla section as *not* pornographic, "because pornography portrays prodigious sexual success," and doesn't involve "impotence and failure" (Slater, 1990,

---

the traditional model of marital love that overcomes the borders of death, cf. Levius 13-19 Morel; Catullus 68.73ff. (Bellandi, 2011, 21ff.); Virgil *Aen.* 6.447-8; Propertius 1.19.7-10.

114 Barchiesi, 1996, 192: "finzione a tema erotico."

115 In the spirit of Cicero *Fam.* 9.22.2 "the speech is made of veiled words, but unashamed in essence" (*totus est sermo verbis tectus, re impudentior*): see Sullivan, 1968, 100: "gross, though delicately handled, sexual material." I fully endorse A. Aragosti's stance (in Aragosti-Cosci-Cotrozzi, 1988, 110): Petronius's dexterity ("agilità narrativa") stands out in indecent passages, where his narrative refrains from lingering on pornography ("evita la lentezza pornografica del racconto").

116 In the erotic tales of the Pergamene Youth (85-7) and the Widow of Ephesus (111-2), both narrated by Eumolpus, we recognise an elaborate variant of the *sermo urbanus*: see Schmeling, 2011, xxviii (also 72-3).

40): does this mean that, if Encolpius and his *fratres* had attacked Quartilla, her maids and the *cinaedus*, the incident would be *ipso facto* called 'pornographic'? I know I'm making this sound very easy, but I would rather suggest that *for different reasons* such scenes may be considered 'not pornographic', inasmuch within them hardly any of the typical features of pornography can be identified: absence of empathy, *dismembering* and commodification of human body.[117] In fact, apart from moralistic and hasty charges on 'pornography' of being a 'vulgar' money-making gamble ("sex for sale"), sensitive readers will probably agree to consider *pornography* as a degrading or exploitative literary work that aims, e.g., at temporarily alleviating stress or sexual tensions: *vice versa*, an 'erotic' work would tend to *tell a story* that involves sexual themes (as 'indecent' or 'obscene' as one wants), combining love with lust: that is, *celebrating*, rather than 'mechanizing', sexuality.[118] As for Petronius, in so far as "the sexual 'shock factor' is undeniably part and parcel of the way" (Rimell, 2002, 1) we read the *Satyrica*, a reader can easily understand why the novel has had "a long history as a banned book (Richlin, 2009, 96)." Nevertheless, I'm inclined to believe that the innovative Petronian language does offer us an elusive, *sensually* permeating experience: all things considered, an erotic one, not at all pornographic. But, as far as the *author* Petronius is concerned, Edward Courtney has cautiously pointed out the danger of bringing his novel "into too close a relationship" to what we know about the character of its author.[119]

I should also assume as hardly arguable in Sullivan's analysis, although coherent with interpretive approaches and criticism in the late 1960s, that psycho-analytical methods may be applied to ancient literary works (to any kind of literary work?).[120] Further-

---

[117] See Steinem, 1983, 219; Ellen Willis, in Nobengo, 2013 (entry posted on march 18).

[118] I would be far from sharing the assertive opinion of Dworkin, 1981, 39: "Erotica is simply high-class pornography; better produced, better conceived, better executed, better packaged, designed for a better class of consumer."

[119] Courtney, 2001, 125: on the relationship between author and narrator, see ch. 2.8.

[120] A contemporary reader, reflecting on Sullivan's eminent stance, may find some of his remarks on voyeurism/scopophilia and exhibitionism as "polarities" in the *Satyrica* (cf. 11.1-3; 24.5-7; 92.6-10; 140.12-13) and still significant; but his methodological primary infer-

more, as Froma Zeitlin has emphasized, by isolating voyeurism and exhibitionism "as the chief perversions" portrayed in the novel, a reader risks missing the multiplicity of sexual possibilities we have been so far exploring: what actually astonishes, in the variety of intercourses, is the "high level of sadism involved," and the very low "level of satisfaction obtained." It's interesting to notice how sex in the *Satyrica* is not rarely depicted either as a source of frustration or as "an assault on an unwilling victim" (Zeitlin, 1971a, 655 n. 59).[121]

Nevertheless, as already noted, the narrator has no restraint in descriptions of sexual activities, whilst his language proves reserved: the word for the male sex organ, *mentula*, is never used in the *Satyrica*.[122] In two cases it is replaced by feminine pronouns: 132.7 *totum ignem furoris in eam converti, quae mihi omnium malorum causa fuerat* ("I turned the entire fire of my anger on the cause of all my troubles"); 132.8 vv. 5-6 *namque illa metu frigidior rigente bruma / confugerat in viscera mille operta rugis* ("My fearful member, colder than the winter's chill, / Shrank to my belly, within a thousand wrinkles hidden"). In most examples, anatomical terms, circumlocutions, euphemisms, and metaphors very attentively take the place of the taboo word *mentula* and its 'moves': *gladius* (9.5 "sword"); *vasculum* (24.7 "small pot"); *vasus fictilis* (57.8 "earthenware pot"); *omnes enim placentaeomniaque poma [...] coeperunt effundere crocum* (60.6 "all the cakes and all the fruit ... began to squirt out saffron"); *inguinum pondus* (92.9 "massive weight of his parts"); *ad inguina mea* (105.9 "my lower parts": cf. 20.2); *funerata pars* (129.1 "that part ... has been laid to rest");[123] *leporem* (131.7

---

ence, that "some literary problems may be elucidated with the aid of psychoanalytical methods" (Sullivan, 1968, 238ff.; 250; 251-3), is highly disputable.

[121] I would instead take issue with Zeitlin's assumption about Encolpius's "ambivalence as a bisexual as indicative of his basic instability" (p. 36).

[122] The unique, raw term *sopio* ("cock, prick") is 'functional' and appropriate to Ascyltos' lewdly painted torso at 22.1: *labra umerosque sopionibus pinxit* ("[the maid] painted his torso and shoulders vermilion"). In Catullus 37.10 the front of a tavern is soiled with drawings in phallic shape (*sopionibus*); cf. *CIL* 4.1700 *ut merdas edatis* ("so that you eat shit") *<q>ui scripseras sopionis* (in *OLD* s.v. 1792).

[123] *Pars* is commonly used to hint at sexual organs, both male and female: Adams, 1982, 45. *Priapea* 37.8-9 (where an injured *mentula* is cured by Priapus: Schmeling, 2011, 492) conveys

"hare"); *bona sua* (134.8 "his goods"); *rigidum cornu* (134.11 "as stiff as a horn"). Even the circumlocution *pygesiaca sacra* (140.5 "sacral sodomy"), for a 'deviant' heterosexual *paedicatio* ("anal intercourse"), doesn't indulge in any sort of obscenity, because it plays on the contrast between ritual sacredness (*sacra*) and technicality (of an adjective stemming from the Greek *pygē*,"stern, backside"): the result is a brand new gimmick, neither dirty nor rude, but ingeniously hilarious: just enough to arouse no disgust at all.[124]

As a matter of fact, aside from the absence of *mentula*, the narrator keeps away from other stronger obscene words of the *sermo pedestris*, like *bulga/cunnus* ("cunt"); *mut(t)o* ("cock"); *futuere* ("to fuck"); *irrumare* ("to impose a fellatio"); *paedicare* ("to sodomize"). Thanks to this expedient, he is offhandedly capable of nourishing – and preserving – an erotic language far less explicit and crude than in Latin inscriptions (*CIL* 4),[125] in authors of short poems (Catullus, Martial, *Carmina Priapea*),[126] and in poets of Roman satire (Lucilius, Horace).[127] Against this background, is Encolpius's atti-

---

a jocular word pun on *pars*: "Priapus, please heal that part of mine, of which you are apparently part" (*fer opem, Priape, parti, / cuius tu, pater, ipse pars videris*).

[124] Courtney, 2001, 225 takes for granted that the Greek novel, where sex is generally "kept within conventional bounds," is the object of Petronian parody, and finds Encolpius's language applied to sex as "notably decorous" (not differently Walsh, 1970, 78): but Barchiesi, 1999, 124ff. and Laird, 2007, 164 show that, as the dating of the *Satyrica* is not yet settled, any conclusive stance about reference to Greek novels is purely speculative (see above, p. 28 n. 21).

[125] Cf. *CIL* 4.3932 *vos mea mentula deseruit* ("my cock deserted you"), *dolete, puellae,* ("do suffer, girls") / *pedicat culum* ("buggers asses"). *Cunne superbe, vale* ("Farewell, my pretentious cunt"); 5291c; 9246; 10678.

[126] *Mentula* occurs 4 times in Catullus and 44 in Martial (Citroni, 1975, 117; Hallett, 2012, 215 n. 7). The motif 'chaste poet vs. lecherous poetry' (cf. Catullus 16.3-8; Ovid *Rem. Am.* 361-2; *Trist.* 2.353ff.; *Priapea* 2.49: Sullivan, 1968, 104, n. 2) echoes in Martial 1.4.8 (*lasciva pagina* vs. *vita proba*: Citroni, 1975, 32-3); on periphrastic reference to the penis in Martial 11.15.8ff., see Kay, 1985, 99 (about "non-euphemistic obscenity," pp. 57ff.; 72ff.; 101). Interesting are the occurrencies (40 out of 83 poems) in *Priapea*: *cunnilingus* (1); *cunnus* (5); *futuere* (3); *irrumare* (5); *mentula* (22); *paedicare* (4). On hendecasyllabic metre, associated with obscenity in Roman poetry, cf. Quintilian 1.8.6; Plinius *Epist.* 4.14.4-5.

[127] On Lucilius, cf. vv. 73; 307 *at laeva lacrimas muttoni absterget amica* ("but with her left hand my mistress wipes the tears from my cock"); 623; 940; 959; 967; 1031; 1058; 1186 Marx: see Mariotti, 1960, 42ff.; 65; 79; 105-6. Horace is intentionally salacious, e.g. in *Serm.* 1.2 (*mutto* at 1.2.68): see Freudenburg, 1993, 193-8 (cf. also *Serm.* 1.3.107 *cunnus taeterrima belli/causa*: "cunt, most nefarious cause of war"). The satirist Juvenal, although never favouring gross sexual terms, is strikingly bewildering and rancorous, e.g. about Messalina's abjection (the *meretrix Augusta*) at *Sat.* 6.114-132: Bellandi, 2003, 41; 146; nn. 353; 357.

tude to sex to be still readily considered as "a fairly standard ancient view" (Sullivan, 1968, 235), or – at the other extreme – as mere "sophisticated, youthful, joking"? (Walsh, 1970, ix).

2.7 CALL ME ENCOLPIUS

In the examination of all the above narrative frameworks (the dialogue Encolpius-Agamemnon; the Quartilla section; the Feast of Trimalchio; Encolpius's love affairs), in spite of the impression of a multifaceted unity conveyed by a first-person narrative, I find it really hard to cope with a major aporia, a baffling dilemma about Encolpius's character: is he *narratively* coherent or inconsistent? We must admit that it is indeed arduous to resist the charm of John Sullivan's influential words: but can we really maintain to this day that Encolpius is "alternately romantic and cynical [...], jealous and rational, sophisticated and naïve," just because the traits of his character are "appropriate responses to the demands of any particular episode," or even because "farce can stand inconsistency"? (Sullivan, 1968, 119).

Broadly speaking, whenever an author employs a first-person narrator, (s)he somehow delegates – to borrow from David Goldknopf – "his most primitive responsibility to a creation of his" within the story: if compared to the "relaxed" attitude of the reader towards a third-person narrative, with the narrating-I a very sort of "querulous interrogation" takes over, because the reader feels an actual pressure behind his "curiosity."[128] Diversely, Susan Lanser has invited us to transcend some tough approaches of structuralist scholarship, drawing attention to those "equivocal" genres of texts, such as poetry, fiction, and drama, that rely on "complex and ambiguous" relationships between author and the narrating-I. About half-way between "attachments" (formed by readers of poetry who tend to link a singular voice within a text to the empirical author's voice) and "detachments" (occurring if the "I" of an author is severed from the multiple "I" of most dramatic works), the narrative fiction occupies a large spectrum of possibili-

[128] Goldknopf, 1969, 13ff. (see Vannini, 2010, 4).

ties, open to a flexible pragmatic and contextual logic, rather than to a formal and structural one.[129]

Could this apply to our Encolpius-narrator? As we have no hold on him, he may very well be a dreadful liar: we readers can only rely on the information *which he volunteers*. In modern fiction, too, a first-person narrator can report on his own inner life, up to the final consequences: without going into specifics, the breathtaking *incipit* of Herman Melville's *Moby Dick*, "call me Ishmael," does pursue a very different novel from a speculative third-person "he was called Ishmael"; or from a trivial "Let us call him Ishmael" (Goldknopf, 1969, 16). How does Petronius's narrative technique actually work? First of all: to what extent can we share the assumption that his technique should be viewed as a device used to create an impression of disorder, "which he felt to be an appropriate representation of reality for his particular age"? (Zeitlin, 1971a, 638). Plainly put: can we presume that the contradictions in the narrator of the *Satyrica* may be regarded as "a mirror of the tensions inherent in the age of Nero"? (Slater, 1990, 46).

Referring to the claim that the peculiar Petronian narrative takes part in the Neronian imagery, greater accuracy should be paid to this matter, beyond the easy recourse to whatever kind of "sociological determinism" (Barchiesi, 1996, 202; my trans.) First of all, regardless of Petronius's fall into disgrace with Nero, reconstructions of clearly defined philosophical or literary circles and lobbies at the emperor's court appear problematic.[130] To put it an-

[129] See Lanser, 2005, 208ff.; 217, whose nuanced analysis underlines some narrow limits of structuralist narratology: the unresolved issue of "identity or non-identity of the lyrical I with the empirical I of the poet" (p. 214); the detachment between author and narrating-I in fiction as "default setting" not to be transgressed (p. 215); the sharp distinction between "fiction and real," whereas – in several cases – nobody can exclude that "the further a homodiegetic narrator wanders from the demands or details of story [...] the more likely that voice is to get authorially attached" (p. 217).

[130] After succeeding Burrus in 62 AD as head of the praetorian guard, Tigellinus awoke Nero's suspicions of Petronius to jealousy, whereas he had until then been highly favoured by the emperor as his most trusted stylistic advisor (*arbiter elegantiae*, "overseer of elegance": Tacitus *Ann.* 16.18.2): the praetorian prefect had charges fabricated against Petronius, connecting him to the Pisonian conspirators, and forcing him to commit suicide in 66 (see Walsh, 1970, 68-9; Connors, 2008, 176; Schmeling, 2011, xiii). Against Sullivan, 1968, 165-86, Connors, 1994, 227 argues that, since there is no evidence of Petronius mocking the poet

other way: if – for the sake of argument – Petronius's "dissidence" from Nero may be just postulated on a biographical level through Tacitus' report, it is methodologically controversial to inquire whether it is perceptibly reflected in the text of the novel.[131] The very Petronian text sounds in turn misleading. Kirk Freudenburg's witticism on this subject is quite fitting: "In the scholarship on Petronius's *Satyrica* Nero is everywhere. In the novel itself, he is nowhere" (Freudenburg, 2017, 107). It is indisputable that quite a few striking parallels, linking Trimalchio to the emperor, do deserve serious consideration: these traits, resembling behaviors ascribed to Nero (Freudenburg, 2017, 108ff), show the boastful dinner-entertainer as concurrently author, director, and actor of his *Cena*; but resorting to the biographer Suetonius, as the main source to excavate for authentic historical details, can become a double-edged sword.[132] In addition to it, attractive evocations of Nero, implied by Trimalchio's ability to "manipulate an audience which, on the surface at least, must enjoy being deceived" (Rimell, 2002, 39), may cause some misunderstanding about the term 'Neronian', quite inflated in prevalent assumptions of Petronian scholarship: occurring as a metaphor of degeneracy or dissipation, life-as-drama, "authorial self-fashioning," and so on, the trademark *Neronian* has lost its chronological connotations, becoming an aesthetic trendy label.[133]

Lucan in order to win favour with Nero, they should not be identified as members of opposing factions.

[131] See Rudich, 1997, 191. On Petronius and Nero cf. Tacitus *Ann.* 16.18.2-20.1 (Syme, 1967-1971, I, 439-40 n. 106; 442 n. 123; II, 718). For an excellent study of Nero's court, and a revision of the standard view of the emperor, especially in relation to the crimes or misdeeds associated with him, see Drinkwater, 2019.

[132] Cf. *Sat.* 29.8 (Trimalchio's first beard stored in the box: Suetonius *Nero* 12.2); 32.2 (the napkin around his neck: Suet. 51); 36.6 (the carver moving the notes of a water organ: Suet. 41); 54.1 (the acrobat falling on Trimalchio: Suet. 12.2); 59.2-7 (the performance of Ajax's madness: Suet. 21.3); 60.1-3 (gifts are let down from the ceiling: Suet. 31.2); 67.7 (the golden bracelet: Suet. 6.4); further examples in Smith, 1975 *ad loc.* Allusions to Nero, familiar to Petronius if he had been in the court circle, could have been found in Suetonius by "any writer in a later age who wanted to impersonate a Neronian courtier": Laird, 2007, 160ff. regards as "disquieting," thus not to be dismissed, the likelihood that Suetonius's *Nero* may be "floated as possible evidence" for the composition of the *Satyrica* in the 2nd century AD.

[133] Laird, 2007, 161. On the topic of "life as a stage," see Conte, 1996, 82 n. 11.

In this context, a further misunderstanding should be cleared up: why should Encolpius's *disordered* experiences imitate a supposedly *disintegrated* Roman life under Nero? Ancient theories of 'mimesis' are even mocked at in *Sat.* 52.1, by means of the paradoxical representation of Trimalchio's vessel: *pueri mortui iacent sic ut vivere putes* ("the boys are lying there so vividly dead that you'd think they were alive"). Furthermore, the very end of the *Cena* shows the trumpeters blaring out so loudly that the fire brigade breaks the front door down, thinking that Trimalchio's house is on fire: an escape from the trap of the banquet is thus granted to the *fratres*, who take to their heels "as rapidly as if there really were a fire" (*Sat.* 78.5-8 *tam plane quam ex incendio fugimus*). We may thus ascertain that, rather than *duplicating* reality, the narrator seems to amuse himself by demolishing his readers' illusions that the *Satyrica* describes 'real' life.[134]

On the issue of Petronian debated 'realism', we may observe that all over the *Satyrica* misinterpretations of reality may cause, on one hand, Encolpius to *confuse real* with literary phantoms, on the other, Quartilla, Trimalchio, Circe, etc. with sex, food, money. Gian Biagio Conte argues that "materialist elements" in the *Satyrica* mark hyperbolic exuberances of characters (Encolpius's voracity for culture, Quartilla's or Circe's mania, Trimalchio's unlimited revelling and flooding wealth): insofar as Encolpius's perspective is illusory, through 'realism', our hidden author restores "the fantasies of the narrator to the proper measure of things."[135] Moreover, whenever gross and incidental details during the *Cena* demand "to be taken as real," they trick readers "by seeming so real" (Freudenburg, 2017, 9ff): notwithstanding such accidents being planned or skilfully manipulated by Trimalchio, we are definitely

---

[134] After Collignon, 1892, 53ff., the foundational Erich Auerbach's 1946 study still stands out: non-stereotypical descriptions of social dynamics and characters in the *Cena* were suggested to coexist with an alleged limitation of ancient 'realism', i.e. with its being confined to comic and satirical *low* areas (cf. esp. pp. 36ff.: see Forenza, 2005, 45): the thesis is accepted by Sullivan, 1968, 102ff.; von Albrecht, 1995, II, 1220-1.

[135] Note the difference between Conte's 1996 "materialist elements" (pp. 180; 183-4) and the *insignificant* details, that produce the "effect de réel," in Flaubert's narrative ("détails inutiles": Barthes, 1968b, 84): cf. Wood, 2019, 73-5.

convinced, in the *Satyrica,* that "illusionism is the other face of realism" (Conte, 1996, 74).

To summarise, no fictional 'chaos' appears to be imposed by its author to the *Satyrica* through Encolpius's voice: the novel is not a work that can be taken as a basic mirror of *Neronian tensions.*[136] The fragmentary condition of the *Satyrica* is not due to an unproven *disintegrating* classical age, that would imply "disjointed/anarchic episodes" reflected by mimetic narrative: its condition is the mere, objective result of the manuscript tradition (Schmeling, 2011, xxxvi). On the basis of this assumption, we may wonder whether, and, if so, how far this (ideological) failure to acknowledge the factual reality of the transmitted text are the result of specific inferential readers' activity, such as the one studied by cognitive narrators, a modern orientation that directly questions the mind and its functions, using narrative as a mode of mental access (Fludernik-Olson, 2011, 3): I'm referring to the concept of the 'narrativity' of a text as naively ascribable to an authorial 'intention'.[137]

It's no coincidence that the mainstream of Petronian criticism, throughout the first half of the twentieth century, has focused on a misleading approach to the functioning of the homodiegetic narration within the actual "shifting back and forth between the views of Petronius and Encolpius" (Goldman, 2006, 2). but ultimately from the vantage point of the *author's role.* Against it, Roger Beck, half a century ago, proposed a different perspective, spotlighting the *narrator's role*: Encolpius's discrepancies might originate not from an inconclusive or conflictual relationship between author and narrator, but from some kind of double personality,

---

[136] Cf. above, pp. 61-2 nn. 130-3.

[137] Noteworthy narrational research, ahead of its time, converge on some orientations of 'cognitive narration' (see Fludernik-Olson, 2011, 17f.). Since it is only in relation to "a plan conceived by man that events gain meaning and can be organized into a structural temporal sequence" (Bremond, 1980, 390), I suggest that the over-interpretation of Petronius's *Satyrica* – as an 'intentional' portrayal of Neronian *disintegrating tensions* – might reflect this kind of storytelling practice, notwithstanding the difficulty to prove that narrative structures are somehow 'wired' in human brains (see Pisanty, 2012, 262). About the disputed question "whether readers' assumptions about authorial intentions should play a role in how narratives are interpreted," see Gibbs, 2005, 247; below, ch. 2.10.

the narrator and the subject of the narration, split between a young, "chaotic and naïve" actor, and an older, "sophisticated and competent" (we may add: retrospectively self-critical) narrator.[138] As we are deprived of the beginning and of the end of the *Satyrica*, we can't exclude that the narrator had somewhere provided the reader with a self-presentation, perhaps an explicit statement of aims, or of narrative purposes, now unfortunately lost.[139] Nonetheless, even keeping to speculation, given the mutilated state of the text, Frank Jones has claimed, with good reason, that old Encolpius's "increased wisdom," throughout a lifetime of adventures, *strengthens* the perceptive distinction between the mature narrator and the naive/acting protagonist (See Jones, 1987, 811ff). Moreover, Gareth Schmeling and Edward Courtney have diversely argued that the chronological gap between narrator and actor makes the reader quite often assume that a more experienced Encolpius is looking back at his 'callow' youth.[140]

Some clear cases seem indeed to reinforce the impression of a temporal distance between narrator and protagonist, by pointing out *both* the act of narrating *and* the narrator's "restricted" ability – as Max Goldman claims – to tell the story (Goldman, 2006, 5). *Sat.* 30.3 *duae tabulae ... quarum altera, si bene memini, hoc habebat inscriptum ...* ("two panels ... If my memory serves me right, one of them had this inscription...") shows explicitly Encolpius's narrative as consisting in recollections of events experienced in the past. The huge number of Trimalchio's deceptive articles of food draws

[138] Beck, 1973, 43ff., emphasizing the frequent resort to verse in Encolpius's storytelling "without any loss of the novel's unity" (55), highlights poems presented as words and thoughts of the *protagonist* (59ff.), and pieces offered as a *narrator* (66ff.). Beck, 1975, 270ff. detects Encolpius's increasingly severe judgements about the *Cena*, from an initial interest until it peaks in nausea (78.5 *ibat res ad summam nauseam*): his language allegedly accounts for impressions of the protagonist cunningly recollected by the narrator (Beck, 1982, 206ff.; cf. Vannini, 2007, 236-7).

[139] Conversely, a narrator-protagonist (as an individual 'existing' outside the context of the narrative) meets the author-figure in Achilles Tatius' *Leucippe and Clitophon*, and tells him the story (Vannini, 2010, 5; Zeitlin, 2012, 106 n. 2); in Apuleius' *Metamorphoses* the narrator of the *Fabula Graecanica* introduces himself to his *lector* at 1.1 (see Jensson, 2004, 206 ff.; Graverini, 2013, 124 ff.): both Clitophon and Encolpius are narrating in the first person and in the past tense (see Courtney, 2001, 36-7).

[140] See Schmeling, 1994-95, 208-9; Courtney, 2001, 37-8.

a narrator's response (56.10): *sexcenta huiusmodi fuerunt, quae iam exciderunt memoriae meae* ("there were countless items of this kind, which have now slipped from my mind"). At 65.1 *quarum etiam recordatio me, si qua est dicenti fides, offendit* ("the very recollection of them, believe me, makes me puke") Encolpius is presenting himself in the vivid act of speaking, or – in the words of Gottskálk Jensson – "as the memories flood his mind."[141]

In a case like 68.4 *servus ..., iussus, credo, a domino suo* ("the slave ... prompted I imagine by his master"), the homodiegetic narrator draws attention to his act of narrating, reinforcing the perception of a narration *after the fact*, and making us readers conjecture that the narrator is not omniscient, his 'restricted' information being marked by modal expressions which assume unproven things, like *credo* ("I suppose/imagine); *nescioquid* ("some/sort of"); *sicut dicebant* ("as they said"); and so forth.[142] About Circe's beauty (126.14 *nam quidquid dixero minus erit*) it's obvious that "any description of mine would be an understatement." The interesting 70.8 *pudet referre quae secuntur* lends itself to slightly different considerations. Walsh and Goldman translate respectively: "I am ashamed to recount the unprecedented performance that followed / I am ashamed to relate what followed," thus assuming that *the events themselves* of the story are (were?) shameful: but I think that it is *the telling in the present* to be here at stake (i.e. *the narrative* of the subsequent events), and to share Jensson's interpretation: "One is ashamed to tell what follows."[143]

---

[141] Jensson, 2004, 45 n. 107 tracks down the idea of " an oral quality" in the narrator's use of *si qua est fides* ("if there is any reliability"), a typical Latin formula for "the emphatic pleading of declamatory speech." By taking a cue from Cicero *Inv.* 1.27 and *Rhet. Her.* 1.8.13 (cf. Quintilian 9.2.58), Jensson regards the *Satyrica* as performance literature, a heap of "recollections" performed by a single actor, and places it in the setting of a Roman rhetoric category called *narratio quae versatur in personis* ("narrative based on characters"): Encolpius, as the only voice organising the text, would impersonate all the other characters, as well as "the person of himself as youth" (pp. 34; 191ff.; *passim*). About Jensson's claim, see Bitel, 2006, 1ff.; Vannini, 2007, 241-2.

[142] See Goldman, 2006, 7ff. (on *Sat.* 6.1; 25.1; 52.20; 113.8).

[143] See Jensson, 2004, 46. Compared to Walsh, 1997, 58 and Goldman, 2006, 5, Ernout, 1923, 70 "J'ai honte à raconter ce qui suit" does seem to grasp the point.

Through narrative comments made at an ironic (or not really amused) distance from the action, the narrator recognises *post factum* the crazy theatrical quality of some situations *of that time* as well as the gullibility of his younger self: there is no shortage of examples. After the double attempt at suicide of Encolpius and Giton as *mimica mors* (94.15), the lovers' quarrel shows up as a *fabula inter amantes* (95.1); by mistaking Chrysis's enticement (effectively on behalf of Circe) for direct advances towards himself, the narrator calls *frigidum schema* (126.8) the "crude ploy" of the flattered but self-deceived protagonist.[144] The humorous pun of 7.1-4, where a stranger is asked *urbanitate tam stulta* by Encolpius if she knows where he lives, underlines the gap between young Encolpius's "heuristic progress from ignorance to knowledge"[145] and the narrator's delighted recognition of the outcome of events. The latter knows very well that behind the apparently noble action of the *anus urbana* there is no divine protection: the protagonist instead, like an epic hero, glimpses a god in human form, but the "second-sighted" *divina* brings him to a brothel (*in fornicem*).... Once this is sorted out, at least in one case, our narrator shows a lack of irony, when recalling an earlier wrong judgement. At 80.1 Askyltos's threat to literally "divide" Giton is taken seriously in Encolpius's recollection (*iocari putabam discedentem. At* ...), whereas it's clear that Askyltos's gag is a mark of his "indulging in rhetorical posturing" (Jones, 1987, 816).

"Evaluative comments" (Courtney, 2001, 39) at some distance from the action can do without irony or burlesque. At *Sat.* 41.5. Encolpius-narrator recalls the reaction of his *alter ego* protagonist, incapable of solving a bewildering 'food-test' of Trimalchio's: *damnavi ego stuporem meum* ("I cursed my stupidity"). The curse is 'coeval' with the event, both episode and remark belonging to the

144 *Schema* (gr. *schēma*) means here "way of putting things, rhetorical trope" (Schmeling, 2011, 477); but the technical term, within a theatrical sphere, may apply to a "dance figure": cf. Euripides *Cycl.* 221; Aristophanes *Pax* 323; Xenophon *Symp.* 7.5; Plato *Leg.* 655[a]; for connotations of "move, feint," cf. Suetonius *Tib.* 43.2; Apuleius *Met.* 4.20.

145 Jensson, 2004, 200ff. analyses tastefully the different "cognitive status" of narrator and protagonist.

context of the *Cena*: Encolpius isn't saying *damno ego (nunc) stuporem (illum) meum* ("I'm now cursing my dullness at the time") or whatever. We are dealing with a 'variation on the theme' of an afterthought that is produced by a bitterly serious reflection of the narrating "I," but not immune to a touch of empathy for the dismayed diner. Encolpius-narrator sensitively recalls *his own comment at the time* on the stupid and rash reaction of his former self, and rebukes his "naivety regarding real life" (Zeitlin, 1971a, 647).

Encolpius-narrator resorts to a peculiar technique, whenever he gives more information than expected, as if he had access to knowledge which he couldn't have had *at the time of the action*.[146] After the dinner-party at Trimalchio's, Encolpius-protagonist dedicates a poem to Giton, but their euphoric night is bitterly cut off (79.8ff.): *sine causa gratulor mihi. Nam cum <u>solutus mero</u> remisissem ebrias manus, Ascyltos ... subduxit mihi nocte puerum et in lectum transtulit suum, volutatusque*[147] *liberius cum fratre non suo ... indormivit alienis amplexibus ...* ("for my self-congratulation proved unfounded. The wine had caused me to relax and I had loosened my drunken embrace. During the night Ascyltos ... removed the boy from my side, and transferred him to his own bed. After sporting in considerable freedom with a brother not his own ... he fell asleep in his stolen embrace..."). As long as the narrator can give more retrospective information "based on his *ex eventu* knowledge" (Goldman, 2006, 8), to what extent is he capable of relating events occurred when the naïve/acting protagonist was asleep? A single swallow does not make a summer... At 97.7 Ascyltos' raising frenzy, in his search for Giton, is described by the narrator with Encolpius protecting Giton on the other side of a

[146] On similar problems, arising in the narrative of Odysseus (cf. Homer *Od*. 9.187-92; 10.135-9; 12.389-90), see Courtney, 2001, 36-7. Through some cases in point in the *Satyrica* (e.g. 15.4; 38.8; 92.10; 140.1-11), Goldman, 2006, 12ff. discusses specific techniques "providing Petronius with the means of creating the particular effect he wants": these types of *alteration* (i.e.: deviation from normal narrative restrictions, whenever a text is furnishing too much information) are analysed according to Genette's 1980 methodology, especially as regards the full-bodied definition of *focalization*.

[147] *Volutari* is a medial-passive form (cf. gr. *kylindomai*), whose sexual connotations are to be found in Propertius, 2.29.36; Seneca, *Contr*. 1.2.13; Plinius, *Nat*. 35.140; Apuleius, *Met*. 9.5.5 (Habermehl, 2006, 11).

door: *interim Ascyltos ut pererravit omnes cum viatore cellas, venit ad meam, et hoc quidem pleniorem spem concepit, quo diligentius oppessulatas invenit fores* ("meanwhile Ascyltos had accompanied the crier on a tour of all the rooms. When he reached mine, his hopes rose higher, because he found the doors more securely barred"). The protagonist's imagination might have been enhanced by an "extended perspective," such as to make him perceive/hear "signs of the excitement" even through the door (Jones, 1987, 815). How does this type of narrator-restricted fiction really work? We may suppose that the reader is playfully made aware of *the very expectation* that the narrator can't really know *what* happened (overnight, in the first example; on the other side of the door, in the second): perhaps, natural logic as well as rational uniformity have been broken, in order to create suspense, since what actually matters is not likelihood, but "textual coherence and narrative tonality" (Genette, 1980, 208).

Strict statistical occurrences or schematic classifications risk jeopardizing our pleasure of reading, as shown by a textual issue at *Sat.* 136.4. Struck by impotence, Encolpius is left alone in the hut of the sorceress Oenothea, in search of a suitable treatment: *cum ecce tres anseres sacri qui, ut puto, medio die solebant ab anu diaria exigere, impetum in me faciunt* ("suddenly three sacred geese – I supposed they were used to demanding their daily rations from the old woman at midday – launched an attack on me"). Some editors (e.g. Müller, 1995) and commentators delete the word *sacri*, alleging that the protagonist isn't told by Oenothea that the geese are sacred to Priapus until 137.2, and that Petronius usually tends to limit the story to what the protagonist knew;[148] editors who instead retain *sacri* (Bücheler, 1862; Ernout, 1958) are followed by scholars who contend that the protagonist *might* have seen the geese coming from the temple (hence "sacred") through the door of the hut (cf. 136.4 *ad casae ostiolum processi*: "I made my way to the tiny entrance to the cottage" [Schmeling, 2011, 528]). All in all, opposites attract. Whatever our choice (in my opinion, *sacri*

[148] On protagonist-restricted perspectives see Goldman, 2006, 9-11.

should not be excised: *lectio difficilior potior*?), in both cases commentators seem to converge on unnecessarily distorting their argument, by favouring a slavish 'natural' logic and neglecting the (even 'abnormal'!) consistency of texture of the narrative. James Wood has wittily pointed out that "our memory selects for us, but not always in the the way literary narrative selects. Our memories are aesthetically untalented" (Wood, 2019, 55).

As far as intriguing narratorial techniques are concerned, with his pioneering enquiry on "speech presentation"in the *Satyrica*, Andrew Laird has noted that some dissimilarities between Encolpius's "angled narration of dialogue" (Laird, 1999, 217) in the *Cena* and in the remaining parts of the novel can be explained regarding the quality of presentation of his own words and thoughts. In the *Cena* a "transparent narrator" is prone to recording what he witnesses, but in the other surviving parts an "agent narrator" usually reports his participation/action in events. It's the reason why in the *Cena* we meet very few direct speeches from Encolpius: direct speech is normally reserved for his interlocutors, whose bold words are thus highlighted, whereas reported speech tends to emphasize the dumb and stunned 'transparent' narrator.[149] I would suggest that some features of this pattern were emerging already in the Quartilla section (16.1-26.6), where the voice of the narrator 'agent', progressively unsteady and fading, withdraws 'offstage': role-playing blatantly 'reported'; theatrical captions proclaimed;[150] Encolpius's speaking/acting participation more and more evanescent; particular emphasis given to the direct speech of 'aggressors'.[151] *Viceversa*, Encolpius's narrating "I"

[149] Laird, 1999, 219ff.; this pattern may originally operate also outside of the *Cena*: at *Sat.* 9.2-5, Giton's direct speech is "relayed to us" through a narrator who "is not so much reporting discourse as overtly constructing it" (pp. 218-9).

[150] Cf. 17.2 *lacrimas ad ostentationem doloris paratas* ("tearful demonstration of grief"); 17.4 *fabulas etiam antecessura latrocinia* ("to outdo the storybooks in your thieving"); 19.1 *mimico risu* ("[resounded] with the laughter of the low stage"); for handclapping, cf. 18.7; 20.6; 23.2; 24.2.

[151] Direct speech acts from the narrator (just two!) are introduced by (awed) courtesy expressions, like "I beg you"; "please" (respectively 20.1 *rogo, inquam, domina*; 24.1 *quaeso, inquam, domina*); whereas the frequent interventions by Quartilla and her maids are authoritative and/or arrogant (cf. 16.3ff.; 17.4ff.; 19.2; 20.6; 21.7; 24.2; 24.7; 25.1).

had erased completely (and significantly) any traces of reported speech in the dialogue with Agamemnon (1.1-5.20), gathering all the energetic narrative effects in a skirmish between two 'agent' antagonists through direct speech: bare 'mimesis'.

Anyway, by contrast with some possible trivialising generalizations about the gap between narrator and protagonist, we should not underestimate that Petronius'ss manipulation of first-person narrative is occasionally such as to cause this divergence narrator/protagonist to be brilliantly (or unconsciously) bridged. When emotional interactions bind the narrator to his past 'self', a reader has a hard time distinguishing comments made by Encolpius – the character- from verbal utterances pronounced *in hindsight* by the 'transparent'[152] narrator. It occurs significantly in the *Cena*: *Sat.* 31.8 *allata est tamen gustatio valde lauta* ("a most elegant hors d'oeuvre had been brought in"); 49.7 *ego, crudelissimae severitatis, non potui me tenere* ("I myself, the hardest taskmaster, could not contain myself"); 78.5 *ibat res ad summam nauseam* ("it was enough to make you spew").[153]

In further predictable instances, when the narrator seems to become one with the protagonist, it goes without saying that the ironic attitude of a 'wiser' narrator would tend to dwindle, or even vanish. In the 'voyeuristic' Quartilla episode, as Encolpius watches the mock marriage between Giton and Pannychis (26.1-3), he is likely to 're-evoke'his resentful attitude assumed *at the time* against Quartilla's role as *pronuba*. The previous temporary excuse, to his taking part in the ceremony (25.7 *ne maiorem iniuriam in secreto frater acciperet, consurrexi ad officium nuptiale*: "I was afraid that the boy would come to greater harm if he were unaccompanied, so I got up to play my part in the ceremony"), seems contradicted by the remark "the boy had clearly offered no resistance, and the girl had not blanched fearfully at the mention of marriage" (26.3 *sine dubio non repugnaverat puer, ac ne puella quidem*

[152] Cf. above, p. 70.

[153] Absence of clear narrator/protagonist distinction is relevant also at *Sat.* 26.9; 29.1; 47.9; 69.9, whereas cases of discrepancy are noticeable at 30.3; 56.10; 65.1; 68.4.

tristis expaverat nuptiarum nomen). All this perhaps shows nuances of self-deception, and removes light-hearted notes from the narrative context: a means for preserving the memory of his relations with Giton "immune from his irony"?[154] Similarly, no ironic narratorial detachment can be found where Giton's beauty is at stake: 91.5 *nam puer etiam singultibus crebris amabile pectus quassaverat* ("his lovable breast heaving with continual sobs"); 93.4 *multaque alia moderationis verecundiaeque verba, quae formam eius egregie decebant* ("he went on at length in this tolerant and modest strain, which so enhanced his good looks").

In this respect, *Sat.* 126.16-8 – with standards of beauty being elegantly made fun of – is perhaps an exception that proves the rule. Frank Jones has properly noted that the description of Circe is here built up "in the light of the worn and romantic imagery":[155]*oculi clariores stellis extra lunam fulgentibus ... iam pedum candor intra auri gracile vinculum positus: Parium marmor extinxerat ...* ("... those eyes were brighter than the stars which twinkle beyond the range of the moon's light ... and her gleaming foot circled with a slender golden and band! Parian marble by comparison lost its sheen"): this type of description, where the composite parts of Circe (sexual ones excluded) are portrayed as sculpted by various artists, notably Praxiteles, does present "a stereotype."[156] In any case, as humorous or parodistic as it might sound, not even here does the representation let us distinguish narrator from protagonist.

2.8 Petronius in disguise?

Inasmuch as the relation between a text and its readers is the field, and the result, of their subjective readings,[157] methodological

---

[154] Jones, 1987, 814. *Vice versa,* A. Aragosti, in Aragosti-Cosci-Cotrozzi, 1988, 132, argues that 26.3 *non repugnaverat puer* might be a foreshadowing, or an early playing down, of the erotic incident, in order to create a gap between narrator and protagonist.

[155] Jones, 1987, 812: this kind of "imagery" had been satirized by Lucilius, 540-6 M and Varro, *Men.* 370ff. B.

[156] Schmeling, 2011, 479.Cf. Ovid *Am.* 1.5.18 *in toto nusquam corpore menda fuit* ("no defect was all over her body"): the detailed description at vv. 19-23.

[157] In narrative theory, "pragmatic" subjectivity tends to exclude objectivity by definition: as being inherent in language use, it corresponds to the idea that an objective statement is either neutral or impossible: see Goldman, 2008, 6.

doubts and caution should overrule assertive certainties. For instance, on the basis of the nature of his narrative, to state that the range of Encolpius's emotions "is wider than in the case of other characters," although obviously chargeable with being *ideological* (as regards definition of *emotions*, selection of suitable passages, interpretation), may be still considered an inference supported by evidence, since Encolpius's fear, anger, joy, and sadness, often recounted, are case by case comparable to his *fratres*'s emotions.[158]

Vice versa, as regards "the humour of Petronius," contending that "the *nostalgie de la boue*, that perhaps dictated this choice of subject [...] contrasts so strongly with some of the literary digressions" (Sullivan, 1968, 215) does sound subjectively *ideological*, as this assessment doesn't appear thoroughly proven. Similarly, such assumptions about Encolpius, as being "genuinely infatuated with the boy" (*scil.* Giton), or about the former's jealousy as "not feigned" (Zeitlin, 1971a, 669 n. 92), need to be tested from somewhat larger theoretical perspectives, and may expose themselves to well-founded rebuttals: primarily, are Encolpius's recollections to be taken at face value? How far should a reader regard him as a trustworthy narrator? In this regard, as far as Beck's distinction between narrator and protagonist is concerned,[159] the fragmentary condition of the *Satyrica* excludes the possibility of any general agreement among commentators and readers: nonetheless, a whole lot of leeway should be granted. For Gareth Schmeling, a statement made by John Winkler about Lucius in Apuleius's *Metamorphoses* may suite Encolpius: "... two sets of characteristics are gradually perceived and assembled – those of Lucius then and those of the narrator now (*actor* and *auctor*)."[160] Quite differently, Victoria Rimell tends to underrate the distinction proposed by Beck, between a sophisticated wiser narrator and a naïve younger

[158] See Jones, 1987, 816 (esp. nn. 27-30). On ideology as "illusory claim to objectivity" see Laird, 1999, 209.
[159] Cf. above, p. 65 n. 138.
[160] See Winkler, 1985, 139, in Schmeling, 1994-95, 208.

self (a distinction maintained by the above mentioned scholars),[161] and finds it almost impossible to "disentangle narrator from protagonist" (Rimell, 2007, 114). I admit it is very likely that cases in which the narrator is *affected* by his own recollections, or concerned by his very act of narration, should imply his losing ironic distance from the younger self;[162] but these instances, as anything but thoroughgoing, are perhaps not to be overemphasized.

As a result of what we have been detecting, I think that instances of a narrator-protagonist 'empathy' can coexist in the *Satyrica* with passages quite clearly focused on a discernible separation between the younger Encolpius and the older one.[163] Obviously, it's not always clear-cut: sometimes remoteness and proximity in the interaction *auctor/actor*[164] tend to overlap. The well-known *Sat.* 41.5 *damnavi ego stuporem meum* ("I cursed my stupidity")[165] shows how the narrator, by using the apparently severed past tense *damnavi*, does not make a clear difference between narration and action in terms of 'now' and 'then' (curse and dullness belong to the event recollected), and replays the accident, say, without a hint of irony: the 'agent' narrator records *and* relives his participation in the past event. At 54.2 Encolpius is likely to be playing both on his own memory and on the reader's one. When Trimalchio *feigns* "a howl of pain" at being hit by the inept slave (54.2), our hero suspects a new trick, because the image of the cook "who had forgotten to gut the pig" (54.3 *qui oblitus fuerat porcum exinterare*: cf. 49.4-5)[166] is still fixed in his mind. But since we readers are well aware that the cook *did not forget* to gut the pig, because we remember that the strategy had been concocted by Trimalchio (cf. 49.8-10), we wonder what's

[161] Cf. above, pp. 65ff nn. 138ff. (on Beck, 1973; Jones, 1987; Courtney, 2001; Jensson, 2004; Goldman, 2006).

[162] Cf. above, p. 71 nn. 152-3.

[163] Coexistence or interchange empathy/detachment affect Barchiesi 1996, 202: "A volte si ha l'impressione che il naratore si immerga ("plunges into") nelle sue esperienze, altre volte che le riveda ("sees them again") con una consapevolezza retrospettiva ("with retrospective awareness")."

[164] This terminology is notoriously applied by Winkler, 1985 to Apuleius' narrative: cf. above, p. 73 n. 60.

[165] Cf. above, p. 36 n 41; pp. 67-8.

[166] Cf. above, p. 36 n. 42-3.

really at stake here. *Whose memory* is actually faltering? Encolpius's or *our* reader-memory (Rimell, 2002, 42 n. 18)? At 92.13, as Eumolpus informs Encolpius of the Roman knight bearing the well-endowed Ascyltos off home from the bathhouse, the narrator remarks: "I kept my mouth shut, pretending that the story meant nothing to me" (*utcunque tamen, tanquam non agnoscerem fabulam, tacui*). I think that, whether or not it may be an example of "fausse naïveté" (Veyne, 1964, 303ff), this narratorial 'hovering' between detachment and complicity is not to be neglected. In short, both sympathy and detachment may complement each other, resulting in a refined and multifaceted connection between the narrator and his former self.[167]

The claimed impenetrability of Encolpius's "flawed, opaque, first-person account" (Rimell, 2002, 11), entirely acceptable as a working assumption, should be explored in much greater detail. There is no doubt that Encolpius – whether gifted with a split or coherent personality; more expressly: whether *transparent* or *agent* – contradicts himself to such an extent, that very rarely can the reader take his words at face value. I have been trying to prove so far that our narrator *does* appear in turn simple-minded and down-to-earth; brutal and warm-hearted; "parasitic flatterer and ingenuous guest" (Walsh, 1970, 81); prone to self-accusation and self-absolution; as a feeble-minded figure of fun and "posing as a clown"....[168] It is equally true that, from a wider perspective, any reader can detect the 'resistance' of the *Satyrica* to definition, by rigorous classical canons:[169] within this framework, Encolpius-narrator's inconsistencies may indeed create an intense uneasiness in a reader's response. It should in fact be added that, speaking also about modern fiction, careful critics have recognised to what

[167] The emotional interaction binding up Encolpius-narrator and his previous 'self' brings to my mind the terms "companionship" and "moral fraternity," used by Henry James for Aspern's recollections of the past (although, differently from Encolpius, he records "all those who in the past had been in the service of art"): see James, 1964, 305.
[168] Rimell, 2007, 115. Barchiesi, 1996, 196 plays with the narrator's personality and opinions: "epicureo, classicista, anarchico, reazionario, avanguardista, cortigiano, sovversivo."
[169] Consider the concerns identified by Schmeling, 1991, 360ff. about Zeitlin,1971a, 633ff.; 676ff.

extent a homodiegetic narrator is, by her/his very nature, "subject to the epistemological uncertainty of life experience."[170]

Notwithstanding all this, uneasiness and disorientation have sometimes prompted scholars to indulge in illusory comparisons to different, or unrelated, literary cultures. Parallels may look captivating, and we cannot but regret that, whenever some scholars set the Petronian novel as a test-case for subsequent modern narratives, resemblances prove to be deceptive. Unlike a "picaro," Encolpius is neither 'untouched' by the false rules of society, nor a cynical or amoral rascal, nor even an outsider escaping punishment for his crimes.[171] Besides, insistence upon "baffling" readers' expectations, as a key to the "meaning" of Sterne's *Tristram Shandy*, is such a truism as to apply to many a 'comic' novel, without necessarily positing the *Satyrica* as a source.[172] Similarly, readers would not bother with a 'Bildungsroman': in the *Satyrica* we are nowhere dealing with an idea of Encolpius's psychological or moral self-education. Nothing hints at the 'formative years' of our hero,[173] like those portrayed in Wolfgang Goethe's late 18th century *Wilhelm Meister's Lehrjahre*: the most we can find in the *Satyrica*

---

170 Olson, 2003, 101. Dr John Watson's attitude towards reality, as a narrating I, may be a case in point. Enthusiastic sidekick and biographer of Sherlock Holmes, he narrates events experienced from a perspective that defines the *round* character of the detective and makes accessible to readers the latter's ability to think about things on a higher plane. By 'filtering out' reality with Victorian prudery, Watson's voice balances Holmes' (admirable) strengths of observation-deduction with his (barely palpable) weaknesses and depression over inactivity, alleviated by cocaine injections (see Buchanan, 2003, 19ff.): "I have noted such a dreamy, vacant expression in his eyes, that I might have suspected him of being addicted to the use of some narcotic, had not the temperance and cleanliness of his whole life forbidden such a notion" (Conan Doyle, 2014, 13).

171 Among the qualities distinguishing the "picaresque novel" of Renaissance Spain (on *The Life of Lazarillo de Tormes*, published in 1554, see Thrall-Hibbard, 1960; Laird, 1999, 211-3), its peculiar ironic or satirical survey of hypocrisies and corruptions of society may be misleading. Following Walsh, 1970, 224-43, Zeitlin, 1971a, 643; 667ff. frames Encolpius's personality in the traditional 'picaresque' features of the lowborn adventurer: her reconstruction of Encolpius's character, obtained 'by subtraction' from Picaro's, is – in my opinion – inconclusive. Schmeling, 1991, 371 n. 52 demonstrates that, as Petronius doesn't write "strong social satire," Encolpius is not to be considered a "proto-picaro."

172 Zeitlin, 1971a, 631 n. 3 gives into this temptation, but eventually resorts to Booth, 1961, 222 for an insightful overview on *Tristram Shandy*'s formal coherence.

173 Encolpius doesn't learn anything from his adventures, his general complaints (cf. *Sat.* 125.4) being "rhetorical poses": Schmeling, 1991, 370.

is a humorous evolution from younger to older, or "from wandering student to novelist," within a setting – comparable to Lucius' recollections in Apuleius' *Metamorphoses* – of "confessions to entertain" (Schmeling, 1994-95, 208-10).[174] Some further examples of brash reading scholarship. For his *Ulysses,* James Joyce has been too promptly regarded as being the only writer to draw inspiration from one of Petronius's characteristic features: the connection of daily reality and 'high' mythical models or archetypes.[175] It's also unlikely that the first century Croton, in the final four episodes of the *Satyrica,* inspired the "ghost city" evoked by Thomas S. Eliot's *The Waste Land.*[176] Finally, Encolpius looks quite far from being a 'countercultural' adventurer on the road, protagonist of well-known (picaresque?) twentieth-century novels, "such as those of Jack Kerouac."[177]

After clarifying some aspects of the interaction narrator-protagonist, a major controversial issue about the first-person narrator applies to the relationship between the *narrator* Encolpius and the *author* of the novel. Once we have established that Petronius is the *historical* author of the *Satyrica* described by Tacitus,[178] its "flesh-and-blood author" (Sternberg-Yacobi, 2016, 338), we can lay aside the empirical Petronius, in order to deal with a peculiar merely *textual function*: the "implied" author, a term introduced more than half a century ago by Wayne Booth (Booth, 1961, 177; 304).[179] This narrative model refers the "implied" term to the authorial character derived by a reader from the text: it is an *image of the author's character*, constructed by the implied reader, its counterpart as the audience presupposed by the narrative itself (Chatman, 1980, 150); the implied author is consistent with all the ele-

[174] I would note that Encolpius's figure, sharing with Trimalchio and Eumolpus the role of *actor*-protagonist, is less "central" than Lucius' character. About Encolpius's "lack of veracity" at *Sat.* 81.3ff. see Schmeling, 2011, 342-3.
[175] See von Albrecht, 1995, II, 1219.
[176] The overstatement concerns 5. *What the Thunder Said*, vv. 331ff.: Walsh, 1970, 76 n. 2.
[177] Sullivan, 1968, 119 is correctly sceptical about such "ideological intentions" on Petronius's side.
[178] On Tacitus, *Ann.* 16.17-20 cf. above, p. 2 n. 5.
[179] About Booth's legacy see Selden-Widdowson-Brooker, 1997, 22-3.

ments of the narrative discourse "that we are aware of" (Porter Abbott, 2002, 77). In the same context, Booth had proposed his concept of "narrator's unreliability," which he held would occur whenever "author and reader are secretly in collusion, behind the speaker's back": the (implied) reader senses a discrepancy between a reasonable reconstruction of the story and the account given by the narrator.[180] In brief, by taking into account a kind of *conspiracy* between the "implied author" and the "implied/ postulated reader," the *rationalized* author portrayed by Booth appears to be included by the reader within a complicity that *excludes* the narrator.[181] As far as our *Satyrica* is concerned, this theoretical framework would have set up the scene for a perceptive essay of Andrea Aragosti and for Gian Biagio Conte's influential study on the "hidden author" in the Petronian novel.[182]

When Booth distinguishes between the virtual author and the empirical one it is relevant to our analysis of the *Satyrica* because it helps us bypass the hastily 'biographical' reading of certain fictional texts (*Satyrica* above all), where peculiarities or moods of the narrator-protagonist were (and not rarely are) attributed to the same qualities of the empirical author, in our case taking Encolpius for the author Petronius: rephrasing a brilliant *boutade* of Booth's, shall we call Petronius when we want to question him about the right interpretation of the *Satyrica*?[183] This misunderstanding about the role of the empirical Petronius, almost as if the author were ready "to speak through Encolpius *in person*" (Sullivan, 1968, 117), has lead some scholars to identify the historical Petronius with the narrator: but H. Porter Abbott has properly admonished that the narrator is usually an instrument, a "device

[180] See Booth, 1961, 343ff.; cf. Chatman, 1980, 233.

[181] This conception, "as an act of authorial communication," has been stressed ever since Booth: see Hansen, 2017, 29 n. 5.

[182] Aragosti, 1979 finely emphasizes that in the market-place episode (*Sat.* 12-15) the reader is capable of recognising literary codes hinted at by the author (comedy, mime, Milesian tale, Menippean satire: pp. 116-7): the narrator, as a *medium*, is an instrument of a two-player game, where the reader is "complicit" ("associate, conspirator") with the author (p. 119). About Conte, 1996 (pref.; chapt. 1-3; 6), see above, pp. 42-3.

[183] In Booth, 1974, 11, the joke was aimed at Voltaire's *Candide*: see Olson 2003, 94.

wielded by the author," who should never be confused with the author (Porter Abbott 2002, 63).

Characters in the *Satyrica* do appear mediated and constructed by the "overtly subjective" first-person narrative of Encolpius as an autonomous Petronian creation, *not* by a satirizing Petronius in the flesh (Laird, 1999, 254): Encolpius is a separate character "whose voice and name organise the text" (Bitel, 2006, 1). In this respect, a reader will eventually approach the narrator each time as a foolish or a sensible puppet, in the hands of a detached, amused, and implicit 'Petronius's (a virtual, silent 'man behind the curtain'), *rather than* as a "Petronius in disguise" (Rimell, 2002, 11). On this matter, Alessandro Barchiesi has timely drawn our attention to John Bramble's appropriate image of the implied author as a "ringmaster," i.e., the director of a circus performance.[184]

Although intensely debated and questioned,[185] Booth's model deserves credit for suggesting the notion of an unreliable narrator as a *function of irony*. If we draw attention to Encolpius's role in the *Satyrica,* inasmuch as irony creates a distance between the actions and the voice of the narrator and those of the implied author, both reader and author are likely to belong to a 'charmed circle', whose values and judgements actually dislodge the *unreliable* narrator, in such a way that a reader can detect several incongruities in the actions and words of the narrator: "behind the naive narrator who in speaking of 'I' exposes himself and his desires, an agreement is being reached between the author and the reader of the text."[186] By recognising this discrepancy as an ironic or humoristic form, a reader should be able to understand, and enjoy, the unspoken message beyond the literal one.[187]

---

[184] Barchiesi, 1996, 196. See Booth, 1961, 64ff.: "an author who stands behind the scenes, whether as stage-manager, as puppeteer, or as an indifferent God, silently pairing his fingernails."

[185] See Pisanty-Pellerey, 2004, 196ff.; Nünning, 2005, 496; Sternberg-Yacobi, 2016, 338ff.; 380 n. 56; *passim*; Hansen, 2017, 29 n. 5; 36 n. 21.

[186] Therefore, "the ideal reader [...] takes shape in the text as a set of values in opposition to those of Encolpius and closer to normality": Conte, 1996, 22.

[187] See Booth, 1961, 93-4; 304-9. Focusing on relevant psychological aspects of irony, even before he knew of Freud's work, in 1908 Luigi Pirandello (*On Humor*: see Illiano, 1960) argued that humour, troubled by contrasts between ideals and reality, contains irony: a *per-*

First-person narrators are frequently, sometimes inevitably ironized by a 'silent' or 'hidden' author, that is by the *virtual* image we modern readers rationalize *from our reading of texts.*[188] Unsurprisingly, in terms applicable to irony in the *Satyrica,* Andrew Laird has clearly shown that authors of countless works of fiction can be "rationalized as being smarter than their created narrators" (Laird, 1998, 199-200). In view of these assumptions, the suggestion that Encolpius might definitely prove to be an "unreliable narrator par excellence" (Rudich, 1997, 186) introduces theoretical reconsideration and updating of the very concept of 'narrator unreliability'.

Since first-person narrative is often treated as a "yet-to-be-validated testimony of uncertain reliability" (Jahn, 2005b, 364), unreliability is commonly considered as *ingrained* in first-person narration: but against all odds, a narrating-I may be often highly reliable. That is, for instance, the case in Jane Eyre's growing retrospective view on her whole life-story; or in the army scout account in Hemingway's *Old Man at the Bridge*.[189] Developing Wayne Booth's statements on this topic, Greta Olson has argued that *textual signals* might help the reader decide whether the narra-

---

ception of the opposite occurs when we find that an ugly old woman is dressed with the obvious intention of arousing male admiration; but all that shifts into a *feeling of the opposite* (as a result of rational activity), when we understand that nothing is more pathetic than such an old woman (see Hughes, 1927, 182ff.). This "mingled amusement and pity" was seen by Pirandello as an "enlargement of the old comic tradition" (Wood, 2005, 14).

[188] The unnamed narrating-I of Graham Greene's 1938 *Across the Bridge*, being conveyed by the con man Joseph Calloway ("he was just an elderly man who kicked his dog and swindled the poor": Greene, 1967, 305), hesitantly underlines some comic scenes: the detectives failing to recognise the suspect; Calloway himself killed by the detectives' car, apparently while trying to save the life of his – till then – maltreated dog; his dying gesture possibly implying a blow, or a loving gesture to his dog. "It was comic and it was pitiable, but it wasn't less comic because the man was dead. Death doesn't change comedy to tragedy" (p. 311): who knows how to represent reality in fiction, when reality, as such, is not accessible? (see Liberman, 1973, 327).

[189] In Charlotte Brontë's novel, the narrator's view is in unison with Mr Rochester's gradually returning eyesight at the end: see Wood, 2019, 15. Jane's narrative, with its "breathless sense of awaiting imminent knowledge" (S. Davies, in Brontë, 2006, xxviii), is the product of a person who can "lead us to the point at which she became the stable self whose voice we have heard all along" (Gibson, 2017, 204; 211ff.). Hemingway's first-person narrator begins as a detached observer, but turns, in the course of the dialogue, into the speech of the painful old man, who is too worn out to flee any further, clinging to his obsession about the destiny of his animals, and having nothing left to live for: "the hot pursuit of immediate reality in which the journalist outstrips the novelist" (see Levin, 1951, 583).

tor is in individual cases "fallible" or "untrustworthy," rather generically "unreliable": some of her inferences, I think, can adjust to Encolpius's narrative. She maintains that misperceptions of a *fallible* narrator appear to be caused by external circumstances, with mistakes being made "consistently"; whereas an *untrustworthy* narrator is usually revealed, thanks to deep-rooted behavioral traits, or prevailing self-interest (Olson, 2003, 101-4).[190]

What shall we do with our Encolpius? Even if one takes obvious differences into account, he conveys the impression of an untrustworthy narrator, like the speaker in Poe's *The Tell-Tale Heart*,[191] or Moll Flanders, or Svevo's Zeno, or even Faulkner's Benjy;[192] whereas Huck (the narrating-I of Twain's *Huckleberry Finn*),[193] or Marlow (from Conrad's *Lord Jim*), might be fallible narrators.[194] I think that we could not imagine different circumstances in which Encolpius, with slightly more information and reflection, would be capable of narrating with unusual clarity, reporting infallibly and consistently. Or rather: would Encolpius narrator be 'absolved' by a reader for his failures and incongruities as a *fallible* one (and hence *redeemable*) would, or wouldn't he rather encounter a reader's motivated scepticism about his (for me) *untrustworthy* and unrepentant

---

[190] On a 'constructivist' approach, opposed to Booth's 'rhetorical' one, see Yacobi, 1981, 119ff. For different approaches to Booth's distinction between reliable and unreliable narrators, see Wallace Martin's and James Phelan's theories, in Phelan-Booth, 2005, 390; regarding the relationship between reader/audience and author in "factual autobiography," as opposed to fiction, see Xu, 2007, 40ff.; 80ff.

[191] In Poe's example the increasingly "expected scepticism" of the narrating *you* causes the dynamics of the narration and "builds up the character of a madman": Hansen, 2017, 40-4.

[192] Zeno Cosini is a "truly unreliable" narrator (Wood, 2019, 15), because he disingenuously *imagines* to be psychoanalysing himself by telling the reader his life-story, as promised to his analyst. In Faulkner's *The Sound and the Fury*, Benjy has his development curtailed to babyhood, and his thirty-three years are present to him "in one uninterrupted and streamless flood" (R. Hughes, in Faulkner, 1967, 9). Further examples in Chatman, 1980, 233ff.

[193] In Mark Twain's novel "the narrator claims to be naturally wicked, while the author silently highlights his virtues behind his back" (Booth, 1961, 74).

[194] As he tries to point out his involvement in understanding tha nature of Jim's dilemma (Kramer, 1966, 263ff.), we may assume that Marlow's "biased and incomplete sources of information" (Olson, 2003, 101) make him a fallible (and thus amendable) narrator. The case of the unnamed first-person narrator of *The Secret Sharer* seems quite different: utterances like "my secret self, my second self, my double" mark his increasing integration with the ambiguous Leggatt, which borders on mental instability and portrays the narrator as clearly untrustworthy.

character? Encolpius's untrustworthiness is due to his narrative unevenness, to his *dystonia*, as it were, from what the story as a whole implies, with his perception being irreversibly conditioned by a fantasy world "steeped in literature." His narrative is compromised by 'lies', but not by mere errors (Schmeling, 1994-95, 207): could a reader ever 'redeem' an addicted mythomaniac narrator?[195] The reader will anyway be ready to evaluate and enjoy, time and again, textual signals stressing the divergence between Encolpius's statements (or attitudes, or value-schemes) and the unrelated or antithetic information provided by the text.[196]

That's more or less what we readers have been laboriously trying to do until now: while urging our poor chap from Quartilla, through Trimalchio and Circe, up to Oenothea and Philomela, we have been mercilessly exposing his postures and inconsistencies… To borrow from James Wood, as "the author is alerting us, reliably, to the narrator's unreliability," the category of storytelling – including our *Satyrica* – can only be comic if we think initially that we know more about a character than he knows himself, "only to be taught that we finally know less about that character than we thought we knew at the outset."[197]

2.9 PRIVATE, SELF-REFLEXIVE, ALMOST SOLIPSISTIC

What is striking in the *Satyrica* is that readers do appear particularly crucial to the creation of Encolpius's character *as narrator*: in his feelings, moves, poses, and oddities, Encolpius turns out to be constructed, time after time, on account of numerous possible

---

[195] Cf. above, p. 42.

[196] See Olson, 2003, 93ff. Hansen, 2017, 39 counts the following "textual signals evoking narrational unreliability": subjective efforts of partiality, absurdities or violations of the logic and the premises the story rests on, changes in the use of pronouns, marked attention towards own reactions, and so on.

[197] Woods, 2005, 8-9. Whenever we think we know more about Encolpius (which quite rarely occurs), we are in the context of the "comedy of correction," i.e. a way of "laughing at" a character, following the tradition of Mōmos, the ancient Greek personification of blame, fault-finding, complaint and reprehension (cf. Hesiod, *Theog.* 211ff.; Aesop, 518; Plato, *Rep.* 487[a]; Callimachos, *Hymn Apoll.* 105ff.; Plutarch, *Hermot.* 20); but as soon as we realise we *know less*, we "laugh with" Encolpius, in the context of a "tragicomedy of forgiveness": cf. pp. 4ff.; 14-16; 82-3; 125-41.

alternatives, according to "readers' varying determinations of intertextuality" (Laird, 1999, 219 n. 18).[198] The late scholar, Don Fowler once reflected upon 'allusion' (Fowler, 1997, 18): is it a way to demonstrate learning? To pay homage to a predecessor? To acknowledge a debt? To borrow lustre from a classic model? We can share his answer, that "these are things done with texts, rather than part of their meaning," and try to imagine how all that may perfectly suit our possible reading of the Petronian novel.

We should however strike a balance between ignoring and overestimating the dense intertextual and allusive perspectives on the *Satyrica*: Petronius's awareness of his Greek and Roman precursors is very clear and by no means surprising (Schmeling, 2011, xxxvii). Within this complex literary structure, we may expect that, at times, the author wishes allusions to be recognised, but that at other times he unconsciously evokes language and motifs from his sources.[199] Such a polychromatic recycling of high and low 'hypotexts' does not always make it easy to distinguish an allusion from a mere topos or commonplace, a conscious evocation of a particular source from a chance combination of words and images.[200]

Whatever the reader chooses to call every single approach to the *Satyrica*, (s)he will either emphasize the interrelationships between texts (proper *intertextuality*),[201] or prefer some supposed au-

---

[198] Coined by Kristeva, 1980, 66 ("any text is the absorption and transformation of another": transl. from the 1969 French edition), the notion of *intertextuality* has been studied as a category of *transtextuality* by the structural narratologist Genette, 1992, 83-4 ("all that sets the text in relationship, whether obvious or concealed, with other texts"), and developed by Idem, 1997, 5 as the focus of the category of *hypertextuality* ("any relationship uniting a text B, which I shall call *hypertext*, to an earlier text A, which I shall call *hypotext*"). For a thorough dissertation on intertextuality, see Moraru, 2005.

[199] Pasquali, 1942 (p. 275 in 1968 edition) distinguished unconscious *recollections* ("reminiscenze") from *imitations* (which the author may wish to elude her/his audience) and *allusions* (which demand an educated reader).

[200] An overview on the general issue in Finkelpearl, 2001, 78-9.

[201] For Conte, 1985, 18ff.; 35ff.; 45-74 intertextuality defines the condition of literary readability, inasmuch as a "poetic memory (the memory of previous texts) is contained within poetic language: in such a way, the role of the writer as conscious imitator is downplayed. For Fowler, 1997, 14ff., no text is read in isolation, but within a matrix of possibilities, constituted by earlier texts (the 'source-texts', to which the 'target-text' is related): Ovid's *Amores* draws upon Propertian love elegy, a Flavian epic upon the *Aeneid*; a Western movie is intertextual with Zinnemann's *High Noon*.

thorial intent (*allusion*),[202] or comment on *references* (quotations), as borrowed utterances consciously referring to the imitator's source.[203] In fact, in several scenes of the *Satyrica,* both explicit and subtle reverberations of passages in the works of Petronius's predecessors presume a highly literate Roman audience,[204] capable of appreciating his unconventional technique, enacted so that his exploitation of earlier (or contemporary) literary models could both intensify the 'melodramatic' dimension of Encolpius's life and function within the context of the first-person narrative (Panayotakis, 2009, 50ff).

Quotations in the *Satyrica,* never accompanied by indications of author,[205] serve different purposes: I would limit myself to poetic examples. Horace, *Carm.* 3.1.1 enlivens Eumolpus's jeremiad about poetry at *Sat.* 118.4. Virgil, *Aen.* 2.44 functions as a proverb in Trimalchio's mouth (39.3); *vice versa, Aen.* 4.34 and 38 downgrades Dido's heroic love for Aeneas in the tale of the Widow of Ephesus (111.12; 112.3) (Schmeling, 2011, 431ff). The parodistic mood peaks at 132.7ff., where Encolpius addresses his treacherous penis in mock-heroic tone, giving shape to an obscene "desecrating" (Schmeling, 2011, x) virgilian *cento*: cf. *Ecl.* 3.83; 5.16; *Aen.* 2.791-3; 6.469-70; 700-1; 9.436.[206]

Between allusion and intertext, Encolpius "employs or parodies elements from every known literary genre":[207] Homer and Virgil predictably take the lion's share.[208] During the *Cena,* En-

---

[202]Applying his theory to poetry as well, Hinds, 1998, 47ff. argues *vice versa* for interventions of one "intention-bearing subject," the alluding poet, in literary discourse: "the production of a poetic text is in some very important ways a private, self-reflexive, almost solipsistic activity."

[203] Terms like *reference, imitation,* or *borrowing* sound, perhaps, as if they were hinting at a scholarly and solemn activity, whereas *allusion* implies "literary play and clever manipulation of the earlier text": Finkelpearl, 2001, 81. For beneficial negotiations between 'intertextualists' and 'cultural critics', see Fowler, 1997, 26ff.; Hinds, 1997, 117ff.; Schiesaro, 1997, 75ff.

[204] The *Satyrica* "seems to elicit, demand and contain an ultra-sophisticated level of literary knowledge" (Rimell, 2007, 116).

[205] For Petronian quotations, and their connection to Greek novelists, see Setaioli, 2013, 193.

[206] Cf. above, p. 51ff nn. 92-7.

[207] Schmeling, 2011, xlvi.Cf. Collignon, 1892, 178 (aptly commenting on Petronius's "persiflage," mockery): "c'est la libre fantaisie d'un esprit moqueur qui s'amuse."

[208] The frequent references to *Iliad, Odyssey* and *Aeneid* in Petronius's novel are detected by Walsh, 1970, 37-39; von Albrecht, 1995, II, 1219.

colpius's examination of the wall in Trimalchio's *triclinium* (*Sat.* 29.2ff.) is comparable to Virgil *Aen.* 6.20-33; the cook, Daedalus (70.2) and the *fratres*' way out of the labyrinth (72.5ff.) to *Aen.* 6.29-30; 72.7; 6.295; 417-23.[209] Encolpius as forlorn *exul* (81.1ff.) might recall Homer, *Il.* 1.348ff.; 21.272; *Od.* 5.299ff; Virgil, *Aen.* 2.749ff.; 4.*passim*.[210] Giton under the bed (97.4) eludes Ascyltos' prying hands as Ulysses, clung to the ram's belly, with Cyclops (Homer, *Od.* 9.424ff.) (Schmeling 2011, 393); even Lichas's ship (101.5ff.) is portrayed as the Cyclops' cave.[211] At 105.9, Encolpius is mockingly recognised by Lichas like Ulysses by Eurycleia in *Od.* 19.467-75; as Polyaenus Encolpius (128.1) cf. *Od.* 12.184.

Hellenistic poetry, Catullus, Horace, as well as elegiac poets (and particularly Ovid), are no less important. Trimalchio's dinner owes much to Horace *Serm.* 2.8.[212] At *Sat.* 79.8ff., Encolpius's lyrical impulse, before Giton's abduction, 'competes' with Propertius (e.g. 1.10.1-6; 2.14.9ff.; 2.15.1ff.) (Habermehl, 2006, 11). Readers not satisfied with correlating the grouping of Homer-Plautus-Virgil to Encolpius's love-pains at 81.1ff.,[213] will resort to the topos of forlorn Ariadne (Catullus 64.132ff.; Ovid *Her.* 10; *Ars* 1.525ff.; *Met.* 8.172ff.; *Fast.* 3.459ff.), Scylla (Ovid *Met.* 8.104), or Medea (Ovid *Her.* 12).[214] Flatterers and legacy hunters at Croton (116ff.) recall *Serm.* 2.5.[215] Circe's reaction to *Polyaenus* Encolpius's failure (128.1) resounds in Ovid *Am.* 1.5.18; 3.7.77;[216] whereas Encolpius's reproach to his penis (132.7ff.) elaborates a folk-tradition of penis-personification: cf. *AP* 11.29; Horace, *Serm.* 1.2; Ovid, *Am.* 3.7; *Priapea* 83.[217] While the hag Dipsas (Ovid, *Am.* 1.8.2-4) is an antecedent of Oenothea (134.1ff.), the latter's reception of Encolpius, the

---

209 Cf. above, p. 38ff nn. 50-3.
210 Cf. above, p. 43 n 61.
211 About Polyphemus in the *Satyrica*, and for the variations on the theme '*anthrum Cyclopis*', see Rimell, 2002, 102ff.
212 Cf. above, p. 6 n. 7.
213 Cf. above, p. 47 n 76-8.
214 Cf. above, p. 47 nn. 79.
215 Cf. above, p. 44 n 63.
216 Cf. above, p. 49 nn. 86-8.
217 Cf. above, p. 53 nn. 100-2.

hero, recalls those of Hecale and Baucis: cf. Callimachus, *Hec.* 230ff. Pf; Ovid, *Met.* 8.631ff.[218]

Further (combinations of) sources may be conjectured for ancient philosophy, historiography, rhetoric, and 'low' drama. Giton's trauma, after Askyltos's attempt to rape him (*Sat.* 9.2-5), explicitly recalls the rape of Lucretia in Livy, 1.58.2.[219] For Trimalchio's *Cena* Plato's *Symposium* is the main Greek reference, not excluding Xenophon's homonymous work.[220] The Cyclops episode of 97.4 can also be interpreted as an adultery mime-scene (See Panayotakis, 1995, 132ff).[221] In the battle on board Lichas's ship (108.7ff.), a reader may be aware of the echo of Roman historians, describing combat (cf. Sallust, *Iug.* 94 and *Cat.*, 58.11) (Schmeling, 2011, 420). The *foedus amoris* between Giton and Tryphaena (113.6) is linked to Latin erotic poetry, whereas Encolpius enclosing in his shirt Giton, ready to be kissed (114.10), recalls Alcibiades' seducing Socrates in Plato, *Symp.* 219[b].[222] Trial-scenes, possibly reflecting the contemporary Roman obsession with rhetoric, are to be found, among others, at *Sat.*, 70.5; 106.1-109.7; 132.9-10: but they might recall opposing sides in the form of rhetoric *declamation* (cf. 1-5),[223] in which historical figures debated how to proceed at some turning points of their lives,[224] rather than speeches delivered by orators at court,

Among irregular, or atypical, 'hypotexts' we can include cues and instances coming from popular and, so called, 'consumer' literature. The *Milesian Fiction* is well represented by three tales, with Eumolpus – by no means fortuitously – as metadiegetic storyteller or protagonist: the Pergamene Youth (*Sat.* 85-87), the Widow of Ephesus (111-112), and – homologous to the latter – the "respectable lady" Philomela (140.1-11).[225] The educated En-

---

[218] Cf. above, p. 54 n. 106.
[219] Cf. also Ovid *Fast.* 2.795-6 (in Laird, 1999, 218-9).
[220] Cf. above, p. 6 n. 16.
[221] On Laberius' and Publilius' mime, cf. above, p. 6 n 16; p. 26 n 16. For use of mime in the *Satyrica* as a stylised representation, see von Albrecht, 1995, II, 1221.
[222] Full discussion in Vannini, 2010, 266-7; 284-5.
[223] See above, ch. 2.2.
[224] See Barchiesi, 1996, 200; Panayotakis, 2009, 59-60.
[225] On *Fabulae Milesiae* see above, p. 9 n. 20.

colpius reacts in his own way to some of these spicy stories and legends, which anyhow *absorb* him: let's consider the *cinaedus'* rude song in the Quartilla episode (16.3); the shaggy dog story of the werewolf (62.6-14); the witches' tale of (63.3-10); the episode of the naked men in the bath-house (92.5ff.).[226] Such anecdotes, reminiscent of widespread licentious collections of escapist literature, do sound impressive, insofar as they show Petronius's remarkable narrative prowess in giving voice both to a dazed and babbling Encolpius and to a discredited swindler like Eumolpus: mimical farse, cheeky tales and jokes, although subliterary texts belonging to 'low' genres, are given stable roles and an unusual literary status in the Petronian novel (Barchiesi, 1996, 201).

Coeval writers might also have been affected by intertextuality, or by parody (as a "species" of intertextuality) (Goldman, 2012, 3). From what survives of the *Satyrica,* however, we cannot know how it actually works: let's just mention the two major poetic essays, the *Troiae Halosis* (*Sat.* 89) and the *Bellum Civile* (119-124.1), both recited by Eumolpus. Petronius's *Troiae Halosis* alleged familiarity with Senecan tragedy has been recently downsized;[227] whereas in the face of clear references to Lucan (cf. *Sat.* 124.1 v. 294 of the *Bellum Civile* and Lucan 7.473), we have no certainty about the epic poet's role in the novel;[228] it's therefore impossible to read Petronius's intentions as regards his *Bellum Civile* as a "flattering or trenchant parody" of Lucan's *Pharsalia.*[229] In both

---

[226] See Aragosti-Cosci-Cotrozzi, 1988, 108; Aragosti,1995, 266 nn. 186-7.

[227] Comparing the texture of Petronius's *Troiae Halosis* (in iambic trimeters) with the technique in Seneca's tragedies leads contemporary scholars not to share Sullivan's 1968, 188 point of view ("the conclusion is hard to resist that the poem is a general imitation and parody of Seneca's tragic style"), since the second book of Virgil's *Aeneid* is accredited as the main point of reference for any further analysis of the Petronian poem: Zeitlin, 1971b, 62ff.; Courtney, 2001, 141; Schmeling, 2011, xlii; 369-70. Nonetheless, possible (parodistic?) allusions to Senecan *Epistulae* and/or *Dialogi* are suggested for *Sat.* 48.3; 58.14; 84.1; 94.11; 96.5; 100.1; 115.16; 141.2 by Schmeling, 2011, *ad loc.*

[228] See Schmeling, 2011, xlii-iii. On speculations about Petronius mocking the poet Lucan, in order to win favour with Nero, see Connors, 1994, 227; 2008, 176 (cf. above, p. 61 n. 130).

[229] Leaving aside the insoluble question of the *Bellum Civile* connection (the poem is in dactylic hexameters) with the Lucanian or Virgilian epic (cf. esp. Zeitlin, 1971b, 56ff.), Rimell, 2002, 78-9 stresses the Petronian choice to trust Eumolpus with the "dramatisation of the difficulty" of writing about civil war.

cases, Gérard Genette would regard this type of parody – if it exists – as "imitative."[230]

In fact, the specific literary procedure of enriching the narrative texture through parody is normally presupposed for the *Satyrica*, rather then proven. In this instance, we do not need to be reminded that our novel may be *also* (but not exclusively) regarded as a 'parody' of the *Odyssey* and the *Aeneid* (Sullivan, 1991/2001, 261). At any rate, burlesque and/or disrespectful Homeric or Virgilian echoes in Petronius shouldn't be considered as "a disparagement of any genre, least of all of the epic, or as despising its heroes" (Schmeling, 2011, xlvi): Odysseus and Aeneas *remain* admirable, and the Virgilian queen Dido, misunderstood by Aeneas, *does endure* sharp suffering. Petronius's "admiration of Virgil does not prevent such parody" (Goldman, 2012, 37): accordingly, I think it would sound too diminishing to consider the *Satyrica* as an "impertinent version of the Aeneid" (Panayotakis, 2009, 53). A reader could perhaps even venture that Petronius's epic poems and Virgil's (or Lucan's) models are so incompatible that *any* Petronian use of these poets "must appear a parody, whether Petronius intended it or not" (Schmeling, 1991, 360): parody may definitely – and cautiously – be regarded as a term unsuitable to "encompass the complexity of Petronius's relationship with his literary predecessors" (Rimell, 2002, 79). But even so, some firm footing may perhaps be gained for what concerns both Eumolpus, as a metadiegetic 'parodist', and Encolpius, as a homodiegetic one.

It comes as no surprise that Eumolpus, the 'sweet singer', shows up at the picture-gallery as a "poet of not inconsiderable genius" (83.8 *non humillimi spiritus*). After declaiming a hexameter poem in the *persona* of a traditional satirist, hostile to vice,[231] his "upright path in life" (84.1 *rectum iter vitae*) abruptly collapses,

[230]An "imitative" parody consists in imitation of a style, taking literary genres or discourse types as its source; whereas in a "transformational" parody, the parodist adapts a hypotext to a new comic purpose: Genette, 1997, 5ff.

[231] *Sat.* 83.10 recalls Horace, *Serm.* 1.1, but Eumolpus's "shabby outfit" (83.9 *tam male vestitus*) indicates a standard device of Roman satire: Collignon, 1892, 253-5; Connors, 1998, 62-3; Rimell, 2002, 63; Goldman, 2012, 28-9.

contradicted by the tale of the Pergamene Youth, where his disguise as tutor and moral advisor is meant to seduce a boy (85-87);[232] in the end, he gives his poetic ecphrasis of the fall of Troy, in response to Encolpius's request (89). This relationship of prose and poetry may suggest a manifold parody (both of satire, epic subjects, tragic diction and of prosimetric structure), perhaps not far from the technique used by Seneca for his *Apocolocyntosis*.[233] Inasmuch as we simply direct our attention to the tendency of our 'mythomaniac' Encolpius to self-glorifying and identifying with heroic roles in epic and tragedy,[234] we will perhaps manage to approach relevant aspects of parody's functioning in the *Satyrica*.

That's why, for example, we won't fail to appreciate the brilliant comic distortion occurring at *Sat.* 105.9, a case of "transformational" parody.[235] A reader easily detects Lichas's epic procedure in unmasking Encolpius: "he trained his eyes directly on my lower parts, extended a formal hand towards them" (*ad inguina mea luminibus deflexis movit officiosam manum*).[236] The sordid tone of the context is raised by a humorous reference to Homer (*Od.* 19.467-75), where the ancient nurse Eurycleia recognises Odysseus, after his twenty years' absence, by the scar on his knee sustained on a wild boar hunting. Beyond (nontheless plausible) similarities to such obscenity and Homeric travesty in the Roman mime (Panayotakis, 1995, 152), a reader is here amused by the gimmick of the narrator but can also enjoy a tasteful parody of the Aristotelian theory of *anagnōrisis* ("recognition") in ancient Greek Theatre.[237]

---

232 The austerity disguise may be a cover for unutterable vices: on Martial, 1.24 see Citroni,1975, 82-5; on Juvenal, 2.3 (and for an insightful overview on the issue) see Labate, 2020, 128ff. (esp. n. 6). About Eumolpus as storyteller – cf. p. 56 nn. 116.

233 See Goldman, 2012, 30ff. On Seneca's *Apocolocyntosis* as "the earliest extant example of any Menippean satire," see Paschalis, 2009; Freudenburg, 2015 provides a basic survey of recent studies of the *Apocolocyntosis*: see p. 105 for 'further reading'.

234 See above, pp. 42-3.

235 See above, p. 88 n. 230.

236 Encolpius proves sexually "well-endowed," as at 129.1 and 140.13 (Sullivan 1968, 75 n. 2); on the erotic *dutiful quality* ("doverosità") of Lichas's gesture, see Vannini, 2010, 171.

237 Cf. Aristotle, *Poet.* 52^{a} 29-33 "recognition [...] is a change from ignorance to knowledge, disclosing either a close relationship or enmity, on the part of people marked out for good

We wish the novel were always so neat and 'readable', but most of the time voice and attitude of the parodist(s) remain those of a cryptic or hidden 'author'. We obviously regret that we don't have a complete text at our disposal: a better understanding of the original Petronian context would clarify many issues.[238] Nevertheless, even if confronted by the uncertain status of our mutilated *Satyrica,* a contemporary reader – probably not unlike Petronius'ss own audience – at times wants to be tricked, "and then made to laugh at himself": "both the feelings give joy" (Schmeling, 1991, 359). An amused reader thus becomes responsive either to Eumolpus, the amoral entertainer and "manic poetaster" (Walsh,1970, 209), or to our whimsical Encolpius... The 'secret collusion' of implied author and postulated reader,[239] once again at stake, is likely to have hit the mark indeed, in order for the comic twists of two complementary and highly untrustworthy narrators to be fully enjoyed.

2.10 LAUGHING *WITH* ENCOLPIUS

Intertextuality seems to be ultimately located in a *reading practice*: its focus on text, and its functional properties, would imply concentrating upon moments of a reader's consumption, according to which meaning is constructed at the point of reception.[240] Does this text/reader interaction presuppose that the (implied) author's role should be *ipso facto* dismissed? We must admit that some of the questions raised by the dynamics of the narrational correlation *author-text/narrator-reader*[241] tend to remain happily un-

---

or bad fortune. Recognition is best when it occurs simultaneously with a reversal, like the one in the *Oedipus*" (Heath, 1996, 18-9).

[238] Goldman, 2012, 37-9 finds it difficult to determine Petronius's attitude toward his source material, because of hurdles erected by the lack "of a clear authorial voice": the deliberate soppression of this voice is alleged as responding "to the structure of power under the literary princeps" (cf. Nero, "both princeps and poet": but on the *Neronian imagery* see above, p. 62 n. 133.).

[239] See above, p. 78 n. 181ff.

[240] See particularly Conte-Barchiesi, 1989, 90ff. About an universalist view of narrative as "intrinsically intertextual," see Moraru, 2005, 259ff.

[241] On text as a 'discourse' addressed by a narrator/speaker to a reader/addressee, see Laird, 1999, 18ff.

answered: anyway, how relevant is the impact of each of the three components on our identifying the meaning, and on the specific evaluation of the *Satyrica*? In general terms, it is difficult not to agree that some approaches of the twentieth century, which insist that *the perceiver* is active, not passive in the act of perception, may be viewed as expressions of mistrust or disruption of objective certainties running through nineteenth-century science:[242] as one would expect, such an emphasis on the observer's active role could not but affect literary theory as well.

Among other theorists, Per Krogh Hansen has recently found "paradoxical" that the rhetorical study of literature, inspired by Wayne Booth (Phelan-Booth, 2005, 389), still entails the implied author as the cause for all dispositions in the narrative, "in an age where semiotics, reader-response criticism and cognitive sciences have done considerable efforts" to show that *the reader* has a decisive effect "on what textual construct means" (Hansen, 2017, 48). I think we can agree that any emphasis on the reader's cognitive capacities would be a beneficial reaction to a redundant dependence on the implied author as a key concept. But further circumspection would be advisable. I have suggested above – disproving an alleged Petronian 'intentionality' as responsible for the fragmented condition of the *Satyrica* – to what extent clues given by cognitive narratology may help us detect an interesting nexus of narrative and mind:[243] cognitive narratologists regard narrativity as not only a quality inherent in a text, but most of all as an attribute *imposed on it* by readers, whose mental approach make them interpret the text as a narrative.[244] In the Petronian case, this

[242] In Selden-Widdowson-Brooker, 1997, 47-8; 153-4 the emphasis is placed on Einstein's theory of relativity (which challenged the belief that objective knowledge was a progressive accumulation of facts); on *Gestalt* psychology (with the conviction that the human mind perceives things as configurations of organized wholes); on Kuhn's idea of apprehending objects not through the senses, but within conceptual limits, as 'frames of reference' brought to the object of understanding.

[243] Cf. above, p. 64 n. 137.

[244] For a general approach to cognitive science see Thagard, 2005.The study of mind-relevant aspects of story-telling practices shows that important refinements continue to be imposed on these focal areas, opening an attractive landscape to future research. Questions encompassed by the term 'cognitive narratology' (first used by Manfred Jahn in 1997) can

cognitive resource has proved to be extremely useful: nevertheless, intentionality aside, why should the implied author *as such* be left for dead?

As a matter of fact, the author's status in narrative theory still tends to remain extremely questionable. In classical hermeneutics the process of understanding a text was known to be regarded as an attempt "to reconstruct an author's intention":[245] but this notion of author was soon challenged by a double offensive: by the American New Critics, dominant in the 1940s and 1950s, and by the French theorist Roland Barthes in the 1960s. On one hand, the concept of a literary text as self-contained, and of textual indications as decisive regarding its meaning, implied the rejection of the personal input of an author.[246] On the other, Barthes's "Death of the Author" propositions strongly took issue with the simplistic idea that the person, life, tastes, and passions of the author serve as a definitive explanation of the text ("as a father to his child"; or as "the subject with the book as predicate"); the text (cf. the analogy *text-textiles*), thus proving "a tissue of quotations drawn from the innumerable centres of culture," rather than from an individual experience, was to be set free from that interpretive tyranny: thus, not by chance, but conclusively, the "birth of the reader must be at the cost of the death of the Author" (Barthes, 1977, 146ff).[247]

---

be traced back to earlier research in the field of literary studies, particularly on reception and reader-response theories (about Iser cf. above, p. 22 n. 3; below, p. 96 n. 261): Jahn, 2005a, 67-71; Pisanty, 2012, 261ff.; Traini, 2017, 248ff.

[245] Jannidis, 2005, 33. Interpreters, aiming at a fusion of their 'horizon' of experience and meaning thereby as to their object of interpretation, would eventually acknowledge the gap between their horizon and that of the text's author: about Gadamer's concept of "fusion" ("Horizontverschmeltzung"), see Ankersmit, 2005, 211.

[246] On this "intentional fallacy" see Wimsatt-Beardsley, 1946. On the parallel exclusion of the emotional effect on the reader, the "affective fallacy," see Wimsatt-Beardsley, 1949 (above, p. 21 n. 1).

[247] After its initial English publication in the American *Aspen-The Magazine in a Box* (= Barthes, 1967: six months before the political uprising in Paris, in May 1968), it had its French launch in «Manteia» (= Barthes, 1968a). The coeval Michel Foucault's essay — *What Is an Author?* (1969), although arguing for the author's function as crucial for many contemporary texts (see Jannidis, 2005, 34), envisaged a dystopian world "where discourse would circulate without any need for an author" (Foucault, 1977, 290), somehow foretelling "anonymous websites and anthrax-laced letters with no return address" (Lanser, 2005, 218).

But in spite of the rapid spread of the death-of-the-author slogan during the 1980s, Barthes's fascinating attack against such an implicitly Romantic idea, of an author "as the solitary, originary, and proprietary creator of literary texts" (Logie, 2013, 494), didn't affect literary criticism. Seán Burke has expertly argued that the notion of the author is not to be dissolved but rather repositioned, in order not to fall into the binary trap of either authorial mastery or authorial banishment.[248] Susan Lanser has advised us to regard the implied author not as a mere body, but as "clothes the body wears," clothes that "can be altered, discarded, tried on, changed before or behind our eyes": differing profiles, fluctuating from extreme personalisation and practices generating "a sense of impersonal form" (Lanser, 2001, 158ff).[249] Wayne Booth, himself, reconsidering the concerns that lead him to develop his 1961 influential concept of an implied author, has humorously saved it from "this or that absurd assassination attempt," and stood up for its actual "resurrection."[250] In this respect, we have had the opportunity to observe that not just the implied author, but the historical author has been sometimes defended and brought into play beyond measure, confirming how a 'legal aid' to the author's role may be wrongly taken to the extreme: as above clarified, John P. Sullivan went as far as even identifying Petronius, the flesh-and-blood author of the *Satyrica*, with Encolpius narrator.[251]

To the role of the narrator in the *Satyrica* I have devoted the preceding sections,[252] but I think it appropriate to insist here on the "Encolpio-centrism" (Beck, 1997, 72) and the attendant distinction between the narrating and experiencing Encolpius. Roger Beck, followed by Frank Jones, has established a research meth-

---

[248] See Burke, 1998, 89ff.; 107-9. In the 1970s, the notion of director-auteur *in cinema* was intensely debated as a consequence of the impact of structuralist and post-structuralist analysis: see Hodsdon, 2017, 18ff.

[249] Since the implied author is "neither an identifiable textual voice nor a demonstrable material being," nor any other textually detectable *persona*, it is a reading effect, i.e. something that "happens in the wake of reading rather than prior to it"; in other words, it is created *from* the text (Lanser, 2011, 154ff.).

[250] See Booth, 2005, 75; on Booth, 1961 see above, p. 77 n. 179.

[251] See above, pp. 78-9.

[252] See above, ch. 2. 7-8.

od[253] that Gian Biagio Conte and Andrew Laird have diversely developed: the former, by highlighting the 'conspiracy' between the implied author and the postulated reader, at the expense of the mythomaniac narrator; the latter, by drawing attention to the readers' determinations of the refined Petronian intertextuality for the construction of Encolpius's character.[254] In this respect, apart from the differing approaches of readers according to their single assessment of intertextuality, allusion or textual references,[255] we may wonder when – and to what extent – the reader comes into play in the *Satyrica*.

Whenever we deal with this issue, we are probably walking into a minefield. Theoretically speaking, insightful semioticians have been speaking out in favour of a flexible interaction author-text/narrator-reader, rather than giving priority to one over the other two. For example, the abstract role of Umberto Eco's *Model Reader* seems to refer to the different types of *Readers* which abounded in literary theory during the 1970s;[256] but, unlike them, Eco lays emphasis on "inferential walks," namely functions which could be extrapolated by readers from the text, or could instead be dependant on cognitive mechanisms to be found outside the text.[257] If the Model Reader seems to be an assembly of interpretive options, authorized by the text to the interpreter, the centre of

---

[253] See above, ch. 2.7.

[254] On Conte, see above, ch. 2.5; on Laird, see above, ch. 2.9.

[255] See above, ch. 2.9.

[256] Wolfgang Iser's 'implied reader' (that "has his roots firmly planted in the structure of the text": Iser, 1978, 34) and Michael Riffaterre's "archilecteur" ('super-reader') are diversely determined on the basis of textual features; Erwin Wolff's "intendierte Leser" ('intended reader') is hypothesised by the author; Stanley Fish's 'informed reader' (partly indebted to Jonathan Culler's 'competent reader') is a postulated one, preceding the text insofar as the same text will be read in different ways by different interpretive communities. On these items see Pisanty-Pellerey, 2004, 197; Rabinowitz, 2005, 30; Schneider, 2005, 482-3.

[257] With *Opera aperta* (1962 = Eco 1989: Varsava, 1995, 89), Eco focused on works of art whose intentionally indefinite structure oblige the users to take upon themselves "the greater part of the production of meaning" (Pisanty, 2015, 39-40); from then on, he investigated what stimulates (or limits) the activity of the interpreter, combining a semiotic approach, dating back to Peirce's model, with a structuralist one: by assuming a text as a chain of devices to be actualised by the receiver, readers are required to complete what is implicit in the text, by adopting their own inferential attitude (on Eco,1979; 1984; 1990; 1994, see Pisanty-Pellerey, 2004, 331ff.; Bianchi-Vassallo, 2015, 7; Elmo Raj, 2015, 329-31).

attention shifts *from the text as such* to the text/reader couple. So, faced with the risk of finding the meaning of the text exclusively through its possible readings, in his theory of 'textual cooperation', Eco repeatedly refuses the notion of the interpreter's unlimited freedom and unrestrained use of a text. Specifically, by distinguishing three types of 'intentions' (*intentio auctoris/operis/lectoris*), he tends to regard interpretation as the fruit of a synthetic fluctuation between the intentions of the text and the reader's, but without reaching any comprehensive conclusion.[258] What interests us most, as regards widespread judgements on the irrelevance of the *intentio auctoris* (shared by most contemporary theories of the text),[259] is that Eco's model doesn't completely remove the author from the act of textual cooperation: the meanings of the text appear thus determined by a tensive interaction between the three *intentiones*.[260]

As regards the *Satyrica*, some scholars have tried to reduce the *supposed* predominance of the implied (or empirical) author, thus running the risk of embracing the opposite excess. This is the case of Niall Slater's prominent reader-oriented interpretation of the Petronian novel, which held the field in the 1990s. His 'reader-response' theory aims at detecting "what happens within the reader during the reading process," and tries to illustrate the Petronian novel in relation to "the reader's own predilections and knowledge" (Slater, 1990, xi; 3). By setting up his stance within Wolfgang Iser's theoretical framework, Slater requires the specific reader of the *Satyrica* to possess some basic literary and cultural skills, labelled the "repertoire": an 'extratextual' reality consisting of references to earlier Greek and Latin works, to social and his-

---

[258] On Eco, 1990 see Pisanty, 2015, 50ff. This topic is prefigured by the Roman juridical distinction, in the interpretation of the *Corpus Iuris Civilis* ("The Body of Civil Law," issued by Justinian in the sixth century AD), between the *voluntas legis* (the content of the Law) and the *voluntas legislatoris* (the interpreter's decision): see Bianco, 1998, 19.

[259] Since Roland Barthes declared the 'death of the author' (see above, p. 92 n. 247), "the reader could be born" (Rabinowitz, 2005, 29).

[260] This kind of extra-textual surplus centered on the author, called "circumstances of utterance," draws attention to the historical period, cultural profile of the speaker, etc. The result is that none of the three intentions should be disregarded giving "the advantage to the other two": on Eco, 1979, 14ff. see Pisanty, 2015, 60.

torical norms, and "to the whole culture from which the text has emerged."[261] Slater's analysis has remarkable merits. It has been acknowledged that important issues are amply illuminated by his captivating investigation on the *Satyrica*: dynamics of role-playing performed by characters, and by the audience *within each* single episode;[262] a definition of the novel as capable of incorporating various types of discourse, "ranging from the serious and classical to the comic and carnivalesque" (Connors, 1991, 2); sound judgements on the presence of epic parody, so as not to overlap onto other literary aspects of the work.

What instead puzzles in Slater's stance is the authoritative, and sometimes constraining pattern of demonstrations, resulting from his triple reading of the *Satyrica*, according to the reader-response method. On one hand, the 'reader' shifts mazily from the empirical to the implied reaction, or from the original contemporary to the modern/universal one (Beck, 1997, 72). On the other, by situating the alleged "meaning" of the *Satyrica* in the audience, rather than in the narrator or the author, Slater's asserted possibility that a text can be "designed to maximize the reader's frustration," or even that an author "can intend *not* to mean something" (Slater, 1990, 236), is contradicted by his very illustration (meticulous and elegant, indeed) that Petronius portrays his characters so effectively: "is this 'not meaning'"? (Beck, 1992, 71-2). Grounded motives of perplexity also concern Slater's stance regarding philological stemmatic criticism. A classicist is familiar with enriching "the text in the act of constituting it," as well as the practice of exercising "his literary sensibility" after resorting to "purely mechanical considerations" (See Slater, 1990, respectively 14, 15, 138). But how can literary interpretation and textual criticism be re-

---

[261] See Iser, 1978, 69ff. Meaning doesn't embody "a treasure that can be excavated through interpretation" (p. 5); the "implied reader" incorporates predispositions laid down, "not by an empirical outside reality, but by the text itself" (p. 34); text and reader are claimed to converge by way of a "situation which depends on both for its 'realisation'" (pp. 68-9); "throughout the reading process there is a continual interplay beween modified expectations and transformed memories" (p. 111). On the 'repertoire' see also Beck, 1992, 69.

[262] Cf. above, p. 23 n. 9; pp. 30-1.

garded as analogous "forms of reading," solely because both base their practice on reading (Slater, 1990, 16)?[263]

As a tentative proposal, I would suggest that whatever orientation one decides to follow as regards the role of the reader, the assumption of a narrator-perspective is still likely to furnish a useful corrective to an *overly unbalanced* reader-response criticism. In fact, since we possess just a fragment of the original *Satyrica*, the 'response' of modern readers cannot fail to be a limited and provisional "approximation to what was and what might be, were the whole accessible" (Beck, 1992, 72).[264] But back to our main topic: apart from this unsatisfactory *hovering* between author, narrator, and reader, how shall we identify and evaluate the reader's perspective in our novel?

A theoretical answer might come from the results of a narrational investigation that, in the last thirty years, has become increasingly popular in the field of Greek and Latin literature (Grethlein-Rengakos, 2009, 1-11).[265] Jonas Grethlein has specifically argued that the tension between the "horizon of expectations" and the "space of experiences" can be reconfigured, on one hand, at a *reception* level, since expectations built up regarding the plot may either prove correct or not in the process of reading; on the other, at a *narrative* level, because, in the temporal evolution of a plot, characters themselves have expectations and experiences.[266]

---

[263] Philology is actually something else. West, 1973, 29ff. thoroughly examines the philological basis of stemmatic analysis (closed and open recension; diagnosis; evaluation of variants): not to mention other requirements, "it must be clear how the presumed original reading could have been corrupted into any different reading that is transmitted" (p. 48). Further reservations about Slater's method in Anderson, 1991, 341; Jensson, 2004, 195ff.

[264] After 24 years, Beck, 1997 confirms the conclusions of his 1973 essay: "a better perspective for integrating the novel is its narrator, not its reader."

[265] On ancient Greek narrative see the pioneering De Jong, 2007-2012.

[266] Grethlein, 2009, 155ff. suggests that human temporality is defined by life *experiences* directing *expectations*, liable to be either fulfilled or disappointed by new experiences: experiences in turn "rectroactively transform the memory" of previous expectations and experiences. This tension features both our *reception* of narrative and *narrative* itself, which is why the readers' *reception* thus "doubles" (p. 157) the tension expectations-experiences from the perspective of the *action* of characters. The application of this philosophical-structuralist model to Herodotus and Thucydides shows that both historians prove to have similar views of human beings *in time*, but they present them in quite different narrative modes, offering divergent reading experiences (pp. 159ff.).

As this narratological groundwork was being established, Gareth Schmeling proposed his study on the reader's attitude towards the Petronian "sense of an ending" (Schmeling, 1991, 353-67). Self-subsistent sections of the *Satyrica*, disappointing and keeping very "observant" readers off balance, prompt them to select a recurrent "readjustment" of expectations: the endings are handled by Petronius in such an unexpected fashion, that a strong tension is created in the reader, who at times covets the "familiar" dimension of the traditional narrative "paradigm," but then "yearns for something new." This lack of interest in the ending "as a purpose" affects both the "absence of purpose and goals" in the novel, and the "aimlessness" of Encolpius: it is no chance that the objective of each story is to conclude with "an outrageous scene or a witty punch-line" (Schmeling, 1991, 359; 364).[267] It's definitely remarkable how Petronius, within rapid shifts in mood, plays with his jolted readers by re-arranging the Aristotelian concept of 'peripeteia', the narrative "reversal."[268]

Diversely oriented in her sensitivity to the reader-perspective, Victoria Rimell has highlighted episodes that echo each other in the text of the *Satyrica*, so that a scholarly reader, capable of paying attention to every detail, should be ready to recognise and connect incidents distant from each other.[269] At 126.13ff., Encolpius is entering into a world of fiction, the mythical Circe-mirage, like students who set foot in court and "find themselves

[267] In the episodes told by Eumolpus, the Pergamene ephebus (*Sat.* 85-87) and the widow of Ephesus (111-112), possible ends of single sections, predicted by the reader, prove "not to be final," with the youth becoming aggressive and the widow becoming the active partner: both stories end "with lightning quickness," and "not in the places the reader had expected" (p. 362); furthermore, both stories could have logically continued – for example – with sanctions against Eumolpus and the widow, but the reader is given "a witty epigrammatic one-liner" (p. 363). Unexpected reality crashes into the *Cena* at 78.7, with the fire brigade as a "swift, daring" final ending (instead of the predictable ending of 74.1). A reader must likewise re-orient himself at 92-96, when Encolpius and Eumolpus try to obtain Giton's favors: the sudden role of Encolpius as *inclusus amator*, locked in by Eumolpus (94.7), is a variation-reversal of the Askyltos-Giton theme at 80.6ff. (p. 367).

[268] Cf. Aristotle, *Poet.* 1452[a] 11: "A reversal is a change to the opposite in the actions being performed, as stated – and this, as we have been saying, in accordance with probability or necessity" (Heath, 1996, 18).

[269] See Rimell, 2002, 147-8. This ideal Petronian reader sounds more attentive than the "alert reader" of Apuleius' *Metamorphoses* (Panayotakis, 2004, 154).

transported into another world" (1.2 *putent se in alium orbem terrarum delatos*). At *Sat.* 129.5, Circe comments on Encolpius's impotence: "doctors say that people who lose their sexual powers are unable to walk" (*negant enim medici sine nervis homines ambulare posse*); similarly, at. 1.1 ("my legs are hamstrung and cannot support my body's weight": *nam succisi poplites membra non sustinent*), the caricatured orator claims that he cannot walk. We could perhaps associate here the allusion to pirates in Encolpius's declamation at 1.3 ("pirates in chains on the seashore": *piratas cum catenis in litore stantes*) – as an example of the absurd training of youngsters in the schools of rhetoric – with the actual courtroom scene taking place on board Lichas's ship at 106ff., when the 'defense attorney' Eumolpus tries to deceive the 'plaintiff' Lichas.[270]

In some other points, readers are prompted to re-analyse their initial readings "or memory of previous passages" (Rimell, 2007, 128ff). At 72.7, when a dog on a chain greets our heroes "with such a din that Askyltos actually fell into the fish-pond," Encolpius recollects his drunkenness, and that he earlier (cf. *Sat.* 29.1) had "recoiled at the sight even of the painted dog" (*etiam pictum timueram canem*).[271] Within this composition-effect ring, relating beginning and end of the *Cena*, a reader will appreciate the further parallelism with the accident of Scylax, the "hulking dog led in on a lead" (64.7 *canis catena vinctus*), described again as the *canis ingens, catena vinctus* at 29.1: incapable of distinguishing real from fake, the double-crossed reader will probably share the whirling sensation experienced by Encolpius. On board Lichas's ship, in the enduring fury of combatants joining battle (the *fratres* for their lives, Lichas and friends for vengeance: cf. *Sat.* 108.9), Giton and Encolpius stage mock suicides, the former with a razor to his manhood, the latter with a barber's knife to his throat (108.10-11). Giton's move recalls the staged death-scene (*mimica mors*) at 94.10-15, where the fake blade didn't obviously mark "any suggestion of

[270] See Panayotakis, 2009, 62.
[271] See above, p. 33 n. 33.

a wound" (*ulla suspicione vulneris*): is Encolpius really forgetting, or pretending to forget the previous episode?[272]

Readers are confronted by a novel where the narrator's recollections almost never clarify, but rather *obscure* reality: frequently invited to reconsider their first impressions, they are actually settled *inside* Encolpius's fictional world by a masterful performance of first-person expanded narration: which is why readers end up somehow *sinking* into ambiguity and conjecture.[273] It goes without saying that readers' reactions can't consist in mere amusement: I believe that the novel "is perhaps more disruptive than entertaining" (Rimell, 2002, 4ff; 33). On one hand, a generalized emphasis on the bare 'ludic' nature of the *Satyrica*, or on a simplistic reading of Petronius's novel as an indecent entertainment, appears quite worn out and misleading.[274] On the other, contemporary readers would hardly be persuaded by complementary approaches centered on Petronius as looking *from above* at the world he depicts,[275] or by perspectives underlining a Petronius'ss so-called 'sophistication', to be seen "in the careful dissociation of the author from the ostensible narrator, who is constantly made the unconscious butt of the author's ridicule and satire."[276] Readers might rather be 'amused', not just by the (intentionally?) satirical or farcical impulse of Encolpius's narrative, but by its enigmatic and baffling features, without partaking in any 'superiority' or 'objectivity' – of either the empirical or the implied author – towards our helpless and clownish narrator. Despite the opposite risk of shifting into a generic or unquestioning 'empathy' for Encolpius, I suppose readers would be ready to accept a double challenge: first, to feel *sympathetic emotion* for the narrator, going along with the "En-

---

[272] The joke is even more amusing if a reader keeps alive the enigma/riddle: is the razor of 108 a sharp one (as having been used on the ship to cut hair and eyebrows of Encolpius: cf. 103.1), or a blunted one (cf. 108.11)? "Is there one razor, or two"? (Rimell 2007, 130).

[273] See above, especially ch. 2.1-4; 2.6.

[274] See above, p. 57.

[275] "Auch Petronius sieht die Welt, die er malt, von oben" (Auerbach, 1946, 53). On Auerbach and ancient 'realism' see above, p. 63 n. 134.

[276] Sullivan, 1968, 258. About misunderstandings due to the idea of Encolpius as a "Petronius in disguise," who observes and satirizes the narrator, see above, ch. 2.8.

colpius outlaw perspective, fogged by drink, drugs, inanity or paranoia" (Rimell, 2007, 114): secondly, in the case of critical assessment, to keep a constructive detachment from the narrator. The complex mingling of emotions, created by the *Satyrica,* in some way *needs* to be ordered by a sensitive and at the same time sagacious reader, whose sympathy doesn't imply blurring or losing her/his capacity of inferential activity. Readers might have recognised and shared, in these pages, the nuanced roles of implied author,[277] untrustworthy narrator,[278] and intertext-addicted reader:[279] but any possible fascination of a contrived 'entanglement', between Encolpius and the reader, has turned out to be deflated and greatly reduced.[280]

As a matter of fact, although placed inside Encolpius's fictional world, and so often lost in the quicksand of its incongruities, readers are *nowhere prevented* from making balanced judgements on the narrator and his world: which means neither proving 'superior' / 'objective' nor collapsing in an undiscerning identification. Readers' involvement *and* detachment can intertwine within a dynamic and very rewarding blend. In the words of James Wood, in a "tragicomedy of forgiveness," like our *Satyrica,* "irresponsibility" is a state in which readers may not always know why a character does something or may not know how to read a passage: but they "must try to merge with the characters in their uncertainty."[281]

---

[277] See above, ch. 2.8.

[278] See above, p. 81 n. 190.

[279] See above, ch. 2.9.

[280] Within Rimell's 2002 great contribution to Petronian studies (Panayotakis, 2004, 154; above, n. 130; cf. Rimell, 2007), what makes us less happy with some of her suggestions may depend on the fact that she tends to emphasize an unrestrained scepticism about the "insoluble" dilemma of Encolpius's personality, and to overdo the reader-involvement in reading the *Satyrica.*

[281] Wood, 2005, 6; 16; p. 82 n. 197.

Chapter 3
DEALING WITH LONG-FOCUS LENSES: FEDERICO FELLINI'S PICTORIAL AFFECTIVITY

—Et Fellini, comment supporte-t-il la gloire?
—Très bien. Il a grossi.

Giulietta Masina to Dominique Delouche (1960)

3.1 IN SEARCH OF SOME 'HYPER-GRAFFITI'

However readers may judge the first-person narrative adopted in Petronius's *Satyrica,* what captures their attention – while moving to Federico Fellini's "free adaptation" of the novel – is that the protagonist's central position, indisputable with the Roman novelist, turns out to be fluctuating and fragmented in *Fellini-Satyricon* (Burke, 2020, 155ff). How should we 'disentangle' ourselves from the mixture of wonderment and unease, linked to the results of closely comparing the novel with the film, that captivates both readers and film-viewers?

It has been clearly demonstrated that Fellini's early movies, where the director applied himself to "well defined main characters," may be regarded as "individualist in emphasis";[1] but after the crucial change with *Otto e mezzo* (1963), these connotations were increasingly reduced, giving rise to a process of "de-individualization" (Burke, 2020, 103): characters, once neatly focused by the author in the '50s, were dissolved or removed over the years. To a certain extent, the very notion of 'protagonist' becomes apparently questionable and risks significant erasure in *Fellini-Satyricon,* as demonstrated by the technical resources – editing, composition of visual space, camera movements, and music – used by Fellini to enact his portrayal of a 'babbling', not rarely disappearing Encolpio.

[1] Burke 1989, 37-8 takes into account: Checco in *Luci del varietà* (1950); Ivan and Wanda in *Lo sceicco bianco* (1952); Moraldo, in *I vitelloni* (1953); Zampanò (I would add Gelsomina), in *La Strada* (1954); Augusto, in *Il bidone* (1955); Cabiria, in *Le notti di Cabiria* (1956); Marcello, in *La dolce vita* (1959). Specifically, Fellini's earliest figures in *Luci del varietà* and *Lo sceicco bianco* are mere caricatures, whereas later figures (starting with *I vitelloni*) are more "rounded characters" (Burke, 2020, 76).

At the outset of the treatment, Encolpio, "with a scoundrelly and aggressive posture," makes advances to a "beautiful married woman" in the middle of the Circus Maximus (thus standing out from the crowd [Zanelli A, 111-3; my trans.]): the scene is deleted in the published screenplay, which shows a distressed Encolpio jerking in despair against the background of a *reddish wall*, thickly scratched by passers-by, "till becoming an abstract decoration of white squiggles" ([Zanelli B, 1.1-9; my trans.]). In the movie (scene 1.1), to the left of a tracking shot, the camera draws back slowly from a brownish wall, where some obscene writings stand out with a large graffiti gladiator, echoing Pompeian images (Pesando, 2010, 198): Encolpio enters the film, first, as a voice-over; then his shadow begins to take shape, silhouetted against the wall, as the camera halts (Bondanella, 1992, 245; 248).[2] The *bituminous or chalky* tones ("toni bituminosi o gessosi") of the graffiti covered wall, led Giorgio Zanchetti to suppose that the painter Antonio Scordia, 'visual advisor' for *Fellini-Satyricon*, might have been inspired – among others – by 'materic' paintings by Cy Twombly, whose canvases, marked by non-figurative scribbles, do resemble scrawled blackboards.[3] Similarly, in the interiors of the *insula Felicles* sequence, some graffiti decorating a back wall suggest the idea of cave dwellers on stage: an ignominious and miserable humanity, swarming in the flats of a sort of a massive ziqqurat filmed from inside (6.107-7.131) (Bartesaghi, 2009, 346). It's not by chance that different kinds and sizes of graffiti will be frequently used by Fellini through very lively variations on the theme. In *Il Casanova di Federico Fellini* (1976), on the wall of Dux Castle's toilet a portrait of the protagonist is plastered over with faecal matter; in

[2] Fellini's special attention to *framing* (the manner in which subjects and objects are 'framed' by the boundaries of the film image) stems from the world of comics and drawings, which, since 1938 (cf. n. 30), let him take into account "the figurative relationship among the characters, the objects, the landscape, and the edges of the frame" (Vanelli, 2020b, 210).

[3] See Zanchetti, 2009, 150-3 on a possible Scordia incentive from Cy Twombly (1928-2011): cf. e.g., *Untitled*, oil paint and crayon on canvas, 1968 (Providence, Museum of Art, Rhode Island School of Design). For *Fellini-Satyricon* the post-cubist painter Antonio Scordia (1918-1988) used to take pictures of archaeological sources, subsequently transposing the material either onto walls, or into easel-format for modern painting collections.

Prova d'orchestra (1979), the protest against the conductor is expressed in anarchic scribbles on the wall; in *La città delle donne* (1980), at a feminist convention, multi-coloured erotic posters, mural inscriptions, and even blown-up pictures of ancient Greek pottery underline mocking threats to male sexuality.

Anyway, besides recognisable meta-cinematic allusions (the opening graffiti like a movie screen), or (involuntary?) references in the opening scene to the Greek-Roman world, from the allegory of the cave in Plato (*Rep.* 7.1), to the origin of painting in Pliny the Elder (*Nat.* 35.151), is it just a coincidence that a wall covered with graffiti serves as a background for the opening credits of Anthony Mann's *The Fall of the Roman Empire*, released just a few years earlier (1964)?[4] Extending the graffiti-topic in Fellini, Rosita Copioli conveniently pointed out that the contingent ambiguity of a piece of graffiti may remind us of a crumbled memory, erratically preserved ("conservata in modo bizzarro"), like a twist of fate.[5] By the power of its 'un-artistic' fragmentation, the allure of graffiti alludes to the survival of low-level traces of the past that cannot be compared to high-level historical, literary, epigraphic, or artistic ones.

On the basis of this assumption, I would go so far as to suggest that such cinematic inter-text, based on a leitmotif, recurring both in other Fellini movies and in his life experience, might allude to the graffiti-idea as a conceptual matrix that encompasses – and somehow transcends – individual films, as a kind of 'hyper-graffiti': an exercise, into which Fellini's mytho-biography and his film-making process seem to converge.[6] In fact, on the one hand,

---

[4] In Mann's movie, the Polish artist, Maciek Piotrowski, was supervisor for 'title backgrounds and murals' (cf. IMDb: *The Fall of the Roman Empire*, 1964 – 'Additional Crew'). Slavazzi, 2009, 61 nn. 6-9 also suggests that Fellini could have been inspired by a piece of graffiti placed under an erotic picture from Jean Marcadé's *Roma Amor* (1963), an art book on Roman painting and sculpture, which Zanelli, 1969, 21 itemised among the scholarly texts piled on the director's desk during the making of the film (Stubbs, 2006, 213).

[5] See Copioli, 2020, 146-7 (my trans.). Graffiti are a component of what Petrucci, 1985, 88ff. calls "scritture esposte."

[6] I here borrow the productive metaphor of 'hyper-film', employed by Marcus, 2002, 170 for Fellini's *Ginger e Fred* (1985), as "the unitary, ongoing creative project that links the artist's

Fellini was quite familiar with twentieth-century cartoons, largely based on graffiti (Copioli, 2020, 147);[7] on the other, drawings had a crucial role throughout his career: *Il libro dei sogni* ("The Book of Dreams") is not devoid of enigmatic and barely explainable fantasies.[8] This semi-unconscious *scribbling of doodles* is best described by the director himself, sustained by his peculiar mixture of modesty, alertness, and dreamy forgetfulness ("smemoratezza"):

> All this unrestrained and inexhaustible graphic trash [...] is a thread at the end of which I find myself in my studio, on the first day of shooting [...] Since I was a child, I have always scribbled on any available piece of paper, in a kind of conditioned reflex, an unconscious effort [...] Since the beginning, draftsmen, caricaturists, painters, even those who draw the Madonna on the pavement, with chalks, have always attracted me [...][9]

Visionary 'hyper-graffiti' ceaselessly continue to create meanings, figures, and reveries, both at a biographical and at a cinematic level. In this respect, beyond individual Fellini films, the wall scribbles in the opening scene seemingly point to a specific abstraction: the perception of something that struggles to take shape, from an amorphous 'aphasia' to a fully articulated expression, i.e. from the 'chaos' of the beginning to the 'cosmos' of a movie in the making... A precious testimony is further given by Fellini, although not concerning this specific film but artistic creation in wider terms:

---

biography to his cinematic corpus at a relatively high level of abstraction, where the author's *life in film-making* coincides, in a sense, with the *film of his life*" (italics Marcus).

[7] On American comics, known to Fellini through Italian magazines, see above, p. 13 n. 27.

[8] Fellini wrote skits and made cartoons for humoristic publications, mainly the *Domenica del Corriere*, the satirical weekly *420* and the bi-weekly *Marc'Aurelio* (1938-1942): see Bondanella, 1992, 11ff.; Kezich, 2002, 25ff.; 34ff.; White, 2015, iv; Bellano, 2020, 59-71. In *Il libro dei sogni* (cf. Toffetti, 2020: above, p. 13 n. 27), a vision of a powerful female bust is "decorated with indecipherable ideograms or hieroglyphs" (22.12.1961); on a large wall at the Salone Margherita, *La Strada* is being screened (April 1968); ancient Roman walls emerge, nestled in modern marbles (3.6.1977); a solid wall apparently belongs to a mental hospital (7.4.1978).

[9] Federico Fellini, in Mollica, 2006, 20-1; my trans.

> That is the archetype of creation which renews itself over and over, the journey from chaos to cosmos, from what is jumbled and elusive to order, statement, completeness.[10]

Furthermore (what is particularly relevant to us), interpreters have not failed to notice that a similar graffiti-covered wall reappears *at the film's end*, through a similar backtracking shot, but with several significant visual shifts.

3.2 Losing and Taking Shape, as the Wind Blows Through

In the opening scene, Ilhan Mimaroğlu's *Prelude for Magnetic Tape XII* anticipates – synchronised with the shot of the wall – Encolpio's monologue. Fellini, usually not interested in sound as purely "mimetic or denotative" (Sisto, 2020, 252), uses the throbbing attack of the electronic composition, as if it were a heart recovering its beat, as appropriate for Encolpio's angry outburst, since Ascilto has taken his beloved Gitone by force ("the Earth's abyss has been unable to swallow me up "… "And who has condemned me to this seclusion?" (my trans.). Mimaroğlu's track shows up as a mysterious and 'liminal' voice producing a sense of suffering: it seems to feature the transition from the *silent darkness* of the opening credits to the *sound light* of the film screening (Sala, 2009, 104 n. 25; 105).[11] In the last scene, a berthed ship is in the background, with a tall bow and a bent stern resembling a bird; after the account of Eumolpo's last legacy, which disposes that his heirs gain possession of his wealth if they are ready to eat his carcass (73.1049-1075), three youngsters – a black guy, the ship's captain, and Encolpio, filmed full-length from behind – move towards the ship, accompanied by the same Mimaroğlu *Prelude* on Encolpio's words "il vento è favorevole" ("the wind is fair," 73.1075-77): as a blowing

[10] Federico Fellini, in Grazzini, 1988, 202 (Joseph Henry's trans.). The opening image of the movie pays visual homage to a "verbal sabotage," which Fellini enacts "by debasing written communication into decor in the form of the graffiti": Van Watson, 2002, 72.

[11] It was no chance that Mimaroğlu's LP *Electronic Music III* (Turnabout tv 34177) was a very recent album, just released in 1967, during the preparation of *Fellini-Satyricon*: see Del Santo, 2009, 110-3.

wind engulfs the music, a crinkled sea is framed from the ship's bow, giving us a glimpse of an islet.

We hear the words of Encolpio in *voice-over*, as a first-person narrator ("I decided to go with them. We left that night. I was a member of the crew. We touched on the ports of unknown cities. For the first time I heard the names of Kelisha, Rectis"); but as soon as his voice fades away in mid-sentence ("On an island covered with high, perfumed grass, a young Greek told us that over the years..."),[12] the scene cuts to a close-up of Encolpio "against a sparkling sea-screen" (Hough-Dugdale, 2020, 245). The slow tracking shot shows the solid wall of the opening now shifting to a final fractured one: three cracked frescoes, recalling first Encolpio and then a number of characters (75.1079-81), all *previously* unsettled cinematographic images throughout the film, are *now* taken out of time into "frozen immobility" (Sullivan, 1991/2001, 271). After coming to life throughout the length of the movie, these "frescoed forms" seem finally to return to their source (Stubbs, 2006, 216):[13] against the background of an imperceptible horizon, a distant sea is almost blended with the sky. The combination of Nino Rota's[14] painful *Melopea* with the gusts of wind underscores both the interruption of Encolpio's narration and the transformation of characters into paintings on fragmented murals, where "everything is frozen and is covered with the dust of ages" (Zanelli B, 1249-53; my trans.). The dissolve into the black ground of the end credits reminds us of the same dark setting from which Encolpio's voice-over had come out of the opening credits against the black background.

---

[12] Cf. scene 73.1078 (trans. Frank Burke, 2020, 156).

[13] The same technique was used by Joseph L. Mankiewicz in *Cleopatra* (1963), where several changes of scene show characters turned into fissured frescoes: it may not be accidental that Italo Tomassi, pictorial supervisor for *Fellini-Satyricon* (cf. below, *Principal Credits*), had collaborated with Mankiewicz as scene painter for *Cleopatra* (see Slavazzi, 2009, 84-5).

[14] Nino Rota (1911-1979), pianist, composer, and conductor, is known for his movie scores for Fellini (from *Lo sceicco bianco*, 1952, to *Prova d'orchestra*, 1979 – except for *Un'agenzia matrimoniale*, 1953), Luchino Visconti, Franco Zeffirelli, and Francis Ford Coppola. About Rota as an actual "sound designer" for *Fellini-Satyricon*, see Del Santo, 2009, 109. Rota's music for Fellini, as capable of blurring, silencing, underlining, or intensifying images, has an open semiotic function, freed from "strict narrative constraints": Sisto, 2020, 255-6.

In the same time frame, Fellini's treatment of voice-over has led to both a different thematic growth and an artistic outcome. In *Toby Dammit*,[15] the immaterial voice-over of the protagonist speaks in the past tense, describing events that have taken place before his violent death.[16] This *narrating-I* first comments on his disquiet vision when landing in Rome, leading him to hope that the plane would reverse its course, and take him far away back home; then, it recounts Toby's fearsome vision in the car on the way to a television studio: the innocent-corrupt smile of a luminous, silent little girl, whose enigmatic white ball bounces against gravity; she had already appeared at his arrival at the airport, and Toby will later identify her as the Devil, answering a journalist in the television interview. No matter if the eerie little girl, as a very likely projection of the protagonist's inner self, reflects Fellini's anxiety regarding mortality, caused by his life-threatening pleurisy attack diagnosed in April 1967,[17] and echoing in some dreams recorded in his "Book of Dreams."[18] In purely figurative terms, the voice-over at the start of the movie is emitted from a disembodied 'spirit', until Toby's name, called by a reporter inside the airport, implies his recovery of a visible human body that leaps off the

[15] *Toby Dammit* (from Poe's '*Never Bet The Devil Your Head*') was finished between February and March 1968. Between June and August (after the definitive failure of *Il viaggio di G. Mastorna* and the release of *Fellini: A Director's Notebook* in USA: cf. below, p. 136 nn. 106-8), Fellini and Zapponi prepared the screenplay of *Fellini-Satyricon*, the filming dates of which were 9th November 1968-20th May 1969 (see Copioli, 2020, 141).

[16] Toby, a British drug-addicted stage actor, agrees to star in a film to be shot in Rome, with the promise of a Ferrari. After a frightening vision of a girl (a radiant 'devil') at his arrival in Rome, he gets drunk at a film award ceremony; failing to recite a Shakespearean monologue, he escapes from the dinner. Now sober, he races with the Ferrari around the city, destroying road signs and guideposts, and stops before a collapsed bridge: passing by his female "devil," he speeds over the edge of the ravine. The car disappears: a suspended wire, dripping with blood, suggests Toby's beheading, and the smiling girl eventually picks up his detached head. On this sort of "horror story" see Bondanella, 1992, 232ff. For an insightful reading of the film, in which Fellini awakens the spectator to the tricks of the cinema, see Sharrett, 2002, 121ff.

[17] Cf. below, p. 117 n. 47.

[18] Cf. above, p. 13 n. 27. From 20 April 1967 to 30 March 1968, Fellini had frequent nightmares dealing with regrets and terrors, linked to his filmmaking: in the significant dream of 19 July 1967, some children are rescued from a car accident, but the driver is beheaded.

screen (Burke, 2020, 135ff).[19] As such, Toby increasingly gets rid of social restraints and professional obligations throughout the film: by eventually crossing the abyss, he isn't confronted by a *physical* death (an absolute silence underscores the scene, where gravity is defeated); nor can we talk of a "suicide of a demented actor" (Bondanella, 1992, 236), but rather of a transformation, within a kind of *symbolic* death and rebirth process.

Since any viewer cannot help but be impressed by Fellini's use of camera movements in concert with treatment of sound, some questions naturally arise. At the end of *Fellini-Satyricon*, on boarding for the final voyage, the postures of Encolpio and the other character *lose* their human shape, but *assume* a transcendental, 'out-of-time' one: they are enhanced by the *same* backtracking as when this dream-nightmare materialised from the scribbled wall in the opening scene, and both scenes are accompanied by the *same* Mimaroğlu's musical score. It should be noticed that, while Mimaroğlu's *Prelude* also occurs in Trimalcione's feast and in the Ermafrodito's temple (as if to highlight cacophonous or dreamlike sequences),[20] Rota's *Melopea* impacts the film significantly in six more peculiar shots, all of them emphasizing either puzzling and trivial incidents, or episodes where tenuous characters express themselves in hypnotic, nearly lost-for-ever languages (Sala, 2009, 97ff).[21] By virtue of these occurrences, the two musical arrangements appear to overload Fellini's narrative with some emphasis

---

[19] The seemingly analogous framework of Billy Wilder's black comedy, *Sunset Boulevard* (1950), with an off-stage commentary provided by Joe Gillis (whose corpse is in the first scene), lends itself to a very different survey: the *entire* thematic content is supported by a voice-over, which diverges from Toby's inasmuch as "the dead-pan tone of *noir* narration" is appropriate to the narrator's character, resigned, sardonic, and unabashed "in telling the shameful tale of his own subjugation" to Norma Desmond and his own death (see Podgorski 2016).

[20] Cf. scene 13.289-301 (mixed with barking dogs, during the performance of actors playing Homeric verses); 53.725-31 (when an amputee visits the Ermafrodito, mixed with dripping water since 729).

[21] Regarding when the melody occurs: cf. scene 7.129 (the sound of a *cetra* swallowed up by the uproar of the *insula Felicles*); 13.246 (during the petty dinner at Trimalcione's); 13.324 (idem); 36.467 (unaccountable words sung by Gitone on board Lica's ship); 49.663 (childish and poignant *melopea* of the girl-slave in the Villa dei Suicidi); 75.1079 (stirred by the wind in the final scene above).

on tentative, pointless, or no longer existing voices: does it mean emphasis on *nothingness*? (Morelli, 2001, 392ff). We may wonder, with Emilio Sala (Sala, 2018, 13ff), whether a different kind of music, unprecedented in the film and not traceable to this ethno-electronic "soundscape" (resulting from the combination of Rota's *Melopea* with Mimaroğlu's *Prelude*), wouldn't have radically changed the 'meaning' of the final sequence.

"There's a lot of wind in Fellini."[22] As part of ambient sounds, the 'Fellinian' wind proves very effective in the final sequence of *Fellini-Satyricon*, as much as everywhere throughout the movie (and in most of his films). Within the classic 'word-centred' films in perfect Hollywood style, with voice and human figure concentrating auditory and visual attention, wind mainly tended (and still tends) to place characters within a given space and a given time (Gianneri, 2017):[23] the story of a traditional "closed film" exhausted the meaning of what it contained, because its emphasis was on narrative tightness; whereas in an "open" form, like Fellini's, the emphasis is "on a lack of restraint and diversity."[24] Through the use of wind, Fellini's camera normally unveils the perceptive scrutiny of an author who – particularly from *Otto e mezzo* on (1963) – moves inside his own staging process, always ready to 'question' it's very *raison d'être*, in tandem with his spectators: the emphasis is on the process of construction, no longer on the product (Burke, 2020, 17). Seen in its effects (due to the opposition between accuracy of sight and inscrutability of the other senses),[25] in Fellini wind is *in constant motion*, sometimes as a saving figure, or as a disturbing element, or as a voice of the subcon-

[22] See Richard Dyer's 2009 introduction to his IKKM Research Project on Vimeo: "The Wind in Fellini."

[23] Cause-and-effect narrativity traditionally depends on "temporal differentiation and sequencing": van Watson, 2002, 74.

[24] On Leo Braudy's distinction between closed and open forms, see Stubbs, 2006, 4ff.

[25] We are reminded by Gianneri, 2017 that since the '60s wind in filmmaking appears as "movimento puro": in Michelangelo Antonioni's *L'avventura* (1960), the wind that strongly sweeps the tiny island of Lisca Bianca seems to be a replica of the restless and bewildered gaze of characters in search of Anna, mysteriously missing.

scious, or as something "liberating."[26] Wind may be harmful: an interesting case in point occurs in a sequence from Fellini's *Roma* (1972), where careless excavations under the Via Appia Antica reveal an underground chamber of a *domus romana,* decorated with frescoes which get irreparably damaged by rushing gusts of wind.

The multifaceted presence of wind throughout *Fellini-Satyricon,* in combination with a grotesque imagery and an "erratic sonic continuum" (Sisto, 2020, 252), sometimes emphasizes the ingenious overtones of a fairy-tale remoteness,[27] as well as the mocking solemnity of ritual and ancient myths.[28] In the fight between Encolpio and Minotauro, Fellini's *montage* of the labyrinth scene (just note Ruggero Mastroianni's refined work on frames jerkily shot by the camera),[29] shows graffiti, murals, low and blind walls with slits, even a high stone relief: by restricting a claustrophobic space, these barren objects ceaselessly assemble in a torrid arena, stunned by the sun, until a wall-trap prevents Encolpio from escaping.[30] In the whole scene, the effect of the fiercely blowing wind is stressed by the noise of Minotauro's iterated hammer strokes, and by the clamour of the chuckling audience during the "Festival of Laughter." Elsewhere in the film, the strong gusts of wind intensify the hyperbolic traits of certain frames, as is the case with the nymphomaniac episode:[31] her husband, closed in silent pain, wanders around like a moronic ghost; the woman squirms uselessly in the cart, imprisoned by leather laces, dull symbols of her subjugating disease (Betti, 1970, 45).

---

[26] Dyer, 2009 draws our attention to Guido's nightmare in the first sequence of *8½*, with the character flowing in the wind to escape from the grip of the traffic: cf. also the decisive presence of wind in *La Strada* (1954) and *Le notti di Cabiria* (1956).

[27] Cf. scene 17.405-26-421 (the widow of Ephesos); 61.980-91; 68.1021-70.1033 (tale and activity of the enchantress Enotea: see above, p. 18 n. 44).

[28] Cf. scene 37.489-515 (the wedding of Lica and Encolpio on the ship: see above, p. 19 n. 50); 58.794-903 (Encolpio's fight with Minotauro in the labyrinth and his défaillance with Arianna).

[29] The editor, Ruggero Mastroianni (1929-1996), collaborated with Fellini, after replacing the legendary Leo Catozzo, from *Giulietta degli spiriti* (1965) to *Ginger e Fred* (1985).

[30] Cf. scene 58-798; 815; 824-6.

[31] Cf. scene 50.676-51.704.

In a couple of crucial incidents, Eumolpo's first legacy to Encolpio and the death of Ascilto, the blowing wind strengthens its creative effectiveness. In the former scene, it intensifies the poignant melancholy of the poet's words: "I bequeath to you poetry, seasons, first of all spring and summer … the wind, the sun, the sea … and the large passing clouds, solemn and light … and sounds, songs, noises! the voice of men, which is the most soothing music…."[32] In the latter, it sharpens the epic atmosphere of Ascilto dying in a clearing on the water's edge.[33] After framing Ascilto twice in a long-shot, the camera moves from the level of the reeds, from a close-up of Encolpio (next to his friend, who seems to be resting peacefully) to an extreme long-shot, where the two youngsters are surrounded by the reeds of the wide field. The soft dissolve on black doesn't perform its "standardised function of indicating the passing of time" (Dyer, 2020, 46), but seems to convey an intense way of 'cuddling' the twosome, almost wrapping them within the silent, 'maternal' embrace of water and earth:[34] a meditative, rather than a purely narrative transition. I am intrigued by the idea of detecting how this scene could have been inspired by the final Po Valley episode of Rossellini's *Paisà* ("Paisan," 1946): the script was totally rewritten by Fellini,[35] so much that the director might have been encouraged by the latter to shoot the sequence (Bondanella, 1992, 48 n. 28), with the camera permanently moving *just above the water* of the swampy river basin, thus admirably capturing the partisans' perspective.

The role of wind in the last scene is no less highly expressive: it enhances and 'seals' the arranged effect of the above-mentioned camera movements and music. As if it were waiting for the arrival of a paralysing silence, where everything comes to an end and from which the film had started, the final wind sharpens the 'par-

[32] Cf. scene 28.422-8, in superb contrast to the run-down revelry of the Trimalcione episode (my trans.).
[33] Cf. scene 71.1034-47.
[34] Death in proximity of water may be enlightening: the Fellinian sea, "as symbol and stimulus of the creative unconscious, is where the *forza generatrice* is concentrated" (Hough-Dugdale, 2020, 245: on the recurring motif of the sea and the shoreline, pp. 242ff.).
[35] See Kezich, 2002, 88.

adox' of an objective oneiric narrative with no connection to Fellini's *private life*, i.e. through an ambiguous detachment from the 'otherness' of the world represented.[36] In a grand scheme, *Fellini-Satyricon* is scattered with excavated and recovered 'fragments', which seduce the film-maker to such an extent that, while he observes them as they are, the film becomes increasingly irresolute and evocative: "Aren't the ruins of a temple far more charming than the temple itself?"[37] Just a few examples. All the works exhibited in the Pinacoteca (scene 10) are in a bad state of preservation: broken remains convey a sense of deterioration, in contrast with the bright sequence; a fragmentary state similarly features the sculptures and artistic treasures, meant for the Cesare, placed inside the hold of Lica's ship (30-38); the Ermafrodito episode takes place in a ruined temple, with a wall seemingly exhumed from earth (53); the very Labyrinth retains defined architectonic models, especially the Cyclopic walls of the Mycenaean Tyrins and Malta temples (Slavazzi, 2009, 77).

Cooperatively with dialogues, music, and ambient sounds (key elements in the post-production process of film editing),[38] framing and camera movements become the most suitable tools for giving shape to this vanished and defunct late Roman world, with which Fellini (as well as us, viewers) has no real relationship. To this "impossible operation" of a "science fiction in reverse,"[39] wind and music somehow add a *sound and time* dimension, whereas the effects of camera movements give depth and openness to *space*: the subsequent amalgam is unique in each sequence. As a matter of fact, within a sort of circular return of the movie on

---

[36] See above, p. 14 nn. 28ff.

[37] Federico Fellini, in Zanelli, 1969, 21 (my trans.).

[38] The *editing* process (performed by a film editor) joins shots and constructs the film story, with its visual and sound elements (cf. *Glossary of Film Terms*, https://www.onlinelibrary.wiley.com). This narration, "by means of interlocking and alternating shots, camera angles, and focal lenghts," corresponds to the *montage*, whereas the *cutting* is the "subtractive operation" of splicing the frames (Vanelli, 2020b, 209).

[39] With the term "science-fiction," Fellini alluded to the impossibility of grasping such remote feelings and motivations: see Luca Canali, in Zanelli, 1969, 59 (cf. above, p. 17 n. 36). Fellini's process reminds Pesando, 2010, 197 of Ray Bradbury's planet Mars in his *Martian Chronicles* (1950).

itself, the journey fades out in the darkness of the opening shot, when Encolpio was a mere shadow: the end credits seem to refer to vacuity, to the mysterious *nothingness* from which the movie emerged like a dream or a nightmare (Sala, 2018, 102-3). So, rather than opening to some kind of hope in the future, Encolpio's final 'evolution' into a portrait seems to be overburdened by the ambiguity of his first-person interrupted narrative. What's more, this change occurs *immediately* after the restoration of Encolpio's sexual potency (through the intervention of Enotea) and after Ascilto's death: a mechanical change, indeed.[40] The transition was smoother, more measured in the 1969 published screenplay: what made Fellini change his mind, as regards Encolpio's reaction to Enotea's potion and drug-trip, in the passage from script to movie? In point of fact, the outcome is that "his potency restored, he pays limited heed to Ascilto's death" (Villa, 2020, 485), and Encolpio's final praise for his friend sounds more like "the self-serving rhetoric of a student who has learned his oratory well" (Burke, 2020, 158). At this juncture, it seems fair to suggest that this (allegedly) optimistic, hasty 'development' of the character leads to an appeal to us spectators for a reflection on the baffling blending of hope with dark nothingness. Are we sure that an *actually* 'reborn' Encolpio is undertaking a voyage of discovery? Discovery of what?

3.3 Dropouts, hippies, rascals

In some paradoxical way, outset and closure tend to converge. What happens throughout the film, during the wandering of our light-hearted Encolpio and Ascilto from one adventure to another, in their contest for Gitone? Judging from Fellini's iterated comments on his movie, this issue affected him and required a lot of effort. Liliana Betti once wondered why Federico was possessed by some kind of "logomania" before and during the making of the

[40] Cf. scene 66.1009-19; 70.1024-33. Note Encolpio's words in 70.1033, after the intercourse with the *maga* ("sorceress"): "We have to be happy, now! I intend to make up for lost time!"; differently, at the screenplay stage, in Zanelli B, 63.1156-79 (pp. 264-6) no words are uttered by Encolpio, who appears to Ascilto *stunned* by what had happened (cf. 64.1180: "stordito da quanto è avvenuto").

Satyricon: an irrepressible craving for "uttering words, asserting, explaining, itemising, soliloquising" about the sense and purpose of his film, elicited by "a heady extroversion" that has no comparison to his comments on previous films (and on following ones). Within the self-protective ritual of his dense "defensive mesh," the filmmaker supposedly aimed at framing and reiterating intentions, demands, and confessions in order to "discharge them of their conditioning power," thus allowing himself to work with uncompromised freedom and willingness (Betti, 1970, 23-4; my trans.).[41] I would share Betti's refined insight. Is Fellini's *fascination with hippies* exposed to this sort of exorcism? This may be the case with statements such as the following, obviously to be taken with a pinch of salt:

> I could say decadent Rome resembles our Rome today, with this grim craving to enjoy life, the same violence, the same absence of principles, the same desperation, the same fatuousness. I could say Encolpio and Ascilto, the main characters in *Satyricon*, are a lot like hippies in that they obey only their bodies, search for new meaning in drugs, and ignore their problems. I could say it, and perhaps I'd venture to say I'm right. Yet all of these more or less convincing explanations aren't worth much in the end. The important thing is that in making this film I'm rediscovering a pleasure, a joyous fervour I feared I'd lost. I think I sense that my will to make movies hasn't run out.[42]

Disregarding for the moment Fellini's *rediscovered pleasure* in making films (a topic that would deserve closer inspection), we may observe that his concern with hippie counter-culture is a complex and long-lasting experience, if we just think that in New

---

[41] In *Fellinikon* (1969), the director and cinematographer, Gideon Bachmann (1927-2016), documented the making of *Fellini-Satyricon*, through interviews in which Fellini explained his methods of creation; with his behind-the-scene documentary, *Ciao, Federico* (1970), Bachmann had Danilo Donati (set and costume designer) and Dante Ferretti (assistant architect) talk about their experiences during the filming of *Fellini-Satyricon*, and about technical aspects of filmmaking (see also Winkler, 2001, 259).

[42] (Christopher B. White's trans.).

York, at the Madison Square Garden premiere in 1970, *Fellini-Satyricon* was warmly received by more than 10,000 young people in the audience of a rock concert, as Tullio Kezich reminds us: "Dropouts, hippies, rascals. Outside it was snowing; inside you seemed to be floating in a cloud of hashish, like on a spaceship [...], with a wealth of the remote past (the images of the film) and the present (the audience)."[43] In this respect, it's quite eloquent that further Fellinian 'declarations of intent' evolve around the suggestion of Encolpio and Ascilto as youngsters *living in the moment*, totally identifying with single irresponsible acts of an existence left to chance:

> Encolpio and Ascilto, these two daredevils, with their ramshackle lives, and their pansexual dreams, resemble a couple of hippies. The similarity really stands out.[44]

At first sight, the new generation's "yearning for profound social transformation" (Villa, 2020, 483) seems to hold a wide appeal in the film. But it's perhaps more than that. It's no secret that Fellini, between *Otto e mezzo* (1963) and *Giulietta degli spiriti* (1965), had experimented a state of consciousness provoked by LSD,[45] thanks to the power of suggestion of Aldous Huxley's *The Doors of Perception*, a work which evaluated psychedelic drugs as facilitators of mystical insight: it was a time when mescaline played a preeminent part in influencing the American beat generation of poets and writers of 1940s-1960s.[46] Either mindful of this, or in not unexpected resonance with it, during his life-threatening illness in April 1967,[47] he experienced a peculiar state of mind:

---

[43] Kezich, 2002, 286 (cf. Paul 2009, 202; Villa 2020, 483): my trans.
[44] Federico Fellini, in Cancogni, 1968, 16 (= Zanelli 1969, 25): my trans.
[45] See Fellini, 1980/2015, 6; 145-6.
[46] Cf. e.g., the implications of the "sacramental vision" in Huxley 1954, 15. On the Beat Generation see esp. Cook, 1994 and Watson, 1998; for a portrait of Jack Kerouac, see McNally, 2003.
[47] Before shooting *Toby Dammit* (1968), Fellini had an allergic pleurisy attack, a rare example of the 'Sanarelli-Schwarzmann syndrome': Bondanella, 1992, 229; Kezich, 2002, 267ff.

> When I felt as if I was dying, objects were no longer anthropomorphized. The telephone that always looked like a big, strange frog or boxing glove was just a phone. But no, it's not like that, it wasn't anything; it's hard to explain. I didn't know what it was because even the concepts of volume, colour, and perspective are a way of understanding reality, a series of symbols to define it, a map, an official primer that everyone can use, and it was exactly this intellectual relationship with objects that suddenly went missing.[48]

All this can perhaps explain why Fellini eventually resorted to mescaline and LSD-25, under medical supervision, in order to treat the syndrome. In a conversation on this subject with Dario Zanelli, it came naturally to shift the focus from Fellini's pleurisy attack on his passionate endorsement of ideas, about the world around, that impressed his interlocutor. These ideas were tied to the generation turmoil and uprising against the 'world of the fathers', which made the filmmaker himself feel strongly attracted to the sense of freedom inspired by the American hippie movement:

> You should explain to me: after all, what did the ideas of the past come out with? Extermination camps, gas chambers, atom bomb ... Well, by Jove, hooray for hippies! [...] Their intransigent refusal to consider even themselves does command my deepest respect [...] How do these guys speak? We view them: they restrict themselves to observing, singing, making love. *But it's the void,* one argues. It could be. But isn't this void better than the 'full' of dumb ideas that has clogged us until now?[49]

Are these utterances reflected by some means in *Fellini-Satyricon*? Or, rather: how far do Fellini's smart storytelling and desire to please interviewers deal with the movie itself? Speaking theoretical-

[48] The recollections of Fellini, 1967, 23-4 form the first chapter of Fellini, 1980/2015, 5 (Christopher B. White's trans.).
[49] See Zanelli, 1969, 14ff. (my trans.).

ly, we should raise reservations about any alleged, or predetermined congruity between intentions and realisations. It's self-evident that any creation *may not be* the consistent fruit of the author's consciousness: due to some kind of 'heterogony of ends',[50] an artistic-directed activity apparently results in aesthetic experiences that end up modifying the original motivational pattern. Within our research area, it's in the scheme of things that a movie can promise much more (or much less!) than it delivers; or that – in simple terms – intentions and cinematic rendering are immeasurable.

At first glance, we are given *the impression* of Encolpio's partial psychological growth through sequences placed in the second half of the film, starting with the triumph of the new Cesare (42.552-561) and the patricians' suicide episode (43.562-49.675). In fact, Encolpio's careless and narcissist complaining attitudes in the first half of the movie (from the beginning to the death of both young Cesare and Lica: 1.1-41.551) seem to be replaced by subsequent initiative and self-sufficiency. From a cursory viewpoint, this occurs when Encolpio – after a long silence – enhances his voice-over by informing us about Lica's ship episode (30.446-450), or about the death of the ruling Cesare (39.521-40.523); not to mention an incident which *might* demonstrate some activation of moral responsibility: his admissions to Enotea both of guilt, for committed crimes, and of impotence (70.1026 "The culprit in front of you committed treason! He killed a man! He profaned a temple! And now he is a soldier without his weapon..."; my trans.).

Upon closer inspection, however, such signs of a personal or moral development turn out to be erratic and ephemeral, and therefore 'suspicious.' Encolpio's first-person narrative in Lica's episode has no following, because in the final sequence, although he temporarily reappears as the story-teller, his voice is cut off in mid-sentence, as already noted.[51] In the Enotea incident, Encolpio's proclamations sound more like a *captatio benevolentiae*, in

---

[50] As a tentative proposal, I venture to apply the well-known term, introduced by the German psychologist Wilhelm Wundt (1832-1920), to cinematic matters.

[51] Cf. above, p. 108 n. 12.

order to win her sympathy and support for the cure of impotence; previously also, his plea for mercy to Minotauro (58.852: "I am not a Theseus worthy of you! Dear Minotauro, I will love you if you save my life. Please, be merciful with Encolpio!"; my trans.) is likely to be motivated by mere survival instinct, rather than by any (embryo of) psychological growth. Evenly relevant, Encolpio doesn't prove to be the arbiter of his own destiny. Whenever luck has a leading role (which occurs mainly in the first half of the film), grotesque or unintentionally comical hints accompany Encolpio's oneiric experience. Having suicide on his mind, he is saved from it by the uproar and rumble, heralding the collapse of the *insula Felicles* (8.164ff.). Being forgiven (and even kissed) by Lica after the wrestling match (36.485ff.), and then spared by Minotauro in the labyrinth (58.856), Encolpio turns out to be a child of fate: on board Lica's ship, where the homosexual marriage with Lica takes place, Encolpio is comically dressed up for the celebration, and taunted by Ascilto (37.493ff.).

On the other hand, it shouldn't go unnoticed that in the second half of the film our hero tends to become a parody object, notably in his apparent "moments of greatest trial and awareness" (Burke, 2020, 157).[52] Just a few examples. When Encolpio addresses Minotauro, some surreal jocularity is apparent (36.850-1: "There should have been a gladiator in my place, I'm only a student! Don't turn on me […] I'm not suitable for this fight!"; my trans.). By the end of the same sequence, the joke played on Encolpio is shared by us spectators with the laughing audience at the "Festival of Myrth" (to which is added Ascilto's mockery), with its climax in his sexual failure with Arianna (58.877-896). In the "Garden of Delights," a mournful Encolpio is introduced to a group of enchantresses by Eumolpo because his friend's "*sceptre* doesn't work," unlike Ascilto's brilliant performances just nearby: as a medical treatment, he is beaten on his buttocks by young girls whispering some kind of gibberish (60.933ff.). During Enotea's cure, tragicomically frightened by the multiplicity of her manifestations, Encolpio watches Ascilto

[52] See also Burke, 2002, 43 n. 13.

in subjective shot from an opening in her cave, but – under drug effects – he can't notice him badly hurt by the ferryman; then he screams a funny "Oh, Mammina!" and eventually throws himself headlong into the half-naked body of the 'Great Earth Mother' (66.1009-70.1030). It's no surprise that Encolpio doesn't make love to Enotea's first manifestation as a beautiful young woman, but to her highly symbolic one as earth mother, similar to "other large Fellini females such as Saraghina" (Burke, 2020, 157), in *Otto e mezzo* (1963). His jubilant cheers after healing reveal blind dullness, and are a vivid contrast with Ascilto's call for help in a faint voice (66.1031), reinforcing our perception of Encolpio's hallucination *as a drug trip*: the result – in terms of film editing and camera movements – is an increasing insensitivity shown by Encolpio to Ascilto's sealed fate (66.1032-33).[53] In Marguerite Waller's words, we spectators can "combine the alternating shots to form a mental picture,"[54] within a process having to do with relating the separate images conceptually: in this regard, the kind of complex and widespread parody that emerges in the last sequences prevents the audience from expecting any moral development or self-determination to be taken seriously from Encolpio. John Stubbs has differently argued: "*Fellini Satyricon* is about the need to begin again"; "Encolpius, the hero of *Fellini Satyricon*, undergoes a process of regeneration"; "Encolpius, in contrast to Ascyltus, will go forward afresh toward the fulfilment of new dreams":[55] but his conclusions appear to me quite controversial.

Not surprisingly, Fellini's sensible use of editing, camerawork, music, and ambient sounds makes us appreciate the growing 'irresolution' of a pretty evocative, rather than exhaustive movie; a peculiarity which the film director was clearly aware of:

---

[53] Cf. above, p. 115.
[54] See Waller, 2002, 109 (about Fellini's technique of 'montage' in *La dolce vita*, 1959).
[55] See Stubbs, 2006 (respectively 211; 219; 222).

> Too many arguments have been advanced about my film. My only concern was stirring up emotions, or atmospheres, rather than sending messages.[56]

From the beginning until the patricians' villa episode (43.562-49.675), Encolpio's theatrical poses are underlined by a very expressive *montage*, resulting from the combination of conflicting shots, between dismayed faces *in close-up* and the compulsive disarray of his gestures *in medium long framing*. First, in the context of a 'play within a play', he tries to rescue Gitone from Vernacchio, pouncing on him on the stage (3.53-74); secondly, in the brothel of the Suburra, he disappears into a sordid tunnel and grabs Gitone out of the old pimp's hands (4.87-6.107); then, in the art gallery, he admires pictures that portray mythological love scenes, rhetorically recalling "all the myths that talk about love," and complaining about a "cruel guest" like his love rival Ascilto (10.191-194). During Trimalcione's dinner, on the one hand, Encolpio ecstatically stares at the mischievous Trifena, as if hypnotized (13.262-266); on the other, stunned by wine and food, he is indifferent to the violence imposed on his friend Eumolpo by the landlord's slaves (13.371). In short, especially after Gitone leaves him for Ascilto (8.158ff.), Encolpio gradually loses control over his life, and tends to appear, once as a wandering ghost (Bartesaghi, 2009, 349), or as a bombastic fabulist, or as a rambling spectator or victim of events.

Vice versa, the second half of the film highlights more lively and dynamic incidents, where movement is created by various *camera angles* and perspectives, congruous with a kaleidoscopic *editing*.[57] When Encolpio takes part in the harsh abduction of the Ermafrodito, his icy and evil glare is filmed *in close-up* as he kills the old interpreter, while the damp walls of the temple obsessively sprinkle dripping water (54.737). In the labyrinth sequence, the attention of spectators is directed by fluid camera movements – that do not

---

[56] Federico Fellini, in Pace, 2009b, 51 (my trans.).

[57] See Vanelli, 2020b, 209. William van Watson, underscoring Fellini's "associative editing," aptly shows how Fellini discards cause-and-effect narrativity, by liberating his camera "from the tidy shot-countershot formations that express it" (Van Watson, 2002, 75).

seem in the least calculated – to Encolpio's jerky acting in the fight with Minotauro: a succession of *subjective*,[58] *panoramic*, and *tracking shots*, in concert with Encolpio's breathing, the blowing wind, the deafening choir of the onlookers, and Ascilto's waving at Eumolpo's arrival (58.785; 794; 829; 870; 897). We spectators are really encouraged to share Encolpio's fear.[59] Specifically, subjective shots of Encolpio, which were almost entirely absent in the first half of the movie, play a major role in the last sequences. Beyond the above labyrinth scenes, in the "Garden of Delights" episode, Encolpio watches Ascilto, who is happily holding a girl, but is in deep distress since after his failure with Arianna the treatment of his impotence proves unsuccessful (60.967); then, in front of Enotea's first manifestation as a beautiful young woman, our hero stares rapturously at her and closes his eyes, elated by the crackle of the fire in the background (66.1014). It's worthwhile remarking that Fellini's use of *subjective shots*, in these moments of Encolpio's altered mental status, provides variety and energy to the erotic scenes which possess the parodic connotations noted by Frank Burke.[60]

Taking into careful account recent perspectives of gender studies, one can observe that the sexual orientation represented in *Fellini-Satyricon* opens a new path to our reading. A sort of 'Edenic' turning point is reached by Encolpio in the patricians' villa. After the suicide of the couple, he and Ascilto – unaware of the event – sneak through a dark part of the house, bump into a Black slave-girl in the dormitory and enter into playful sexual intercourse with her (49.637-660). Beyond the superb *montage* of the sequence, centred on the contrast between the pathos of the tragedy and the idyllic lightness of the erotic scene,[61] we may remark that this is the only incident where Encolpio's coitus with a *real* woman is successful in the whole movie, although his and Ascilto's threesome with the girl soon changes "into a twosome between the two young men"

---

[58] In a 'subjective POV' (point-of-view), the camera position is close to the line of sight of the character (here Encolpio): cf. *Film Term Glossary*, in *https://www.elginisd.net*.
[59] See Stubbs, 2006, 221.
[60] Cf. above, p. 120 n. 52.
[61] "A tragedy, which will be quickly converted to comedy": Sullivan, 1991/2001, 262.

(Waller, 2020, 313), which eventually *expels the woman*. This (partial) exclusion recalls analogous, more substantial ones. Marguerite Waller emphasizes the fact that whatever in *Fellini-Satyricon* is associated with the 'female', or with 'intersex' persons, is destined to be excluded or suffer capitulation. As well as the 'expulsion' of the Black slave-girl (49.660-668), the female actress playing the emperor is assassinated (scene 40.522-536); Lica, sexually identified as Encolpio's 'bride' (37.489ff.), is beheaded by the new Cesare (41.547); the demigod Ermafrodito is wildly abducted by our heroes and dies from lack of water (54.732-57.784).[62] To these examples I would suggest adding the nymphomaniac episode (50.676-52.711): the suffering caused by her pathology refers to a well-established ancient Roman tradition, based on two divergent, but complementary stereotypes of misogyny: female *fragility* (implying a paternalistic disregard for an 'inferior' needing protection, lat. *tutela*) and *incontinence* (induced by men's fear of her 'uncontrollable' life force, which requires male restraint).[63]

The absence of a real heterosexual partner for Encolpio – regardless of his failure with Arianna (58.877-896) – stands out at the end of the film, at the peak of the strong parody of the character's alleged psychological 'development': in fact, his initiatic sexual relationship with Enotea, as a mere archetypal earth mother (70.1026-1033),[64] is consequently lacking any concrete, emotional ardour. Why is this sorceress/earth goddess portrayed as *a full-figured black woman*? Within the scope of recent 'decolonial studies', which open a fascinating landscape to new lines of inquiry, Shelleen Greene has shown that researching Fellini's biography and works may reveal

---

62 Waller (2020, 314) applies to the structure of Fellini's film the term 'heteronormative masculinity' (used in 'queer theory'), "strongly associated with whiteness": cf. the "conspicuously blonde, blue-eyed British actor" Martin Potter, playing Encolpio. As regards Lica, he "makes a sham of patriarchy" by dressing as a bride and marrying Encolpio, and his decapitation corresponds to a form of "displaced anatomical castration": see Van Watson, 2002, 77.

63 About these implications in Juvenal, the Roman Satirist (esp. *Sat.* 6), see Bellandi, 1995, 35, respectively on the Roman concepts of *infirmitas sexus* and *impotentia muliebris*.

64 Cf. above, p. 121.

reflections not only upon the Italian colonial legacy,[65] but also upon "the articulation of an Italian 'white' racial identity."[66] So, within the hellish representation of the ancient past in *Fellini-Satyricon*, which so deeply diverges from the Fascist vision of the grandiose Imperial Rome, the journey of a blue-eyed and blond-haired Encolpio, to have his virility restored by a black woman, culminates with a face-to-face encounter with the frightening figure of an African earth goddess, who appears "elongated and distorted" (Stubbs, 2006, 28) by means of the camera placed near her feet: in this idea of blackness as mere hallucination, we spectators cannot properly distinguish between an African femininity, constructed – in Greene's words – by Encolpio's "white imaginary," and Africa itself as a "geography of conquest." As a kind of "revisionist historical film," *Fellini-Satyricon* takes an additional parodic twist in the last sequences and responds to the triumphal movies "produced during Italy's silent and Fascist eras" (Greene, 2020, 340).

Unlike his disastrous heterosexual relationships,[67] the affection of Encolpio's lovemaking with Gitone cannot be compared with any other moment of sexual intimacy, not only in *Fellini-Satyricon*, but in the whole of Fellini's film production (Burke, 2020, 343). Early in the film, when the camera moves to the Encolpio's silent flat (8.132-136), we spectators are impressed by the abrupt transition from the shot of the roaring and frightening *insula Felicles* and from Nino Rota's melancholic *Cetra* (both *a visual and sound cut*). Against a background of the slight sound of lapping water, En-

---

[65] On Fellini's short stay at Tripoli in 1942, to work as screen-player of the never completed *Knights of the Desert*, see Kezich, 2002, 73. Ennio Flaiano (cf. above, p. 1 n. 3) was a precious link for Fellini to Fascist Italian colonialism: his remarkable 1947 novel *Tempo di uccidere* recollects his experiences as an army officer during the Italo-Ethiopian war of 1935-36 (see Greene, 2020, 334).

[66] Greene, 2020, 332. A film like *Scipio Africanus* (1937) demonstrates how the establishment of the Italian East Africa (formed in 1936 through the union of Somalia, Eritrea and the newly occupied Ethiopian Empire) was meant to create an actual successor of the Roman empire (339).

[67] As noted above, (cf. p. 45 nn. 69-70), Encolpius's heterosexual flops in Petronius's *Satyrica* should not be overestimated. Although the fragmentary nature of the text makes our conclusions tentative, references to Encolpius's successful performances with women – in missing sections of the novel – are still available in the bits of what once was a much larger work (cf. above, p. 3 n. 7).

colpio and Gitone hug each other passionately and fall asleep: their loving moments are marked by soft *dissolves on black*, as if indicating an intense passing of time during the night, before the sudden intrusion of Ascilto and his fight with Encolpio over Gitone (8.137ff.).[68] Fellini's prowess is here demonstrated by an inspired directorial intuition. Gitone, whose self-centered passivity makes him mute for the entire duration of the film,[69] maliciously smiles at his suitors, and chooses Ascilto uttering his only words in the whole movie: "Con te" ("With you…": 8.157). Michel Chion brilliantly suggests that Giton, keeping quiet during the quarrel, actually plays the game: his strikingly hoarse and vulgar voice, clashing with his thin, 'ephebic' appearance, perhaps reveals that we never possess our object of desire…[70]

Shall we then suggest that the most 'rewarding' aspects of Encolpio's masculinity are inherent in homosexuality, rather than in heterosexuality? It's a fact that his 'masculine' acts are either spoiled at the start by some congenital 'weakness', or committed to reiterated failure: he treacherously kills the interpreter of the Ermafrodito in his sleep (54.734-738); he is terrified and about to be murdered by the raging thief, but is eventually saved by a strong Ascilto (54.781-784); defeated by Minotauro, he proves impotent with Arianna (58.802-891). It's also a fact that homosexuality, elsewhere in the film, might *appear* related to emotional immaturity (Gitone), depravity (Trimalcione), or effeminacy (Lica): but this is just a tiny part of the truth. In fact, a closer scrutiny of Fellini's focus on 'masculinity', and on his parody of Encolpio's alleged 'growth' in the last quarter of the movie, helps us descry different perspectives.[71]

---

[68] Unsurprisingly, in the Petronian novel the protagonist's attachment to Giton is the unifying theme, and Encolpius's narrative is marked by the constant fear of being interrupted in his intercourse with Giton: anyway, in spite of the latter's regular and predictable betrayals, the narrator declares himself devoted to his beloved (cf. above, p. 48 nn. 81ff.).

[69] The distance from Petronius'ss character is relevant: cf. below, p. 153.

[70] See Chion, 1993, 96: a mute character like Giton "est parfois aussi, plus rarement, l'*objet du désir*, dans la mesure où on n'arrive pas à vraiment le posséder"; Giton is a sort of "monstre," who speaks"d'une voix obscène et basse" (p. 123).

[71] On 'masculinity' in Italian cinema, and in particular on Fellini's *La città delle donne* (1980), see Rigoletto, 2014, 34-44. In his analysis of "male disempowerment and vulnerability" (p.

A wide-ranging investigation on 'gender' is an area of film and cultural theory for which Fellini's movies have been most problematic.[72] It has been pertinently suggested that his films and drawings are engaged in deepening the "opacities" of gender relations, "exploring the mystifying tyrannies of a sex/gender system" in which Fellini himself was entangled (Waller, 2020, 312). On these assumptions, Frank Burke's farsighted "gay-positive reading" (Burke, 2020, 347) of *Fellini-Satyricon* shows that, after Encolpio's failed attempt with Arianna in the labyrinth episode, the successive scenes are based on his *forced adaptation* to heterosexuality, rather than on an inner, aware improvement of some sense of identity: his 'pharmacological' treatments – at the "Garden of Delights" and with Enotea – are just *external* influences (strongly ironised as such) that push him to take a *culturally induced* sexual orientation, not at all a natural one. In the final sequence there is no place for an Encolpio's 'congenital' maturation process. We have seen that Enotea, as a creation in Encolpio's mind-change (fostered by drug taking), is an abstract symbol. This can explain, on the one hand, how Encolpio's rejection of a concrete intimacy with a 'real' woman stems from his 'acquired' heterosexuality; on the other, why his pronouncements of freedom in the final sequence can be a target of Fellini's clear parody:[73] as we suspected, Encolpio's voyage of discovery to Africa is neither a conquest of an authentic emancipation nor an enjoyment of a mature emotional life.

---

2), it's noteworthy that "inadequate male subjects" appear already in Neorealist films and melodramas of the 1940s and 1950s, whereas "male sexual vigour" – celebrated in the propaganda films of the fascist period, and "so central to the representation of masculinity in Hollywood cinema" – is often ridiculed in *Italian-style comedies* of the 1950s and 1960s (pp. 4-5).

[72] See Burke, 2020, 342; 347. Fellini's contribution to women's visibility, through characters played by Giulietta Masina (*La Strada*, 1954; *Le notti di Cabiria*, 1956; *Giulietta degli spiriti*, 1965), was focused on by feminist theory in the 1970s., whereas conventional male stereotypes, in the representation of women through polar opposites ("spirit/sexuality," "Madonna/mistress," "virgin/whore"), occur within the films themselves, from *La dolce vita* (1960) to *La città delle donne* (1980): see pp. 332-41. Surliuga, 2020, 192ff. emphasizes that, in Jungian terms, Marcello Mastroianni was Fellini's 'feminine', non-assertive *anima*, while Giulietta Masina was his *animus* ("active, assertive, and resilient").

[73] Cf. above, pp. 120 n. 52; 123 n. 60.

Obviously, the fact remains that the last sequence of the film *objectively* reflects the current 1960s optimism about a desirable evolution of the social order, and about the replacement of oppressive capitalism "with social forms more conductive to emancipation" (Burke, 2020, 161).[74] But insofar as Encolpio's sailing for Africa may be "a nod to the possible social revival promised by the 1960s counter-cultural moment" (Greene, 2020, 340), Fellini's parody of Encolpio's 'initiation' acquires full force and effect. Once again, the Fellinian self-deprecation overcomes the (surmountable) obstacles of his cheated interviewers. As "a great storyteller, off-screen as well as on-screen" (Waller, 2020, 311), he still floors and amazes us spectators, by making fun of his own witty and idiosyncratic proclamations of interest in Encolpio's sense of 'freedom', inspired by the American hippie movement.[75]

3.4 Depthless instability of a *fresco*-movie

In an unpublished digression on «Il Corriere della Sera», Ennio Flaiano gave shape to some kind of daydream concerning *Fellini-Satyricon*:

> Fellini's Satyricon / The cheerful and esoteric sadism of Bosch and the medieval cruelty [...] / The wholesale Markets. Testaccio, Rome living like a hippo in his own juice / Woman is exclusively Sorceress. Enchantress, Prostitute, Harlot, Nymphomaniac, Whore and servant in a brothel [...] / Children with wax faces, ambiguous, scoundrels destined to grow up and outrun their fathers [...] / Cruel, in desperation / One can't live in Italy for fifty years without being moved and eventually surprised.[76]

The words of such an emotionally involved witness reverberate, among others, in the understanding of a contemporary scholar like Shelleen Greene: "The ancient Rome of the film is a place of poverty, crime, excess, ribald humour, debauchery, and sudden,

[74] Cf. above, p. 20 n. 51.

[75] Cf. above, p. 117 nn. 45ff.

[76] See Flaiano, 1982, 13 (he died in 1972: cf. above, p. 1 n. 3): my trans.

iniquitous death" (Greene, 2020, 339). Death is relevant in the film. It ranges from the staging of Trimalcione's own death, an actual "Totenspiel,"[77] to the real, wicked death of several characters: the albino Cesare, Lica, the patrician couple, the Ermafrodito with his two guardians, the thief, Ascilto.[78] Opposed to the Fascist establishment's monumental invocation of the imperial Roman past, the hallucinatory vision concocted by Fellini is fostered by a sense of impending doom and by images of disfigurement, sometimes inspiring aversion or distaste. Up to the limits of hypertrophy, what keeps us spectators off balance is the depraved, deformed 'carnality' of *Fellini-Satyricon,* effectively heightened by very heavy make-up (Taddei, 2000, 305). At any time in the movie a phantasmagorical multitude shows up: hunchbacks, gimps, cripples, injured and overweight people, dwarfs, fleshy women,[79] transvestites, pimps, wrinkled prostitutes, buggerers and catamites, brutal robbers. No wonder Fellini's visual strategy, with its plethora of "statues and faces surfaced from the rinds of time" (Grazzini, 1977, 300; my trans.), has elicited recourses to easy tags, which end up labelling its gallery of *freaks,* once in the category of Hieronymus Bosch's demonic 'grotesque,' once of Pieter Brueghel's comic-caricatural one.[80] For other scholars, besides recurrent judgments on Fellini's "decadent-baroque vein" (Bongioanni, 1970, 97), his peculiar combination of violence and serenity in *Fellini-Satyricon* – with no distinction between the drama and the dream, all being dream – has been pushed in a "surrealistic" direction, halfway "between de Chirico's metaphysics and Magritte's surrealism" (Moravia, 1978, 165). Even the painter Francis Bacon has been brought up for his "charm of deformity and restless self-representation" (Gargiulo, 2016, 122; my trans.).

---

[77] See Sütterlin, 1996, 205. At sc. 380-387 Trimalcione contemplates his mausoleum, comfortably nestling on a convenient stretcher.

[78] On Eumolpo, mummified in the middle of a beach, see Brunet, 2002, 36-7.

[79] On the mythical and "monstrous nature" of woman in Fellini's films, as well as on the "archetypical fantasy" of large women portrayed in his drawings , see Bellano, 2020, 68.

[80] John Stubbs's emphasis on applying to Fellini's cinema a historic-artistic term like "grotesque" appears to me an oversimplification (see especially Stubbs, 2006, 23ff.).

Anyway, most of Fellini's disfigured portraits are crammed into five self-contained episodes of the film: the *Suburra* (sc. 4.81-6.120); the interiors of the *insula Felicles* (7.121-131); Trimalcione's dinner (13.235-372); the temple of the demigod Ermafrodito (53.712-731); the "Garden of Delights" (60.910-979) (Moravia, 1978, 166). This remark invites spectators to reflect on the entire construction of *Fellini-Satyricon*. The treatment-screenplay-movie transitions demonstrate that no link, or clear narrative blocks, are likely to be rigidly determined in advance:[81] which corroborates Fellini's stylistic inclination to place episodes next to each other in a *fresco*, rather than to 'sculpt' psychologically defined, dynamic, and layered characters.[82] One can even argue that we are dealing with characters like papier-mache sculptures,[83] a statement fairly close to Bernardino Zapponi's intentions:[84]

> The movements of characters became more puppet-like, rarefied […] elusiveness was to drag on in anxiety.

The result is that insofar as Petronius properly *narrates*, thanks to Encolpius's permanent presence and recollections, Fellini – with Encolpio's tenuous presence and puppet-like characters – simply lets things *show up*, enhancing the gaps in Petronius's fragmentary novel: if cinema, as such, *exhibits*, Fellini actually *lingers* (Brunet, 2006, 2; my trans.). What is lost in depth and substance, is achieved in terms of vivid spectacular quality. Federico gives a *pictorial* shape to a setting where almost *flat* characters,

---

[81] See above, ch. 1-3.

[82] Eumolpo is an exception who proves the rule. In Cancogni's 1968 interview (p. 16), Fellini highlights Eumolpo's main traits: "He is a poet, but very doubtful about his mission; he is a sycophant, but whenever he struggles for poetry he reveals dignity […] In the last sequence, when his heirs babble around his carcass ready to eat it, he seems to be saying, with a wry grin on his face: eat poetry, not my remains […] He is a scholar of our time: cynical, idle, at the service of the mighty, but with an absolute confidence in poetry" (my trans.). He is a free man, almost idealised by Fellini (Bongioanni, 1970, 108 n. 6; Luca Canali, in Pace, 2009b, 48). Unsurprisingly, Eumolpo's role was played by the outstanding stage actor, Salvo Randone (see Pace, 2009a, 36; 39), the only professional in the cast, together with Alain Cuny (Lica).

[83] "Sculptures en carton-pâte" ; Grisolia, 2006, 73.

[84] Cf. above, p. 15 n. 32.

surrounded by deformed walk-on actors, interact in a sort of scenic structure: fixed frameworks and stage-shaped scaffoldings appear to endlessly repeat a theatrical pattern, where the three-dimensional representation is transformed into a two-dimensional one.[85] Anyhow, in this respect, we should distinguish this broader *theatrical* perspective from peculiar sequences where an explicit play-within-a-play is at hand: let's just bear the comic Vernacchio episode in the *Suburra* (sc. 3.18-80) in mind, or the labyrinth performance during the "Festival of Myrth" (58.785-896). In both scenes we spectators are simultaneously amused by a surrealistic show and by a cheering audience *on stage*.

What matters most, Marco Vanelli has shown that *Fellini-Satyricon* and *La dolce vita* (1960), "as social portraiture," might be considered two "*fresco* films that are related to one another" (Vanelli, 2020b, 210). For both movies, although diversely oriented and artistically achieved, Fellini used in fact the new wide screen CinemaScope, ratio 2.35:1,[86] and (with a few exceptions) long focal length lenses, from 75mm up to 150mm.[87] The simultaneous application of CinemaScope format and telephoto lenses was a challenge delivered by Fellini to cinematographer Otello Martelli at the time of *La dolce vita*; but they were used in *Fellini-Satyricon* as well, with Giuseppe Rotunno as director of photography: Martelli's advice concerning *La dolce vita*, reported by Richard Dyer, can be thus applied to *Fellini-Satyricon*. Within some kind of a bet, Martelli used to jokingly quarrel with Fellini about the use of

[85] "Die Darstellung seiner (i.e. *des Regisseurs*) Imagination begrenzt er nun im fast zweidimensionalen Raum des Theaters": Sütterlin, 1996, 210.

[86] The 'aspect ratio' (or 'format') of an image is the ratio of its width with its height, expressed by two numbers separated by a colon (common formats used in cinema are 1.85:1 and 2.39:1). Fellini's previous films were in the standardized Academy ratio (1.37:1), which was replaced, in "the miracle year" 1953, by wider formats, such as 1.6:1, 1.75:1, 1.85:1, until the CinemaScope ratio 2.35/2.55:1 – almost twice as wide as the Academy one – established the widescreen format in motion pictures (see Bordwell-Thompson 1997, 477-82; Chrissochoidis, 2013, 9-11; 47ff.).

[87] A 'long-focus lens' makes distant objects appear magnified, with the effect of compressing the distance between objects. Long shots normally required a 50mm lens; conversely, Fellini chose a long focal length (75mm-150mm), which was used for portraiture and close-ups (see Dyer, 2020, 36). For some 'anomalies' in *La dolce vita*, with use of 'wide-angle' lenses (or 'deep focus') as forerunning *Otto e mezzo* (1963), see Pravadelli, 2017, 230; 242.

lenses for camera movements and tracking shots: Federico, overlooking the normal 50mm lens, boldly required a long focal length (75mm-150mm), usual for portrayals and close-ups, *but not* for long shots or when movement was involved: with the consequent risk of producing flutter, i.e., an out-of-focus effect. Fellini, who demanded a perfectly focused character and disregarded the depth of field,[88] answered Martelli's (feigned) objections: "Who cares?" The facts proved him right (Paul, 2009, 213). In fact, since focal length lenses put characters in focus and keep the detail of the background defocused and 'blurred' (with no separation of foreground and background), the subsequent *flattening* effect (Paul, 2009, 213) turns out to be congruous with the horizontality of the new wide screen, and generates a "depthless and unstable" image quality.[89] Fellini himself once commented:

> You can read a complete story in a fresco. I love paintings that show several views at the same time.[90]

All this suits the *pictorial* dimension of *Fellini-Satyricon* perfectly, as one of its most apparent structural and functional features: in such a way, the enigmatic *painted wall-effect*, that we have detected by comparing the opening graffiti with the final scene,[91] can be considered part of an extensive *fresco-effect*: a connecting link among the narrative blocks of the film. The combination of a two-dimensional space restriction (theatrical *frontality*) with a painted-on-fresco fragmentary construction (pictorial *stillness* and *simulta-*

---

[88] The 'depth of field', achievable with a wide-angle lens, is the distance between the nearest and the furthest objects that are in an *acceptably* sharp focus: a minimum depth of field obviously compresses the distance between objects.

[89] See Dyer, 2020, 37 (cf. also 44-5). A well-known exception is the episode of Anita Ekberg wading into the Trevi Fountain in *La dolce vita*. Fellini's use of a wide-angle lens (as opposed to a long-focus one) hid the narrowness of the square and increased its spatial range (see Pravadelli, 2017, 242): *vice versa*, in *Fellini-Satyricon* the depth of field is excluded, or strongly limited, by the use of long-focus lenses, causing the loss of what we have termed a "three-dimensional representation" (cf. above, p. 131 n. 85), to the advantage of the *pictorial* quality of the framing.

[90] See Federico Fellini, in Liehm, 1984, 177 (cf. Dyer, 2020, 74 n. 14).

[91] Cf. above, ch. 3.1-3.2.

neity) is quite apparent in the setting of specific backdrops for single visual units.[92] Let's reconsider[93] how Fellini coped with his difficult task, taking the role of

> an archaeologist piecing together fragments of ancient vases, trying to guess what the missing parts looked like [...]

and how deeply he had been working on his *imaginary* reconstruction:

> the ancient world is a lost world and my ignorance of it leaves me with no connection to it other than a fantastic, imaginative one, nurtured by hypotheses and impressions severed from facts and historical knowledge.

It sounds obvious, but imagination does not create "fragments": a few shards do remain from the past, and our "archaeologist" is actively ready to make sense of (to exercise his imagination on) these fragments, adjusting them to the whole thing. But there is much more. Not only does *Fellini-Satyricon* proceed 'in fits and starts' as a purely cinematic choice: its fragmentary pace is characterised also by deep contrasts from the perspective of content, i.e. by thematic and stylistic *counterpoints*. In fact, spectators following Encolpio's adventures come very frequently across scenes confronting scenes, and episodes confronting episodes, within a strong tension between two polarities, and even between elements of the same scene or sequence.[94]

As far as *female figures* are concerned, within Fellini's acclaimed polarity *Madonna-mistress*,[95] the protracted framing of the prosti-

---

[92] For some of which Brunet, 2006, 4 uses the term *micro-events* ("microeventi").
[93] Cf. above, p. 14.
[94] See Brunet, 2002, 59ff.; 2006, 3-4. In a complementary way, the *specularity* of some characters attracts our attention. About their appearance, young Cesare and Ermafrodito, both albinos, refer to each other: the former is marked by some health disease (cf. Zanelli B, 32.604 = Bartesaghi, *aud.* 40.525); the latter is "a frail creature, trembling [...] moans slightly, like a puppy" (cf. Zanelli B, 47.822 = sc. 53.718-722).
[95] Cf. above, p. 127 n. 72.

tutes in the *Suburra* brothel and of the lustful nymphomaniac and Arianna[96] conflict with the fast close-up of the "sweet and submissive" patrician bride who commits suicide (Zanelli B, 35.664; my trans); Enotea's multiple, bewildering manifestations are no longer a mystery.[97] As regards *environments,* on the one hand, spectators are baffled by a recurrent framing imbued with suffocating gloom: the "asylum climate" (Zanelli B, 3.74 [= sc. 3.18ff]: my trans.) in the Vernacchio episode; the dreadful darkness of the *Suburra,* where Encolpio and Gitone wander around like ghosts; the hellish collapse of the *insula Felicles;* the oppressive, marshy air of the avenue leading our heroes to Trimalcione (Zanelli B, 12.248 [= sc. 11.205]); the frightening ship's hold where Lica gathers a crowd of young men "slimy with sweat, who resemble leaping fish caught in a huge haul" (Zanelli B, 213-5 [= sc. 29.437ff]; my trans.); on the other, clarity and brightness are conveyed by the 'cut' (a sudden jump in camera angle and location) from the collapse of the *insula* to the large image of the picture gallery visited by Encolpio (Zanelli B, 11.234ff. [=sc. 10.191ff]); or by the transition from the triumph of the new brutal Cesare to the pure, classic lines of the patricians' villa (Zanelli B, 34.653 [= sc. 43.562-564]).

As for polarities *inside the same sequence,* I would dwell on a couple of indicative examples, the Ermafrodito and the widow of Ephesos sequences. In the first, the camera moves in the temple, placed in the middle of a forest, (Zanelli B, 47.816-818,) from the shot of an old man in close-up, whose image is reflected in a puddle of water, to the silent murder of the guardian;[98] later, after a dissolve from black on an increasingly stony and barren area (where the frail creature will be killed by the heat of the sun),[99] a full-shot of Encolpio, looking for water in a desert basin, appears to stem from *White Crackle,* a "dry-point on paper" of the 'polyma-

---

[96] Cf. respectively: sc. 6.107ff.; 50.676ff.; 58.868ff.
[97] Cf. above, pp. 121; 124.
[98] Cf. sc. 53.712; 54.732-738.
[99] Cf. sc. 55.744.

terialist' painter Alberto Burri.[100] As opposed to the passage from forest to desert, a symmetrical process, consisting in a "miracle of pigmentation," occurs in the widow of Ephesos episode (Snyder,1978, 168ff): the"chalky, stark whiteness" of the woman's face, at first comfortless (Zanelli B, 21.466 [= sc. 17.405-410]), is gradually converted to a "chromatic radiance" after she embraces the guard, eventually choosing life rather than death (Zanelli B, 23.474). At first sight, Encolpio, leaving the rotten corpse of Eumolpo (just as the widow 'leaves' her husband's carcass), *evolves* into colour from a state of whiteness, i.e. "from an indistinct shadow on a white wall [...] to a brilliantly coloured portrait at film's end" (Snyder, 1978, 168): but I'm afraid I can't share this stance. I find it difficult to substantiate (about Encolpio's alleged "transformation of shadow and disembodied 'word' into a concrete life-supporting system") such statement as: "by Encolpio's humble acceptance of the demands of the creative forces in Oenothea's hovel [...] he is made whole and is reborn into the world" (Snyder,1978, 169; 185).[101] We have above argued that these comments, taking Encolpio's *moral evolution* for granted, appear to clash not only with the combination of montage, framing, camera movements, and musical arrangement, but mainly with the clear parody covering the second half of Fellini's film.[102]

3.5 THE ANCIENT WORLD AS SEEN WITH THE TERRORS OF TODAY'S MAN

Which faces to give Encolpio and his fellow travellers? Fellini wasn't sure it was worth it to focus on celebrities of that time. An underlying clarification was needed:

---

[100] Cf. sc. 55.761, and Alberto Burri, *Cretto bianco*, 1971 ('incisione a secco su carta'), in Zanchetti, 2009, 160-1.

[101] About the "generative pattern," discovered by Snyder in the film as regards "the metaphoric qualities of actual colour generation in the narrative" (pp. 171ff.), see Bondanella, 1992, 244, who supports Snyder's idea of a *colour generation* accompanying Encolpio's decision "to affirm life and to experience personal growth."

[102] On Encolpio's just *apparent* indicators of "both personal and aesthetic development," see Burke, 2020, 155; 163 n. 10.

> What is fascinating in the story [...] is the opportunity to narrate, to represent characters endowed with a pre-christian psychology, therefore outside our concepts and ways of judging [...] Let's take a practical case: the choice of faces. Whenever we watch a face, we judge it, albeit unintentionally. We can't help it. Between us and human reality there is a filter of moral judgments, of a Christian, Catholic morality, which we obviously apply to images [...] Well, I would like to overlook being a Christian, I aim at re-examining the world of that time, with the eyes of that time.[103]

The question was about choosing "guys that appear to have breathed another air, eaten other food, ingested poisons," i.e. "faces inhabited by other thoughts." An almost unknown theatre actor, the British Martin Potter, was eventually cast as Encolpio.[104] As regards minor characters (chosen from *Testaccio* slaughter house men, bit-players from *Cinecittà*, shopkeepers, caterers, peasants, greengrocers, and gypsies), the screenwriter Bernardino Zapponi recollected Fellini's actual obsession with faces to be selected: on his large envelopes, stuffed with photographs, some of the signs said: "Rotten faces"; "Beautiful cougars"; "Freaks."..[105] Anyhow, in those months the problem of acting leads Federico to a new strategy of filmmaking, and consequently to a new conception of casting, during the filming of *Fellini: A Director's Notebook* (1969).[106] After ascertaining the inadequacy of Marcello Mastroianni as protagonist of *Il viaggio di G. Mastorna*,[107] Fellini quits the

---

[103] Federico Fellini, in Zanelli, 1969, 26-7 (my trans.).

[104] On the choice of Hiram Keller as Ascilto and Max Born as Gitone, see Zanelli, 1969, 34-5 (my trans.).

[105] Bernardino Zapponi, in Zanelli, 1969, 85 (my trans.). Photographer Tazio Secchiaroli (1925-1998: the inspiration for Fellini's Paparazzo in *La dolce vita*) collected 100 black-and-white photos taken in 1968 on the shooting of *Fellini-Satyricon* (cf. Secchiaroli, 2001): each of them is accompanied by Latin extracts of Petronius's novel.

[106] Commissioned in 1968, for television, and broadcast in 1969 by NBC in the United States, this documentary (shot in 16mm) is a cinematic 'explanation' both of the recently abandoned project *Il viaggio di G. Mastorna* and of his work in progress *Fellini-Satyricon* (cf. Winkler, 2001, 258-9).

[107] In Cavazzoni, 2008 we can read the screenplay (in the 1994 original Italian typescript preserved at 'Diogenes Verlag AG', Zürich) of the never-made movie *Il viaggio di G. Mastorna*, the story of a cello player who must learn how to cope with death. Supposed to come

Mastorna project and thereafter, through *I Clowns* (1970), *Roma* (1972), and *Amarcord* (1973), he will resort to unprofessional actors with appropriate faces "in place of the familiar personae and skills of trained actors": a cinema of "character and depth" becomes one of "image or surface."[108]

Aside from "moral judgments" on characters, another consideration may have contributed to Fellini's requirements for a new kind of casting: in a movie designed and realised as the documentary of a dream,[109] actors should not become accurate characters, but would have to remain "apparitions": that is, ambiguous, *painted* images (Moravia, 1978, 167). And if Fellini has so deeply drawn on his unconscious, it may follow that in ancient characters he encounters the projections of his moods and feelings:

> the ancient world as seen with the terrors of today's man.[110]

By locating in them his metaphysical fears, his artistic desires and discomforts, he seems to be perceiving that the eternal condition of man involves a sharp sense of the transience of life, which passes like a shadow (Grazzini, 1977, 299). An example comes to mind. Coinciding with a close-up of Encolpio about to kill himself, the collapse of the *Insula Felicles* is foretold by a "dull rumble" that frightens its inhabitants, who shout with one voice producing a sound "like the buzzing of frenzied bees" (Zanelli, B 8.218 [= sc. 8.166ff.]; my trans.): the huge, dizzying cavity, with its Dantesque concentric hell-pits, collapses onto a world of miserable and defenceless beings (Pace, 2009a, 27), wiping away stairways, horses, and people in an instant – amidst sand falling from the walls and piles of rubble. In a manner of speaking, the content and the cli-

after *Giulietta degli spiriti* (1965), it consists of "notes, a tentative script, an incomplete set for the first scene, a few shots in *Fellini: A Director's Notebook,*" and not much else: see Carrera, 2020, 129-39.

[108] Burke, 1989, 43. On the two exceptions, Salvo Randone as Eumolpo and Alain Cuny as Lica, see above, n. 587. Fellini's recourse to a celebrity will occur again for *Il Casanova di Federico Fellini* (1976), with Donald Sutherland as protagonist.

[109] Cf. above, p. 13 n. 27.

[110] See Federico Fellini, in Zanelli, 1969, 73 (my trans.).

mate of the film, its proper "Stimmung," can be looked upon as broadly *religious*.

How does this special religiosity become active in *Fellini-Satyricon*? Fellini's fondness for a particular montage and framing conveys a funereal impression of unhappy creatures, who appear to expel their terror of death by devoting their days to revelry, devastated by greed and profligacy. While lurking in claustrophobic nights or dawns, inflamed or murky air, passageways, caves, cells, or labyrinth-like spaces,[111] camera movements occasionally catch faces disfigured by make-up and tinged with languor and melancholy: they suddenly stop and pose, look at the lens, and *watch us spectators*, appearing almost amazed to glimpse "survivors of their sinking" in the dark (Grazzini, 1977, 300; my trans.). Which is to say that in some moments of the film – apart from Encolpio in the last scene, stuck in stillness for a few seconds before being pinned to the mural – several background artists, marked by physical deformities or obscene postures, abruptly fix their stunned face upon us, as if upon witnesses (aren't they a reflection of ourselves?) of their own defeat.

It's true that we have become accustomed to this kind of 'breaking of the fourth wall' since Federico's earlier movies. Destroying the traditional mediation between audience and film, he used to bring us into play through characters directly addressing us spectators, somehow *speaking* to our "soul, mind, and values" (Vanelli, 2020b, 213). By living in a spiritual dimension – so as to seal a possible final 'rebirth' – some of those characters focused on the camera eye, and acknowledged our presence as an invisible but present audience, somehow transcending "realms and barriers."[112] *Vice versa*, in *Fellini-Satyricon*, the gaze into the camera has

---

[111] 'Open' spaces (bearing in mind that the film was almost entirely shot at Cinecittà Studios: cf. above, p. 13 n. 24) are extremely rare: Encolpio's awakening on the beach before Lica's ship episode (sc. 29.429ff.); the nymphomaniac sequence in the desert landscape (50.676-52.711); the performance with Minotauro and Arianna at the "Festival of Myrth" (58.785ff.); the final boarding for Africa (73.1049ff.).

[112] It occurred with Cabiria (*Le notti di Cabiria*, 1956), Paola (*La dolce vita*, 1960), the Cupid figure (*Le tentazioni del dottor Antonio*, 1962), Giulietta (*Giulietta degli spiriti*, 1965): but the

absolutely different implications, if we only examine sequences drenched in anguished desolation and characters *abandoned by God* (Pace, 2009a, 30). Certain figures look as if they were captured in snapshots, or painted portraits, and, for a brief moment, are taken out of the meaningless flow of events, suspended in an abrupt freeze frame: they look at the lens as if hoping to *validate* their own presence.[113] With mournful grimaces, they seem to suggest a dimension where – shortly afterwards – they won't exist any longer, as if they were on the brink of a chasm.

Within this perspective, I suggest that some kind of deep, idiosyncratic religiosity underlies the entire *Fellini-Satyricon*, in the form of both an existential despair and an atmosphere (or tension) of death. This sense of death, as the other side of unbridled sexuality, marks faces emerging from the dark (with no distinction between major and minor roles), out-and-out *masks* clinging to sensual intoxication with the vitality of dying animals: "spots of shadows and lights" (Taddei, 2000, 307; my trans.). One may wonder what really *lies hidden* beneath the Fellinian deformation of faces and incidents. Federico gives us a glimpse into how humans perhaps don't *consist in* those disfigurements: there must be something that escapes an overall identification, since every single framing of disfigured faces – every single desperate gaze into the camera – suggests its opposite, a kind of yearning for lost integrity. Are deformities to be seen as glimmers of *religiosity* surfacing from the film?

Anxiety and disorientation run across the whole movie, caused by senseless violence, superstitions related to heinous rites, brutal robberies, homicides: but if despair and bewilderment do not properly entail a genuine *religious* desire as such, they can still pave the way to (some form of) it, by at least explaining Fellini's sense of turmoil and dismay confronted by

"discovery" of the camera eye, and the eyes of the viewers, is extraordinarily effective in the cases of Cabiria and Paola: see Burke, 2020, 90-1; 98-9.

[113] I would resort to a consideration made by Barthes, 1980, 129, on photography: "L'effet qu'elle produit sur moi n'est pas de restituer ce qui est aboli (par le temps, la distance), mais d'attester que cela que je vois, a bien été."

a world that no longer believes and however needs to believe.[114]

It has been suggested[115] that a Fellinian meditation on spiritual transcendence is embodied in the magic atmosphere of the Enotea sequence, under the captivating influence of Apuleius' *Metamorphoseon Libri*;[116] or, in some respects, in the calm lightness of Encolpio's final departure for Africa: but I take issue with this interpretation. In these episodes, one clearly detects a certain amount of parody, which undermines the reading, in concert with the *unsettling death* of Ascilto, to which Encolpio "pays limited heed" (Villa, 2020, 485): we have repeatedly argued our reservations as to the idea of Encolpio's 'growth' and transformation in the last quarter of the movie.[117] The theme of redemption or 'regeneration' recurs in various ways in earlier films: *La strada* (1954); *Il bidone* (1955); *Le notti di Cabiria* (1956); *Giulietta degli spiriti* (1965);[118] predictably enough, the theme doesn't entail any psychological or religious (model of) redemption throughout *Fellini-Satyricon*, where there is no hint of either a Christian sense of death-and-rebirth or of an afterlife. An artist is obviously not the only interpreter of his own art (Bongioanni, 1970, 123), but Fellini's stated intentions to 'signal' Christ on the horizon (Zanelli, 1969, 60; 62) are contradicted by a "pre-Christian film made from a post-Christian perspective" (Burke, 2020, 165).

The absence of an after-life perspective doesn't mean the absence of any need for purification. As an example of the incongruities of the pagan age represented in the film, for an ancient historian, like Santo Mazzarino, the sense of hope for a miracle may be found in a poetic, successful scene: the framing of the old shepherd, who asks for grace in the temple of the Ermafrodito, and reflects his face in a stretch of water.[119] Much discussion is instead caused by

---

114 Federico Fellini, in Zanelli, 1969, 16 (my trans.).

115 Among others, by Pace, 2009a, 31ff.

116 See above, ch. 1.2.

117 See above, my conclusions of ch. 3.1 and 3.2.

118 See Bondanella, 1992, 109-10 (Zampanò); 118-9 (Augusto); 129 (Cabiria); 307 (Giulietta).

119 See Santo Mazzarino, in Zanelli, 1969, 57-8, referring to sc. 53.715.

the claim that Fellini's conception of antiquity may be regarded as similar to the one dating back to the Christian Middle Age, when antiquity was portrayed as an era of "fallen and corrupt nature," brimming with physical and moral monsters, "not yet redeemed and saved" (Moravia, 1978, 165-6). To such a simplistic interpretation, it might be objected that the Christian religion is not only centred on a moral system, but also on a doctrinaire and metaphysical apparatus; in any case, Fellini's *religiosity* can't be trapped within strict theological paradigms (Bongioanni, 1970, 119ff).

In other respects, however, Fellini's efforts didn't succeed in evading a (perhaps inevitably) *moralistic* approach to the pagan world, an approach fuelled by the recourse to a non-Petronian source that accompanied his reading of the Latin novel: Jérôme Carcopino's *Daily Life in Ancient Rome*.[120] A filmmaker like Fellini, eager to remain aloof[121] from a Roman world in many respects enigmatic and unfathomable, was interested in the pictorial descriptions of this figurative textbook. To this extent, information derived from Carcopino proved to be skeleton notions, which were fleshed up by Zapponi and Fellini, and became hefty episodes: *fragments* eventually took shape.[122] Here are some fitting examples.

Early in the movie, after Encolpio and Ascilto argue about Gitone in the bluish-coloured interiors of the *Thermae*, Vernacchio's crude, buffoonish farce is inspired by Carcopino's description of Roman mime and pantomime.[123] In the *Suburra* district, the "almost African narrow roads" of the screenplay might be an echo of Carcopino's suggestions of "roaring multitudes," that overcrowd "the square and market place of Jemaa el-Fnaa in Marrakech";[124] moreover, the cosmopolitan character of Rome, with people "crowding in

[120] Which he must have checked out in the Italian 1942 edition: see Brunet, 2002, 40ff.
[121] Cf. above, p. 14 nn. 28-9; 17 n. 36.
[122] See Brunet, 2002, 41-2 (my trans.); Pace, 2009a, 27. General views on some matters – regarding ancient history -have evolved, and new material has filled in the temporal gap throwing "new light on specific issues" (Soldevila, 2004): but Carcopino's bright reconstruction of daily life in ancient Rome is still a vivid picture of backstreet and domestic life, in spite of some awkward moralizing passages (about women, sex, and religion) or erasures (embarrassing topics like homosexuality), which bear witness to the author's lifetime.
[123] Cf. Zanelli B, 3.63ff. (= sc. 3.18ff.); see Carcopino, 1942, 362.
[124] Let's compare Carcopino, 1942, 84 with Zanelli B, 4.147.

from the *provinciae* with their different idioms, customs and habits" (Carcopino, 1942, 92; my trans.) is revived by the Fellinian image of roads animated by "droves of shadows who walk huddling, in an uninterrupted intertwining of different languages and dialects."[125] The very *insula Felicles,* rising above the monuments of the 'adoptive' emperors (AD 96-192) "like a skyscraper" (Carcopino 1942, 45) is depicted as "a proletarian skyscraper" by Federico's assistant Liliana Betti:[126] Fellini's camera significantly goes up to the upper floors, revealing its imposing *ziqqurat* shape.[127] Last but not least, on account of its quality of historical representation, the marriage between Encolpio and Lica on the ship, a clear rewording of the Giton-Pannychis marriage in Petronius,[128] deserves special attention: not just cues, but even literal resumptions of Carcopino's text marked the screenplay and remained intact in the movie.[129] In a few words: apart from Vernacchio's incident (entirely made-up by Fellini), the other three Petronian sequences, which were nothing more than bare backgrounds for actions in Petronius's narrative (*Suburra; insula Felicles;* the Lica-Encolpius wedding), in Fellini took a rich *visual texture* thanks to Carcopino's essay, expanded in such a way as to become scenographic protagonists.

The fact remains that Carcopino's reading of antiquity, through an ideological grasp of right or wrong, was particularly noticeable in his description of Roman marriage, woman, and family: as a major non-Petronian source, it ends up prevailing in *Fellini-Satyricon* over the strong tension we have observed between polarities light/bright-dark that mark the structure of the movie.[130] All this implies that Fellini's moralistic approach — resulting from his use of Carcopino's descriptions and comments — contradicts the initial

---

[125] Cf. Zanelli B, 4.149 (my trans.). Within Fellini's "polyglot delirium," different and specific languages blur into one another and "degenerate into pure sound": Van Watson, 2002, 72.
[126] See Betti 1970, 42; my trans.: cf. Zanelli B, 7.185ff.
[127] See sc. 7.131.
[128] Cf. *Sat.* 25-26.3: cf. above, pp. 5 n. 12; 30 n. 25; 72 n. 154.
[129] Parallels between the wedding ceremony in Carcopino 1942 and Zanelli B, are collected by Brunet 2002, 55-6: cf. Carcopino pp. 130 (= Zanelli B, 33.633; 634); 131-2 (= 33.639; 640; 643; Bartesaghi *aud.* 37.489-512).
[130] Cf. above, p. 133 nn. 94ff.

choice of filtering the moral judgments of a Christian, Catholic morality applied to images. We can suggest that Federico's purpose in *overlooking his being a Christian,* and of "re-examining the world of that time, with the eyes of that time,"[131] has generated a very fruitful artistic inconsistency. Ester Brunet deserves credit for being (to my knowledge) the first scholar to highlight – by detecting some significant Fellinian incongruities – the important elements of Carcopino's essay, which Federico's imagery splendidly developed into visual contrasts: virtuous vs. vicious women and *domus* (ornate villa) vs. *insula*; inefficacy of traditional religion and openness to Eastern mysticism. Ultimately, Fellini's claimed estrangement and detachment are thwarted by an unintentional moralistic approach: "he doesn't stage hopelessly *different*, but *crazy* and corrupt characters" (Brunet, 2002, 65; trans. and italics mine).

3.6 From *Satyrica* to *Fellini-Satyricon*

> When we say that a character is "alive" we mean that an author has succeeded in detaining us in the world of the novel, not that we expect to meet the character in the supermarket.
>
> David Goldknopf (1969)

The realm 'represented' in the movie, against the background of which Encolpio lives his daring adventures, is one that Fellini was eager to

> keep watching with some kind of wonder and awe: like a speleologist who penetrates down to the bottom of the earth, or plummets through, like a sea diver.[132]

It's no surprise that in view of the impossibility of reaching the core of that world, the director's attitude ends up converging with the work of scholars of classical antiquity: as hard as they try, even academics of the highest quality can only endeavour to *get*

---

[131] On Fellini's intervention in Zanelli, 1969, 26-7 see above, p. 136 n. 103.

[132] Federico Fellini, in Zanelli, 1969, 59 (my trans.).

closer to their forebears and to their personality through a variety of disciplines: archaeology, palaeography, textual criticism, history, philosophy, costume history. Hence its cryptic inaccessibility; i.e.: its manifest "sense of detachment."[133] Around the same time, a classical philologist like Martin L. West pointed out that a greater part of our knowledge of antiquity comes to us from what the ancients wrote: "in almost all cases, those writings have survived, if they have survived at all, only in copies many stages removed from the originals, copies of which not a single one is free from error. Often the errors are so great that it is no longer possible to tell what the author meant to say" (West, 1973, 7-8). In our case, Fellini's "wonder and awe," *confronting the unknown*, appear to raise more questions than they answer.

Since the 1969 release of the film, some classicists had been puzzled above all by its "syncopation of events" and its "drastic redistributions of incidents among the characters"; in a word, by how unfaithful it is to Petronius'ss novel.[134] Among the most influential scholars, the American Erich Segal (Segal, 1971, 56-57) claimed that Fellini misunderstood the pagan mentality portrayed by Petronius, because he had "left the Church, but the Church has never left him": one may object that, regardless of the fact that a work of art should be investigated on its own terms, Catholic culture is doubtlessly a relevant part of Fellini's upbringing, to be born in mind by film critics, but it can't explain his artistic intentions and achievements in such a clumsily, as it were, deterministic way.[135] On the other hand, Segal wondered "why Fellini so misrepresented Petronius," by turning Petronius's "hilarious reminder" to live each moment to the fullest, into a warning of the inevitability of death: he supposedly took "a work that sang *carpe*

[133] Luca Canali, in Zanelli, 1969, 58-9 (my trans.).

[134] Noteworthy reviews and articles on Fellini's film are collected by Sullivan, 1991/2001, 259 n. 1 (his essay appeared in 1991: cf. editor Winkler's note p. 258).

[135] Such axiomatic sternness has often met the reception of Fellini's movies: of course none of them, including *Fellini-Satyricon*, can be understood without reference to his Catholic cultural background; as much as, for instance, Carl Th. Dreyer and Ingmar Bergman's films are to be interpreted, respectively, in the light of Lutheran Scandinavia or Søren Kierkegaard's philosophy (see Bongioanni, 1970, 102).

diem[136] and made a film that croaked *memento mori*." We can share his latter statement, as far as the gloomy atmosphere of Fellini's film is concerned; but as for the criticism regarding Petronius, we may respond that part of Segal's assumptions on the *Satyrica* has been called into question over the years, particularly in the context of the relationship author-narrator and the tone of the novel. As I've been trying to argue,[137] the peculiarities or moods of the narrator-protagonist Encolpius shouldn't be *ipso facto* attributed to the *empirical author* Petronius Arbiter, apart from the fact that the identification itself of the historical Petronius, *arbiter elegantiae* ("arbiter of elegance"), with the author of the *Satyrica* has been recently called into question.[138] So it may be safer to assume, on one hand, that Petronius himself, as an intellectual and an empirical author, *could* have been an Epicurean, possibly willing to implement the *carpe diem* tenet, which Segal cared so much about; but on the other, there is no cue that Epicurus' philosophy necessarily shapes the "fundamental structure" (Slater, 1990, 85 n. 82) of the *Satyrica,* justifying the *carpe diem* tenet, as a trademark for the novel (or rather, as a support for Segal's author-narrator overlap thesis).

However, Segal's belittling criticism of the film – an understandable stance, in the heat of the moment, as a classicist's reaction to the release of the movie – would need to be tested from more extensive theoretical perspectives, analysing the transition from a literary medium to a visual (and "aural") one (Paul, 2009, 210). Film language is essentially different from language in literature; nevertheless, the most important components of the narrative (plot, repetition, events, characters) are central concepts in film theory too, although literature and film vary greatly as to the

---

136 The Latin aphorism "pluck/seize the day," taken from Horace *Odes* 1.11, dates back to the Greek Epicurus (341-270 BC), whose philosophy had the purpose of attaining happiness (*eudaimonia*) in life, through freedom from fear (*ataraxia*) and absence of pain (*aponia*).

137 See above, ch. 2.8, esp. p. 78 nn. 183ff.

138 The identification of Petronius Arbiter (cf. Tacitus *Ann.* 16.17-20) with the author of the *Satyrica* (which implies dating the novel to the reign of Nero, specifically AD 66), is disputed by Laird, 2007, 164: cf. above, p. 2 n. 5; p. 59 n. 124.

form of presentation.[139] On closer inspection, the virtual image, whom we have ascertained as the *implied author*[140] of the *Satyrica*, does not appear either hilarious nor "festive" in tone, as the American critic apparently claims. The *Satyrica* never appears to be plainly *joyful*: more precisely, it feels ironic and parodic, but not basically *hilarious*. Similarly, *Fellini-Satyricon* never appears jocular ("scherzoso"),[141] but – whenever it is parodic – there is a painful, tragic backdrop underlying even its 'farcical' sequences. At this stage, we can perhaps smooth out some roughness, by removing any alleged clear-cut discrepancy between a carelessly *entertaining* Petronius and a *funereal* Fellini. In fact, although the origins and the realisation of the two works differ considerably, *both the novel and the film* reveal an underlying sadness, a kind of premonition of death, a refined ability to smile: which implies that, in spite of Fellini forcing himself to detach himself from the Roman world,[142] the result of his *Fellini-Satyricon* is – in some respects and to a limited extent – in partial *consonance* with Petronius's world. Likewise, as regards his repeated claims that analogies could be found between ancient and modern (Paul, 2009, 214-6), Fellini has perhaps provided the paradox of antiquity, felt at the same time as remote and abiding, i.e., alien and timeless. The film director himself underlined unconscious analogies between Petronius's world, portrayed in his film and contemporary society:

> As I am a man, who, one way or another embodies many deep incongruities of our society, it is inevitable that I have included current elements in my film, without perhaps being aware of doing so. We might say that Petronius'ss society is declining, and that a new Christian era will follow, with an absolutely unfamiliar language, one that leaves men in deep bewilderment. The

---

[139] See Lothe, 2000, 8; 151. On Jakobson 1959 theory of "inter-semiotic translation" see Dusi, 2015, 181ff.; 195ff.; da Silva, 2017, 71-5: cf. above, p. 20 n. 52.

[140] On Booth's definition of 'implied author' cf. above, p. 77 nn. 179ff.: as we know, its character is inferred and constructed by the 'implied' reader from the text, as an *image* of the empirical author.

[141] Luca Canali, in Pace, 2009b, 46.

[142] Cf. above, ch. 1.2.

> same bewilderment, perhaps, the same lust for life, the same grungy anxiety we experience today, feeling that some great change is taking place, a change we are not prepared for [...] these confusing forms may today be symbolised by the rebellion of young generations, as they were yesterday symbolised by the early Christians.[143]

This position is echoed by Luca Canali, the Latin language consultant for *Fellini-Satyricon*, who reminded us that both Petronius and Fellini, although in different forms of presentation, felt "the conditions of breakdown and redemption" in the dramatic ambiguities of their age.[144] As regards Petronius, the irony, the "disillusionment" and the "bitter smile" of the novel reveal traces of an upper class novelist, who was part of a social *milieu* defeated by the triumph of "business bourgeoisie," freedmen and "urban mob" (lat. *plebecula*), before and during Nero's age; the social life imbalances, marked by "material luxury and artistic sophistication" (Sullivan, 1991/2001, 265) *may* have some common points with Fellini's world of the late sixties, where a prosperous society, endowed with cultural vitality, finds itself weakened to its foundations and reveals that some of its ethic values are enfeebled or failing.[145] As evidence of the multi-faceted irony of the Petronian novel, we have above argued how readers, surrounded by Encolpius's fictional world, end up *sinking* into the realm of ambiguity:[146] the same readers, not simply *amused* by satirical and farcical incidents, are rather *baffled* by the enigmatic features of the *Satyrica*, by the absence of a "positive ideology" (Conte, 1997, 386; my trans.) from its narrative. Here's why Victoria Rimell's comment on the novel, qualifying it as "more disruptive than entertaining" (Rimell, 2002, 33), resonates quite well with Luca Canali's sociological approach.

---

[143] Federico Fellini, in Zanelli, 1969, 62-3 (my trans.).

[144] Luca Canali, in Zanelli, 1969, 62 (my trans.). On "disconcerting" analogies, between Petronius and Fellini, see also Paul, 2009, 208.

[145] Luca Canali, in Pace, 2009b, 47; my trans.; on this subject, see also Cristofoli, 2013, 90ff.

[146] Cf. above, p. 100 n. 273.

Undeniably, some specific analogies between the novel and the film might be recognised, in episodes changed or added by Fellini, in terms of visual 'equivalence' to the atmosphere of his model. For instance, it's self-evident that Petronius's *intertextual* familiarity with Latin poets of the past wouldn't have been grasped by the spectators of the film: more importantly, allusive (or satirical) references to Virgil, *in primis*, and to the tragic and epic poets of Nero's age, Seneca and Lucan,[147] were impossible to convey on the screen. Fellini resorted to a cinematic device that may be taken as an example of what Dudley Andrew would call an *intersemiotic* mode of "fidelity and transformation."[148] The film director, dealing with such a demanding *transposition* of Latin epic and tragedy into his movie, replaced literary episodes with 'political' ones, i.e.: with three sequences which he believed to be inherent in (or compatible with) Nero's age, which were: the death of the young Cesare – Lica's subsequent beheading – the triumph of the new emperor.[149] What matters most, is that the result of this transformation is before everyone's eyes. A strong visual appeal emphasizes the overcast atmosphere of the scenes that precede the suicide of the patrician couple: a turning point in the transition from the "death of the old order"[150] to the second half of the film.

Nonetheless, 'resemblances' between the movie and the Latin novel should not be taken at face value. The examples of Fellini's intersemiotic mode of 'equivalences', that we have touched on (emerging both from 'changes' at the treatment stage, and 'expansions' of the screenplay and movie ones),[151] show how Fellini *transforms* whatever is 'Petronian' into something, that is always new and surprising, by making it cryptic, bewitching, as well as deformed: a disfiguring disease will not leave anything intact (Copioli, 2020, 143-4). Eumolpo is *not* Eumolpus. He is no longer a

---

[147] On intertextuality in the *Satyrica*, see above, ch. 2.9.

[148] See Dudley Andrew, in Lothe, 2000, 87: "it is assumed that the task of adaptation is the reproduction in cinema of something essential about an original text."

[149] Cf. above, pp. 18 n. 42; 19 n. 47.

[150] Burke, 2020, 160. Lica, the emperor, and the patricians end up killed in a row: cf. sc. 40.522-45.612.

[151] Cf. above, ch. 1.3.

swindler, an opportunist and pander, disguised as a charming inventor of fables, nor an amoral entertainer, even less a manic poet hack:[152] Fellini lends dignity and moral standing to an intellectual who refuses to compromise, capable of confronting the arrogance and pettiness of the *nouveau riche* Trimalcione,[153] and ready to 'bequeath' the freedom of poetry and nature to Encolpio.[154] Similarly, Ascilto *outlives* Askyltos, who disappears in Petronius after *Sat.* 97.10, replaced by Eumolpus, as the second love triangle's vertex.[155] Despite being Encolpio's love rival, he is an example of overflowing and altruistic masculinity, by rescuing his friend from mortal dangers and eventually facing death; while a self-centred Encolpio, under the effect of Enotea's drugs and potions, pays no heed to Ascilto's death.[156] For his part, the Petronian Lichas from Tarentum, an old enemy of Encolpius (in love matters), plays a farcical role in the comedy of errors at *Sat.* 100.3ff., and is finally reconciled with Encolpius and Giton by Eumolpus: *none of that* in the Fellinian Lica, heinous slave-holder and effeminate employee of the emperor (both of them brutally killed).[157] Just as importantly, the dissolute Petronian sorceress and priestess of Priapus at Croton, Oenothea (*Sat.* 134.1-6), "she whose god is wine" (Schmeling, 2011, 596) has very little to do with Enotea, Fellini's archetypal earth mother who 'cures' her unintentionally funny patient Encolpio.[158]

This is the reason why, as far as the first half of the movie is concerned, I think we can only partly share John P. Sullivan's assumption that *Fellini-Satyricon* turns out to be "astonishingly true to his model" (Sullivan, 1991/2001, 264). It's undoubtful that many of the Petronian scenes, which take place at night, amidst dirty dwellings, dark bathhouses, and brothels, are transposed by Fellini (notably in the opening sequences of the film) to locations satu-

---

[152] Cf. above, pp. 22 n. 5; 23 n. 7; 88 n. 231; 90.
[153] Who falsely claims verses belonging to the poet T. Lucretius Carus: cf. sc. 13.362ff.
[154] Cf. scene 28.423ff. For Eumolpo in Fellini cf. above, p. 130 n. 82; see also Pace, 2009a, 36ff.
[155] Cf. above, p. 22 n. 5.
[156] Cf. above, pp. 115; 121 n. 53.
[157] On Lica cf. above, pp. 19 nn. 50-1; 124 n. 62; 129.
[158] Cf. above, pp. 119; 124-5.

rated with foggy air, and with brownish or reddish colours that suggest dust and mud: even water is transformed into the sordid, "subterranean flow of a sewer" (Moravia, 1978, 166). But the 'Stimmung' is different. If we equate Petronius and Fellini as possessing a "longing for degradation" and a feeling of "*nostalgie de la boue*" (thus levelling out the diversity), on one hand, we risk overstressing Petronius's alleged 'decadence',[159] and underestimating his subtle sense of humour; on the other, we end up disregarding Ester Brunet's excellent point about Fellini's 'creative' inconsistencies (thanks to the strong visual/aural virtue vs. vice contrast), between his claimed detachment, or estrangement, from the social ambience of the novel and his unintentionally moralistic approach.[160]

In a like manner, parody and irony should be interpreted with caution, distinguishing the 'specifically cinematic' *Fellini-Satyricon* content from the narrative peculiarities of the *Satyrica*: any strict comparative reading would otherwise end up by calling attention to some (purely apparent) similarities between novel and film. As we know, Gian Biagio Conte found a *mythomaniac* infatuation with mythological and epic heroes in Encolpius, intoxicated by Greek and Roman literature: all of which explains our hero's impulse to self-glorify, and *dramatize* the miserable reality of his everyday life.[161] Irony here creates a distance between the actions and the voice of Encolpius-narrator and those of the *hidden* author, to the point that both reader and author establish a *charmed circle*, i.e. a kind of complicity that *excludes* the protagonist-narrator and makes a mockery of him. Contrasting with the Petronian novel, where this wide-ranging and 'systematised' irony is an integral part of its inner structure,[162] we have emphasized that, in the cryp-

---

[159] Sullivan, 1991/2001, 265-6 notes that the *Satyrica* was defined by Huysmans as one of the favourite works of Des Esseintes, in his 1884 novel *À rebours*; but he over-stresses the "desire for sexual degradation" of both Circe and the widow of Ephesos in Petronius (p. 267).

[160] See above, pp. 149ff nn. 120-31.

[161] Conte's 1996 analysis developed and applied well-known concepts (introduced by Wayne Booth) to the *Satyrica*: see above, pp. 78 n. 182; 79 n. 186.

[162] Parody, as *reinterpretation* of literary genres and cultural myths in Petronius's novel (an actual encyclopaedic *summa*) is not surprising in a new era, inaugurated by Ovid's *Meta-*

tic elusiveness of Fellini's film, parody is to be found only in the last quarter of the movie, from the labyrinth episode onwards,[163] and – more importantly – is addressed to a fragmented and *failed* first-person narrator, or *controversial* protagonist.

Now we come down to it. Encolpio's 'phenomenology' shows how the Fellinian readjustment of a character can be extremely distant from Petronius's model: in this respect, it won't make much sense to speak of a film director *adopting the mood* of a novelist. Unlike the Petronian Encolpius, the indisputable protagonist and homodiegetic narrator, the credibility of the Fellinian Encolpio throughout the film is first of all prejudiced by the character's *absence* from some notable events in the movie, whether the scenes were freely adapted from Petronius, expanded, or invented by Fellini and Zapponi.[164] Encolpio *goes missing* in the following scenes of the final script:[165] Eumolpo in Trimalcione's kitchen (scene 14.373-379); Quartilla's story of the Widow of Ephesus (16.404-27.421); Lica's beheading (41.537-551); the triumphal procession of the new emperor (42.552-561); the suicide of the patricians (43.562-45.612); Ascilto's intercourse with the nymphomaniac (50.690-51.704). Encolpio's absence is already strikingly relevant in Zanelli's 1969 screenplay.[166] Moreover, as we have been arguing so far, Encolpio apparently misses the coherent centrality – despite their respective differences – of Guido (*Otto e mezzo*, 1963), Juliet (*Giulietta degli spiriti*, 1965), or Toby (*Toby Dammit*, 1968):[167] all of which is likely to be consistent with the fact that Fellini himself, never mentioning Encolpio as *the* protagonist, in actual fact, considered *both* Encolpio *and* Ascilto as his "main characters," and

---

morphoses (AD 8), and continued by Pliny the Elder (AD 23-79) and Quintilian (35-100): see Conte, 1997, 388 n. 2.

[163] Cf. scene 58.785ff.

[164] See above, ch. 1-3.

[165] As explained above (pp. 2 n. 6; 17 n. 36), I follow Bartesaghi's 2009 audiovisual screenplay, i.e. its final version.

[166] In Zanelli B, Encolpio is absent from scenes 14 (Trimalcione's farmhouse: *scene deleted in the film*); 16 (Eumolpo savagely beaten by Trimalcione's slaves and cooks); 32.603-626 (emperor's murder); 33.627-652 (Lica's murder); 34-38 (suicide of the patricians); 43 (procession of the new Cesare); 44.790-794 (cart of the nymphomaniac).

[167] See Burke, 1989, 37-8 (above, p. 103 n. 1).

paired up "these two dare-devils" as "a couple of hippies."[168] I would even venture to suggest that the only successful *round* character, and co-protagonist with our two youngsters in the film, is Eumolpo, who was, in fact, played by a professional stage actor.[169] To make matters worse, inasmuch as Encolpio very rarely exceeds the limits of a *flat character*,[170] he only experiences *apparent* phases of a personal or moral 'development' that, in actual fact, proved to be false, and even targeted by Fellini's parody.

Nowhere is the discrepancy between Petronius and Fellini most evident than in erotic infatuation and sexuality. As shown by scholarly literature, within a light-hearted treatment of sex throughout the *Satyrica*,[171] sexual intercourse quite often proves unpleasant and disappointing: it's true that sex is often depicted either as a source of frustration or as "an assault on an unwilling victim";[172] but generally, within the framework of a long-established Greek-Roman tradition, marked by a "frank acceptance of the physical side of life,"[173] the attitude of Petronius (as the *hidden author*) to sex, at the expense of the amazed narrator, is made pleasant and playful through a celebration of Eros as a survival instinct *in all its facets*. So much so that irony and amoral disenchantment[174] make it possible to combine (a unique case in Roman literature) obscene episodes with the narrative instrument of a plain style: that is, indecent actions described by a clean phraseology.[175]

Going even more into detail, we have remarked that Encolpius appears fairly unsuccessful when making love, although in missing sections of the *Satyrica* some of his heterosexual relations are

---

[168] Cf. Fellini, 1980/2015, 164-5; Fellini in Cancogni, 1968, 16, above, p. 117 n. 44.

[169] Cf. above, p. 130 n. 82. On "round" and "flat" characters, see Wood, 2019, 89; 99.

[170] An exception might be found in his loving moments of intimacy with Gitone: cf. especially sc. 8.132-136.

[171] Cf. above, ch. 2.6, p. 57 nn. 117ff.

[172] Cf. above, p. 58 n. 121, on Zeitlin, 1971a, 655 n. 59.

[173] Cf. above, pp. 44-5, on Sullivan, 1968, 232.

[174] See Conte, 1997, 385-6.

[175] Cf. above, ch. 2.6, esp. p. 56 nn. 114-6.

likely to have been gratifying.[176] *Vice versa,* within the film, successful masculinity "tends to be associated with homosexuality" (Burke, 2020, 343), rather than with heterosexuality: on the one hand, Encolpio's affection for Gitone in the movie follows and enhances the protagonist's attachment to Giton as the unifying theme in the Petronian novel;[177] on the other, there is a remarkably strong divergence between movie and novel on the level of characterization. Gitone is mute[178] and passive for the entire duration of the film; whereas Encolpius's boy-love in Petronius is a cunning mediator between him and Askyltos – a maliciously enterprising, talkative, and even witty orator.[179]

There is a good deal more to it than that in *Fellini-Satyricon*'s approach to sex. Petronius's psychological insight into characters is sacrificed in the movie to Fellini's claimed *dreamlike effect*:[180] his cinematic perspective results in a "feral attachment to life," which can abruptly change into "disgust, denial, and a desire for death" (Moravia, 1978, 167). In just two incidents, the sexual drive shows up as joyful abandonment, yet with a melancholy background: in Encolpio's lovemaking with Gitone, at scene 8.132-136, and in the sexual intercourse of Encolpio and Ascilto with the Black slave-girl, at 49.637-660.[181] Otherwise, sexual craving and physical decay almost always intermingle: sex is felt, with a sort of non-pagan terror, as a compulsion that annihilates, since inner motivations are reduced to a zero degree of elementary lust (Taddei, 2000, 305). We have above highlighted the sense of decomposition deriving from the stunned gaze into the camera of disfigured faces, and the

---

[176] Cf. above, p. 45 nn. 68-70; 177. Undoubtedly, Circe's reactions at Croton to Encolpius's défaillance in Petronius (*Sat.* 128.1; 132.2-5) resound in Arianna's attitude towards Encolpio's failure at the peak of the "Festival of Myrth" (sc. 58.877ff.): but it is an isolated case of 'resemblance'.

[177] In the *Satyrica,* in spite of Giton's regular and predictable betrayals, the narrator claims himself (and *feels* as well?) devoted to his beloved (cf. above, p. 48 nn. 81-2.).

[178] For the only exception, see Michel Chion's observations above, p. 126 n. 70.

[179] His verbal interventions are copious and interesting: cf. 9.4-5; 80.4; 93.4; 102.14-16; 105.7; 114.11.

[180] Cf. above, pp. 13 nn. 27ff; 137.

[181] Cf. above, pp. 123-4.

impression of impending end in Fellini's peculiar *religiosity*.[182] Against the rhetoric of Fascist imperial stones and dazzling marbles, Fellini sets foggy, sagging, and figuratively suffocating interiors.[183] This is perhaps the reason why, in a film where life-death tensions run through sequences saturated with moral and physical deterioration, even sexual impotence (the tragic-comic manifestations of which were instead handled by Petronius with amused irony)[184] becomes a target of grotesque and biting, but never liberating, *cathartic* parody. Encolpio's dysfunction in Fellini, identified by reiterated, clownish misadventures, is the object of an unsettling parody, that strengthens Encolpio's status as "far more a creature of luck than self-determination" (Burke, 2020, 157): his final ruinous and failed 'development' will lead him, through drug treatment, to a *specious* voyage of discovery to Africa, after he mentally *removes* his friend Ascilto's death.[185]

Anyway, differences between the novel and the film are not limited to this. While reading the *Satyrica*, we have become accustomed to a narrating voice as inherent to the role of fully-fledged recollecting protagonist. We have above ascertained that the fragmentary condition of the *Satyrica* is a merely objective result of the manuscript tradition, not a 'Neronian' example of an unproven *disintegrating* classical age: which would imply the misleading idea of disjointed episodes, or chaotic Encolpius's adventures, reflected by a supposedly mimetic Petronian narrative.[186] Nevertheless, the ubiquitous and manipulative storyteller's voice of the extant novel has been antithetically assessed by scholars. Some academics have underscored Encolpius's double personality, the narrator and the subject of the narration, split between a young, naïve

---

[182] Cf. above, ch. 3.5, in particular p. 137 nn. 110ff.

[183] Cf. above, pp. 124-5, on Greene, 2020, 339-40.

[184] For Encolpius's impotence in the novel (cf. "the heavy wrath of Priapus" at *Sat*. 139.2 v. 8), cf. above, p. 53 n. 105.

[185] Cf. above, conclusions of ch. 3.2.

[186] About the deceitful term "Neronian," connected to the assumption of Encolpius's *disordered* experiences, as imitated by an allegedly *disintegrated* Roman life under Nero, cf. above, p. 61 nn. 130ff; 250ff.

actor, and an older, self-critical narrator;[187] for some other critics, the *Satyrica* should be regarded as a piece of *performance literature*, i.e. an assemblage of recollections performed by a single actor, Encolpius, whose single voice would impersonate – among all the other characters – "the person of himself as youth."[188] From the perspective of some further analysts, Encolpius, as a *transparent* narrator, appears sometimes inclined to recording what he witnesses, whereas in other episodes, as an *agent* narrator, he usually reports his participation or action in events.[189] In closing, according to overcautious commentators, within a constant confusion between the real and the artificial (a mixture that is likely to prevent readers from distinguishing when, or where, Encolpius is narrating straight or pretending), such a collision between a wiser narrator and a chaotic younger self would make it impossible to *disentangle* narrator from protagonist.[190]

On a completely different level, the voice-over in *Fellini-Satyricon* is directly related to Encolpio as *hardly a central* character.[191] A couple of scenes show the groundlessness of any impression of Encolpio's psychological or moral growth: when he interrupts a long silence and enhances his voice-over by informing us about Lica's ship episode (scene 30.446-450), or about the death of the ruling Caesar (39.521-40.523), such *seeming* initiatives are not acted upon, and any possible personal development turns out to be erratic and ephemeral. This is confirmed in the final scene. After beginning to narrate the stages of his journey to Africa, his voice fades away in mid-sentence ("On an island covered with high, perfumed grass, a young Greek told us that in the years..."): his image turns into the frozen immobility of a fissured fresco, as the random chaos of life "is now given a timeless quality"[192] by

---

[187] Cf. above, pp. 64ff, on slightly different readings by Beck 1973; Jones 1987; Schmeling 1994/5; Courtney 2001; Goldman 2006.

[188] Cf. above, p. 66 n. 141, on the *narratio quae versatur in personis* ("narrative based on characters") in Jensson 2004.

[189] Cf. above, p. 45 nn. 70-1, on Laird 1999.

[190] Cf. above, pp. 42; 73-5; 101 n. 280; 292; 298; 460, on Rimell 2002; 2007.

[191] Cf. above, pp. 151-2.

[192] Sullivan, 1991/2001, 271. On the voice-over in the last scene, cf. above, p. 108.

the slow drawing back of the camera, which reveals Encolpio as a mere fragment among others, *removed from time*.[193] Far from implying a 'transformation', as in the case of Toby Dammit's *symbolic* death and rebirth process,[194] Encolpio's teetering and fluctuating voice-over appears incapable of promoting any identification between his character and us, as spectators, as if it were *our own voice*: unlike the Latin voice of Petronius's Encolpius, it is never a "voix englobante" (Chion, 1993, 56). Yet, beyond any reservation or perplexity, not all theoretical questions – concerning the intersemiotic book-to-film translation[195] – can receive definite answers. We are perhaps able, at best, to detect no more than "a precarious analogy between the attempts at first-person narration offered by films and the novel's first-person narration."[196] Even more so, if we deal with a film like *Fellini-Satyricon*, a complex and elusive example of "cinema of the seer," defined not by action but by "purely optical situations."[197] It will depend upon each of us spectators to decide whether a *free adaptation* from Petronius had already been shot ten years before, with the title *La dolce vita* (Del Buono, 1970, 18). In which case, how shall we resist, with Dario Zanelli (Zanelli, 1969, 13), the urge to regard *Fellini-Satyricon* as *Il viaggio di G. Mastorna* into Hades at the time of Nero?

---

[193] With regard to the "distinction between experience and representation of experience" in Fellini's work (Burke, 2002, 30), Toby and Encolpio can diversely *articulate* their experience. Through the device of voice-over narration Toby is capable of "getting right the second time what did not work the first"; conversely, Encolpio disappears in the end, transformed into a fresco, escaping "somewhere beyond the bounds of the film" (32).

[194] Cf. above, pp. 19-20.

[195] Cf. above, pp. 20 n. 52; 148 nn. 148; 151.

[196] Brian McFarlane, in Lothe, 2000, 89.

[197] Gilles Deleuze, in Pravadelli, 2017, 241-2.

BIBLIOGRAPHY

1. PETRONIUS ARBITER. GREEK AND LATIN LITERATURE. LITERARY THEORY AND CRITICISM

Adams, J.N. (1982) *The Latin Sexual Vocabulary* (Baltimore).

Anderson, G. (1991) 'Review N. Slater (1990)', *CR* 41: 340-1.

Ankersmit, F. (2005) 'Hermeneutics', *RENT*: 211-2.

Antoniadis, Th. (2013) 'Beyond impotence. Some unexplored Ovidian dynamics in Petronius'ss sketch of the Croton episode' (*Satyrica* 126.1-140.12), *Trends in Classics*, 5: 171-91.

Aragosti, A. (1979) 'L'episodio petroniano del *forum* (*Sat.* 12-15): assimilazione dei codici nel racconto', *MD* 3: 101-19.

Aragosti, A. (ed.) (1995) *Petronio Arbitro. Satyricon* (Milano).

Aragosti, A., Cosci, P., and Cotrozzi, A. (1988) *Petronio: l'episodio di Quartilla (Satyricon 16-26.6)* (Bologna).

Auerbach, E. (1946) *Mimesis. Dargestellte Wirklichkeit in der abendländischen Literatur* (Bern).

Barchiesi, A. (1996) '*Extra legem*: consumo di letteratura in Petronio, Arbitro', in Pecere, O. and Stramaglia, A. (eds.) (1996) *La letteratura di consumo nel mondo greco-latino* (Cassino), 189-208.

Barchiesi, A. (1999) *Traces of Greek Narrative and the Roman Novel*, in S.J. Harrison (1999), 124-41.

Barthes, R. (1967) 'The Death of the Author', *Aspen. The Magazine in a Box*, 5-6.

Barthes, R. (1968a) 'La mort de l'auteur', *Manteia*, 5: 12-7.

Barthes, R. (1968b) 'L'effet de réel', *Communications*, 11: 84-9.

Barthes, R. (1977) *Image, Music, Text* (*trans.* S. Heath) (London).

Barthes, R. (1980) *see below, sect. 2.*

Beck, R. (1973) 'Some Observations on the Narrative Technique of Petronius's, *Phoenix*, 27: 42-61 [= Idem, in S.J. Harrison (1999), 50-72].

Beck, R. (1975) 'Encolpius at the *Cena*', *Phoenix*, 29: 271-83.

Beck, R. (1982) 'The *Satyricon*: satire, narrator, and antecedents', *MH* 39: 206-14.

Beck, R. (1992) 'Revew Slater, N. (1990)', *Phoenix*, 46: 69-72.

Beck, R. (1997) 'Afterword to Beck (1973)', in S.J. Harrison (1999), 72-3.

Bellandi, F. (ed.) (1995) *Giovenale. Contro le donne (Satira VI)* (Venezia).

Bellandi, F. (2003) *Eros e matrimonio romano. Studi sulla satira VI di Giovenale* (Bologna).

Bellandi, F. (2011) 'Colpi di fulmine e patologie d'amore da Omero a Catullo: qualche considerazione', *Bollettino di Studi Latini*, 41: 1-30.

Bellandi, F. (ed.) (2021) *Giovenale. Satira 9* (Berlin/Boston).

Bessone, F. (ed.) (1997) *P. Ovidii Nasonis Heroidum Epistula XII Medea Iasoni* (Firenze).

Bianchi, C. and Vassallo, C. (2015) 'Introduction. Umberto Eco's Interpretive Semiotics: Interpretation, Encyclopedia, Translation', *Semiotica*, 206: 5-11.

Bianco, F. (1998) *Introduzione all'ermeneutica* (Roma/Bari).

Bitel, A. (2006) 'Review G. Jensson (2004)', *BMCR* 01.33.

Bodel, J. (1999) 'The Cena Trimalchionis', in Hofmann, H. (ed.) *Latin Fiction: The Latin Novel in Context* (London), 38-51.

Bodel, J. (2003) '*Captatio* at Croton: Petronius and Horace', in J. Pucci (ed.) (2003) O qui complexus et gaudia fuerunt: *Essays Presented to Michael C. J. Putnam by his Brown Colleagues on the Occasion of his 79th Birthday* (Providence), 1-15.

Booth, W.C. (1961) *The Rhetoric of Fiction* (Chicago).

Booth, W.C. (1974) *A Rhetoric of Irony* (Chicago).

Booth, W.C. (2005) 'Resurrection of the Implied Author: Why Bother?', in J. Phelan and P.J. Rabinowitz (2005), 75-87.

Bremond, C. (1980) 'The Logic of Narrative Possibilities', *New Literary History*, 11: 387-411 (= 'La logique des possibles narratifs', *Communications*, 1966, 8: 60-76).

Brontë, Ch. (2006) *Jane Eyre* (intr. S. Davies) (London).

Buchanan, R. (2003) '«Side by Side»: the Role of the Sidekick', *Studies in Popular Culture*, 26: 15-26.

Bücheler, F. (ed.) (1862) *Petronii Arbitri Satirarum Reliquiae* (Berlin).

Burke, S. (1998) *The Death and Return of the Author: Criticism & Subjectivity in Barthes, Foucault & Derrida* (Edinburgh).

Burkert, W. (1991) *Mito e rituale in Grecia. Struttura e storia* (Roma/Bari: UC-Regents 1979).

Callebat, L. (ed.) (2012) *Priapées* (Paris).

Caughie, J. (ed.) (1981) *Theories of Authorship* (London).

Chatman, S. (1980) *Story and Discourse. Narrative Structure in Fiction and Film* (New York).

Ciappi, M. (1998) 'Contaminazioni fra tradizioni letterarie affini di ascendenza tragica nel racconto ovidiano del mito di Procne e Filomela (*Met.* 6.587-666)', *Maia*, 50: 433-64.

Citroni, M. (ed.) (1975) *M. Valerii Martialis Epigrammaton Liber I* (Firenze).

Clarke, J.R. (1998) *Looking at Lovemaking. Constructions of Sexuality in Roman Art 100 B.C.-A.D. 250* (Berkeley/Los Angeles/London).

Codoñer, C. (1995) 'Encolpio visto por el narrador', in Callebat, L. (ed.) *Latin vulgaire-latin tardif IV. Actes du 4e colloque international sur le latin vulgaire et tardif (Caen, 2-5 septembre 1994)* (Hildesheim-Zürich), 701-14.

Collignon, A. (1892) *Étude sur Pétrone; la critique littéraire, l'imitation et la parodie dans le Satiricon* (Paris).

Conan Doyle, A (2014) *A Study in Scarlet* (London: 1887).

Connors, C. (1991) 'Review N. Slater (1990)', *BMCR* 02.14.

Connors, C. (1994) 'Famous last words: authorship and death in the Satyricon and Neronian Rome', in Elsner, J. and Masters, J. (eds.) *Reflections of Nero. Culture, History, and Representation* (Chapell Hill/London), 225-35.

Connors, C. (1998) *Petronius the Poet. Verse and Literary Tradition in the* Satyricon (Cambridge).

Connors, C. (2008) 'Politics and spectacles', in T. Whitmarsh (ed.) *The Cambridge Companion to the Greek and Roman Novel* (Cambridge), 162-81.

Conte, G.B. (1985) *Memoria dei poeti e sistema letterario* (Torino: 1974).

Conte, G.B. (1996) *The Hidden Author. An Interpretation of Petronius's* Satyricon (Berkeley/Los Angeles/London).

Conte, G.B. (1997) *Letteratura latina. Manuale storico dalle origini alla fine dell'Impero Romano* (Firenze).

Conte, G.B. and Barchiesi, A. (1989) 'Imitazione e arte allusiva. Modi e funzioni dell'intertestualità', in G. Cavallo, P. Fedeli, and A. Giardina (eds.) *Lo spazio letterario di Roma antica* (Roma), 81-113.

Courtney, E. (2001) *A Companion to Petronius* (Oxford).

D'Amanti, E.R. (ed.) (2020), *Massimiano. Elegie* (Milano).

De Jong, I.J.F. (2007-2012) *Studies in Ancient Greek Narrative* (I-III, Leiden).

Drinkwater, J.F (2019) *Nero: Emperor and Court* (Cambridge).

Dworkin, A. (1981) *Pornography: Men Possessing Women* (New York).

Eco, U. (1979) *The Role of the Reader: Explorations in the Semiotics of Texts* (Bloomington/London).

Eco, U. (1984) *Semiotics and the Philosophy of Language* (Bloomington/London).

Eco, U. (1989) *Open Work. Form and Indeterminacy in Contemporary Poetics* (Cambridge, MA).

Eco, U. (1990) *The Limits of Interpretation* (Bloomington).

Eco, U. (1994) *Six Walks in the Fictional Woods* (Cambridge, MA).

Elmo Raj, P.P. (2015) 'Text and Meaning in Umberto Eco's *The Open Work*', *The Context*, 2: 326-31.

Ernout, A. (éd.) (1958) *Pétrone: Le Satiricon* (Paris).

Ernout, A. (1974) *Morphologie historique du latin* (Paris).

Fantham, E. (1989) 'Mime: The Missing Link in Roman Literary History', *CW* 82: 153-63.

Faulkner, W. (1967) *The Sound and the Fury* (intr. R. Hughes) (London).

Fedeli, P. (1981) 'Petronio: il viaggio, il labirinto', *MD* 6: 91-117.

Fernandelli, M. (2016), Chartae laboriosae. *Autore e lettore nei carmi maggiori di Catullo (c. 64 e 65)* (Cesena).

Finkelpearl, E. (2001) 'Pagan Traditions of Intertextuality in the Roman World', in D. MacDonald (ed.) *Mimesis and Intertextuality in Antiquity and Christianity* (Harrisburg, PA), 78-90.

Fish, S. (1980) *Is There a Text in This Class? The Authority of Interpretive Communities* (Cambridge, MA/London).

Fludernik, M. and Olson, G. (2011) 'Introduction', in Olson, G. (ed.) *Current Trends in Narratology* (Berlin/New York), 1-33.

Fordyce, C.J. (ed.) (1961) *Catullus* (Oxford).

Forenza, E. (2005) 'Alcune note sul realismo di Auerbach', *QDIUB* 2005: 35-50.

Foucault, M. (1977) 'What Is an Author?', in J. Caughie (1981), 282-91.

Fowler, D. (1997) 'On the Shoulders of Giants: Intertextuality and Classical Studies', *MD* 39: 13-34.

Franzoi, A. (ed.) (2014) *Le elegie di Massimiano* (Amsterdam).

Freudenburg, K. (1993) *The Walking Muse: Horace on the Theory of Satire* (Princeton).

Freudenburg, K. (2015) 'Seneca's Apocolocyntosis: Censors in the Afterworld', in S. Bartsch and A. Schiesaro (eds.) *The Cambridge Companion to Seneca* (Cambridge), 93-105.

Freudenburg, K. (2017) 'Petronius, Realism, Nero', in S. Bartsch, K. Freudenburg, and C. Littlewood (eds.), *The Cambridge Companion to the Age of Nero* (Cambridge), 107-20.

Gasti, F. (2020) *La letteratura tardolatina. Un profilo storico (secoli III-VII d.C.)* (Roma).

Genette, G. (1980) *Narrative Discourse: an Essay in Method* (New York).

Genette, G. (1992) *The Architext: An Introduction* (Berkeley).

Genette, G. (1997) *Palimpsests. Literature in the Second Degree* (Lincoln, NE).

Gibbs, R.W. (2005) 'Intentionality', *RENT*: 247-49.

Gibson, A. (2017) 'Charlotte Brontë's First Person', *Narrative*, 25: 203-26.

Goldknopf, D. (1969) 'The Confessional Increment. A New Look at the Narrating-I', *Journal of Aesthetics and Art Criticism*, 28: 13-21.

Goldman, M.L. (2006) '*Anseres [sacri]*: Restrictions and Variations in Petronius's Narrative Technique', *AN* 5: 1-23.

Goldman, M.L. (2008) 'Point of view in Ancient Narratives', (Nashville, TN: unpublished manuscript).

Goldman, M.L. (2012) 'Literary Parody in the Age of Nero', (Nashville, TN: unpublished manuscript).

Gonoji, M. (1998) 'Encolpius, the unreliable narrator of *Satyricon*', *JCS* 46: 88-97; 181-83.

Graverini, L. (2013) 'Come si deve leggere un romanzo: narratori, personaggi e lettori nelle Metamorfosi di Apuleio', in M. Carmignani, L. Graverini, and B. Todd Lee (eds.), *Collected Studies on the Roman Novel – Ensayos sobre la novela romana* (Brujas Córdoba), 119-39.

Graves, R. (1979) *I miti greci* (Milano: London 1955).

Greene, G. (1967) 'Across the Bridge', in Ch. Dolley (ed.), *The Penguin Book of English Short Stories* (Aylesbury), 302-12.

Grethlein, J. (2009) 'Philosophical and Structuralist Narratologies-Worlds Apart?', in J. Grethlein-A. Rengakos (2009), 153-74.

Grethlein, J. and Rengakos, A. (eds.) (2009) *Narratology and Interpretation. The Content of Narrative Form in Ancient Literature* (Berlin/New York).

Habermehl, P. (2006) *Petronius. Satyrica 79-141. Ein philologisch-literarischer Kommentar, Band I: 79-110* (Berlin/ New York).

Hallett, J.P. (2012) 'Anxiety and Influence: Ovid's *Amores* 3.7 and Encolpius's Impotence in *Satyricon* 126 ff.', in M.P. Pinheiro-M.B. Skinner-F. Zeitlin (2012), 211-22.

Hansen, P.K. (2017) 'The Dynamics of Unreliable Narration: Implicit and Omitted Authors, Double narratees and Constructive Readers in First Person Ureliable Narration', in S.S. Grumsen, P.K. Hansen, R. Andersen Kraglund, and H.S. Nielsen (eds.), *Expectations. Reader Assumptions and Author Intentions in Narrative Discourses* (Copenhagen), 28-53.

Hardie, Ph. (2002) *Ovid's Poetics of Illusion* (Cambridge).

Harrison, S.J. (ed.) (1999) *Oxford Readings in the Roman Novel* (Oxford).

Heath, M. (ed.) (1996) *Aristotle. Poetics* (London).

Heinze, R. (1899) 'Petron und der griechische Roman', *Hermes*, 34: 494-519.

Hinds, S. (1997) '«Proemio al mezzo»: Allusion and the Limits of Interpretability', *MD* 39: 113-22.

Hinds, S. (1998) *Allusion and Intertext. Dynamics of Appropriation in Roman Poetry* (Cambridge).

Holzberg, N. (2006) *Der Antike Roman. Eine Einführung* (Darmstadt).

Hubbard, T.K. (ed.) (2003), *Homosexuality in Greece and Rome. A Sourcebook of Basic Documents* (Berkeley/Los Angeles/London).

Hughes, M.Y. (1927) 'Pirandello's Humor', *The Sewanee Review*, 35: 175-86.

Illiano, A. (ed.) (1960) *Pirandello on Humor* (Chapel Hill).

Iser, W. (1978) *The Act of Reading. A Theory of Aesthetic Response* (Baltimore/London).

Jahn, M. (2005a) 'Cognitive Narratology', *RENT*: 67-71.

Jahn, M. (2005b) 'Narrative Situations', *RENT*: 364-66.

Jakobson, R. (1959) 'On Linguistic Aspects of Translation', in R. Brower (ed.) *On Translation* (Harvard), 232-39.

James, H. (1964) *The Aspern Papers* (London).

Jannidis, F. (2005) 'Author', *RENT*: 33-4.

Jensson, G. (2004) *The Recollections of Encolpius. The* Satyrica *of Petronius as Milesian Fiction* (Groningen).

Jones, F. (1987) 'The narrator and the narrative of the *Satyrica*', *Latomus*, 46: 810-9.

Kay, N.M. (ed.) (1985) *Martial. Book XI* (London).

Kennedy, G. (1978) 'Encolpius and Agamemnon in Petronius's, *AJPh* 99: 171-8.

Kent, R.G. (ed.) (1958) *Varro on the latin language, I, Books 5-7* (Cambridge, MA/London: 1938).

Kerényi, K. (1962) *Gli dei della Grecia* (Milano: Zürich 1951).

Kirk, G.S. (1984) *La natura dei miti greci* (Roma/Bari: Harmondsworth 1974).

Kramer, D. (1966) 'Marlow, Myth, and Structure in *Lord Jim*', *Criticism*, 8: 263-79.

Kristeva, J. (1980) *Desire in Language. A Semiotic Approach to Literature and Art* (*trans.* Th. Gorz) (Oxford).

Labate, M. (2020) *Petronio. Ricostruzioni e interpretazioni* (Pisa).

Laird, A. (1998) 'Review G.B. Conte (1996)', *JRS* 88: 198-9.

Laird, A. (1999) *Powers of Expression, Expressions of Power. Speech Presentation and Latin Literature* (Oxford).

Laird, A. (2007) 'The True Nature of the *Satyricon*?', in M. Paschalis, S. Frangoulidis, S. Harrison, S., and M. Zimmerman (eds.), 'The Greek and the Roman Novel', *Ancient Narrative Supplementum*, 8: 151-67.

Lambert, M. (2004) 'Review Hubbard, Y.K. (ed.), *Homosexuality in Greece and Rome. A sourcebook of Basic Documents*, Berkely/Los Angeles/London 2003', *CR* 54: 439-41.

Lanser, S. (2001) '(Im)plying the Author', *Narrative*, 9: 153-60.

Lanser, S. (2005) 'The "I" of the Beholder: Equivocal attachments and the Limits of Structuralist Narratology', in J. Phelan-P.J. Rabinowitz (2005): 206-19.

Lanser, S. (2011) 'The Implied Author: an Agnostic Manifesto', *Style*, 45: 153-60.

Lee Clark, K. (2019) *Giton's Performance of Status in the* Satyrica *of Petronius* (Seattle).

Levin, H. (1951) 'Observations on the Style of Ernest Hemingway', *The Kenyon Review*, 13: 581-609.

Liberman, M.M, (1973) 'The Uses of Anti-Fiction: Greene's *Across the Bridge*', *The Georgia Review*, 27: 321-y28.

Logie, J. (2013) '1967: The Birth of *The Death of the Author*', *College English*, 75: 493-512.

Lothe, J. (2000) *Narrative in Fiction and Film* (Oxford).

Lübker, F. (1989) *Lessico ragionato dell'antichità classica* (Bologna: Leipzig 1882[6]).

Maass, E. (1925) 'Eunuchos und Verwandtes', *RhM* 74: 432-76.

Mariotti, I. (1960) *Studi luciliani* (Firenze).

Moraru, Ch. (2005) 'Intertextuality', *RENT*: 256-61.

Müller, K. (ed.) (1995) *Petronius, Satyricon Reliquiae* Stuttgart 1995⁴.

Murray, P. (1996) *Plato on Poetry. Ion; Republic 376e-398b; 595-608b* (Cambridge).

Nobengo, A. (2013) 'The Difference between Erotica and Pornography', in *Feminist Theory and Fiction -Course Blog* (WordPress.com).

Nünning, A. (2005) 'Reliability', *RENT*: 495-97.

Olson, G. (2003) 'Reconsidering Unreliability. Fallible and Untrustworthy Narrators', *Narrative*, 11: 93-109.

Palmer, A. (2005) 'Realist Novel', *RENT*: 491-92.

Panayotakis, C. (1995) *Theatrum Mundi. Theatrical Elements in the Satyrica of Petronius* (Leiden).

Panayotakis, C. (2004) 'Review V. Rimell (2002)', *AJPh* 125: 152-5.

Panayotakis, C. (2009) 'Petronius and the Roman Literary Tradition', in J. Prag and I. Repath (2009), 48-64.

Paschalis, M. (2009) 'Seneca's *Apocolocyntosis* and Petronius's *Satyricon*', in M. Paschalis, S. Panayotakis, and G. Schmeling (eds.), *Readers and Writers in the Ancient Novel* (Groningen), 102-14.

Pasquali, G. (1942) 'Arte allusiva', in Idem (1968), *Pagine stravaganti* (II, Firenze), 275-82.

Peri, G. (2007) *Discorso diretto e discorso indiretto nel* Satyricon. *Due regimi a contrasto* (Pisa).

Petersmann, H. (1999) 'Environment, Linguistic Situation, and Levels of Style in Petronius's *Satyrica*', in S.J. Harrison (1999), 105-23.

Phelan, J. and Booth, W.C. (2005) 'Narrator', *RENT*: 388-92.

Phelan, J. and Rabinowitz, P.J. (2005) *A Companion to Narrative Theory* (Oxford).

Pinheiro, M.P., Skinner, M.B., and Zeitlin, F. (eds.) (2012) *Narrating Desire. Eros, Sex, and Gender in the Ancient Novel* (Berlin/Boston).

Pisanty, V. (2012) 'Narratologia e scienze cognitive', in A.M. Lorusso, C. Paolucci, and P. Violi (eds.) *Narratività. Problemi, analisi, prospettive* (Bologna), 261-78.

Pisanty, V. (2015) 'From the model reader to the limits of interpretation', *Semiotica*, 206: 37-61.

Pisanty, V. and Pellerey, R. (2004) *Semiotica e interpretazione* (Milano).

Porter Abbott, H. (2002) *The Cambridge Introduction to Narrative* (Cambridge).
Prag, J. and Repath, I. (eds.) (2009) *Petronius. A Handbook* (Oxford).
Rabinowitz, P.J. (2005) 'Audience', *RENT*: 29-31.
Richlin, A. (2009) 'Sex in the *Satyrica*. Outlaws in Literatureland', in J. Prag and I. Repath (2009), 82-100.
Rimell, V. (2002) *Petronius and the Anatomy of Fiction* (Cambridge).
Rimell, V. (2007) 'Petronius's lessons in learning - the hard way', in J. König, and T. Whitmarsh (eds.) *Ordering Knowledge in the Roman Empire* (Cambridge), 108-32.
Rosati, G. (1999) 'Trimalchio on Stage', in S.J. Harrison (1999), 85-104.
Rudich, V. (1997) *Dissidence and Literature under Nero. The Price of Rhetoricization* (London/New York).
Schaeffer, J.-M. and Vultur, I. (2005) 'Mimesis', *RENT*: 309-10.
Schiesaro, A. (1997) 'L'intertestualità e i suoi disagi', *MD* 39: 75-109.
Schmeling, G. (1991) 'The *Satyricon*: The Sense of An Ending', *RhM* 134: 352-77.
Schmeling, G. (1994-95) '*Confessor gloriosus*: a Role of Encolpius in the *Satyrica*', *WJA* 20: 207-24.
Schmeling, G. (2011) *A Commentary on the* Satyrica *of Petronius* (Oxford).
Schneider, R. (2005) 'Reader-Response Theory', *RENT*: 484-86.
Selden, R., Widdowson, P., and Brooker, P. (1997) *A Reader's Guide to Contemporary Literary Theory* (Harlow).
Setaioli, A. (2004) 'I due "epigrammi" di Trimalchione (Petr. *Sat.* 34.10; 55.3)', *Prometheus*, 30: 43-66.
Setaioli, A. (2011) Arbitri Nugae, *Petronius's Short Poems in the* Satyrica (Frankfurt am Mein).
Setaioli, A. (2013) 'L'uso della citazione poetica in Petronio e negli altri romanzieri antichi', *Prometheus*, 39: 188-206.
Setaioli, A. (2018) 'L'impotenza di Encolpio. Una messa a punto', *Prometheus*, 44: 197-201.
Shen, D. (2005) 'Diegesis', *RENT*: 107-8.
da Silva, A.C. (2017) 'On Jakobson's Intersemiotic Translations in Asterix Comix', *Comparatismi*, 11: 71- 81.
Slater, N. (1990) *Reading Petronius* (Baltimore/London).
Smith, M.S. (ed.) (1975) *Petronii Arbitri Cena Trimalchionis* (Oxford).

Soldevila, R. (2004) 'Review J. Carcopino (2003) *Daily Life in Ancient Rome: the People and the City at the Height of the Empire* (New Haven)', *BMCR* 03.23.

Solin, H. (2017) 'Onomastica petroniana. Il senso nascosto dei nomi nel *Satyricon*', *Il Nome nel Testo*, 19: 315-29.

Steinem, G. (1983) *Outrageous Acts and Everyday Rebellions* (New York).

Sternberg, M. and Yacobi, T. (2016) '(Un)reliability in Narrative Discourse. A Comprehensive Overview', *Poetics Today*, 36: 327-498.

Sullivan, J.P. (1968) *The 'Satyricon' of Petronius. A literary study* (London).

Sullivan, J.P. (1991/2001) 'The Social Ambience of Petronius's *Satyricon* and *Fellini-Satyricon*' [= Idem (1991), *The Bucknell Review*, 35: 251-8], in M.M. Winkler (2001), 258-71.

Sütterlin, A. (1996) *Petronius Arbiter und Federico Fellini. Ein strukturanalytischer Vergleich* (Frankfurt am Main).

Syme, R. (1967-1971) *Tacito*, I-II (Brescia: London 1958).

Thagard, P. (2005) *Mind. Introduction to Cognitive Science* (Cambridge, MA/London).

Thrall, W.F. and Hibbard, A. (1960) *A Handbook to Literature* (New York: 1936).

Traina, A. (1973) 'Riflessioni sulla storia della lingua latina', in F. Stolz, A. Debrunner, and W.P. Schmid (1973). *Storia della lingua latina* (Bologna: Berlin 1966), i-xxx.

Traini, S. (2017) 'La struttura assente e il principio di immanenza. Qualche riflessione sul metodo semiotico', *RIFL* 11: 245-54.

Vannini, G. (2007) 'Petronius, 1975-2005: bilancio critico e nuove proposte', *Lustrum*, 49.

Vannini, G. (2010) *Petronii Arbitri "Satyricon" 100-115. Edizione critica e commento* (Berlin/New York).

Varsava, A. (1995) 'Review U. Eco (1994)', *The International Fiction Review*, 22: 89-90.

Veyne, P. (1964) 'Le "je" dans le *Satyricon*', *REL* 42: 301-24.

von Albrecht, M. (1995) *Storia della letteratura latina. Da Livio Andronico a Boezio* (Torino, II: Bern-München 1992).

Walsh, P.G. (1970) *The Roman Novel. The 'Satyricon' of Petronius and the 'Metamorphoses' of Apuleius* (Cambridge).

Walsh, P.G. (1997) *The Satyricon* (Oxford).

West, M.L. (1973) *Textual Criticism and Editorial Technique* (Stuttgart).

Williams, C.A. (2010) *Roman Homosexuality. Ideologies of Masculinity in Classical Antiquity* (New York/Oxford: 1999).

Wimsatt, W.K. and Beardsley, M.C (1946) *The Intentional Fallacy* (Lexington).

Wimsatt, W.K. and Beardsley, M.C (1949) *The Affective Fallacy* (Lexington).

Winkler, J.J. (1985) Auctor et Actor*: a Narratological Reading of Apuleius' Golden Ass* (Berkeley).

Winkler, M.M. (1997) 'Review A. Sütterlin (1996)', *Petronian Society Newsletter*, 27: 8-9.

Winkler, M.M. (ed.) (2001) *Classical Myth and Culture in the Cinema* (Oxford).

Wood, J. (2005) *The Irresponsible Self. On Laughter and the Novel* (London).

Wood, J. (2019) *How Fiction Works* (London: 2008).

Xu, D. (2007) 'Intratextuality, Extratextuality, Intertextuality: Unreliability in Autobiography versus Fiction', *Poetics Today*, 28: 43-87.

Yacobi, T. (1981) 'Fictional Reliability as a Communicative Problem', *Poetics Today*, 2: 113-26.

Zeitlin, F. (1971a) 'Petronius as Paradox: Anarchy and Artistic Integrity', *TAPhA* 102: 631-84.

Zeitlin, F. (1971b) '*Romanus Petronius*: A Study of the *Troiae Halosis* and the *Bellum Civile*', *Latomus*, 30: 56-82.

Zeitlin, F. (2012) 'Gendered Ambiguities, Hybrid Formations, and the Imaginary of the Body in Achilles Tatius', in M.P. Pinheiro, M.B. Skinner, and F. Zeitlin (2012), 105-26.

2. Federico Fellini. Film Studies

Alonge, G. (2020) 'Ennio, Tullio, and the Others: Fellini and His Screenwriters', in F. Burke, M. Waller, and M. Gubareva (2020),165-76.

Bartesaghi, G. (2009) '*Fellini-Satyricon*. La sceneggiatura audiovisiva', in R. De Berti, E. Gagetti, and F. Slavazzi (2009), 319-540.

Barthes, R. (1980) *La chambre claire. Note sur la photographie* (Paris).

Bellano, M. (2020) 'Fellini's Graphic Heritage. Drawings, Comics, Animation, and Beyond', in F. Burke, M. Waller, and M. Gubareva (2020), 59-77.

Betti, L. (1970) *Federico A.C. Disegni per il Satyricon di Federico Fellini* (Milano).

Betti, L. (2015) 'A Revealing Book', in F. Fellini (1980/2015), 288-96.

Bondanella, P. (ed.) (1978) *Federico Fellini. Essays in Criticism* (Oxford).

Bondanella, P. (1992) *The cinema of Federico Fellini* (Princeton).

Bondanella, P. (2002) *The Films of Federico Fellini* (Cambridge).

Bongioanni, M. (1970) 'Fellini Satyricon', *Cineschedario*, 27: 97-128.

Bordwell, D. and Thompson, K. (1997) *Film Art. An Introduction* (New York).

Brunet, E. (2002) *Tramandare-tradire: le fonti letterarie e iconografiche del* Fellini-Satyricon (Venezia).

Brunet, E. (2006) "Tramandare-tradire": storiografia e senso dell'antico nel *Fellini-Satyricon, Engramma,* 49: http://www.engramma.it/ engramma_revolution/49/049_saggi_brunet.html.

Burke, F. (1989) 'Fellini: Changing the subject', *Film Quarterly*, 43: 36-48.

Burke, F. (2002) 'Federico Fellini: Realism/Representation/Signification', in F. Burke and M. Waller (2002), 26-46.

Burke, F. (2020) *Fellini's Films and Commercials. From Postwar to Postmodern* (Bristol/Chicago).

Burke, F. and Waller, M. (eds.) (2002) *Federico Fellini. Contemporary Perspectives* (Toronto/Buffalo/London).

Burke, F., Waller, M., and Gubareva, M. (eds.) (2020) *A Companion to Federico Fellini* (Hoboken, NJ).

Cancogni, M. (1968) 'Cinema-I Maestri: Federico Fellini: buon viaggio Eumolpo', *La Fiera Letteraria*, 35: 16-7.

Carcopino, J. (1942) *La vita quotidiana a Roma all'apogeo dell'impero* (Roma/Bari: Paris 1939).

Carrera, A. (2020) '*Il viaggio di G. Mastorna*: Fellini Entre Deux Morts', in F. Burke, M. Waller, and M. Gubareva (2020), 129-39.

Cavazzoni, E. (ed.) (2008) *Federico Fellini. Il viaggio di G. Mastorna. Scritto con la collaborazione di D. Buzzati e B. Rondi* (Macerata: Zürich 1994).

Chandler, C. (1995) *I, Fellini* (New York).

Chatman, S. (1980) *see above, sect. 1.*

Chion, M. (1993) *La voix au cinéma* (Paris: 1982).
Chrissochoidis, I. (2013) *CinemaScope: Selected Documents from the Spyros P. Skouras Archive* (Stanford).
Comparetti, D. (1941) *Virgilio nel Medio Evo*, I-II (Firenze).
Cook, B. (1994) *The Beat Generation: the Tumultuous '50s Movement and its Impact on Today* (New York: 1971).
Copioli, R. (2020) *Gli occhi di Fellini* (Firenze).
Cristofoli, R. (2013) 'Contesti storici di un viaggio in un tempo estraneo', in G.L. Grassigli and J. Reinhardt (eds.), *Fellini-Satyricon. Tra memoria, racconti e rovine: un sottosuolo dell'anima*, Napoli, 85-102.
De Berti, R. (2009) 'Riflessi di *Fellini-Satyricon* nella stampa periodica illustrata contemporanea', in R. De Berti, E. Gagetti, and F. Slavazzi (2009), 253-99.
De Berti, R., Gagetti, E., and Slavazzi, F. (eds.) (2009) *Fellini-Satyricon. L'immaginario dell'antico-Milano, 6 marzo 2007* (Milano).
Del Buono, O. (1970) 'I due Federici', in L. Betti (1970), 5-21.
Del Santo, M. (2009) '"Tra i nostri mari e i nostri alberi vaghiamo, immersi nella miseria". Il *Preludio* a un viaggio nella "sconosciutezza"', in R. De Berti, E. Gagetti, and F. Slavazzi (2009), 109-14.
Dusi, N. (2015) 'Intersemiotic Translations: Theories, Problems, Analysis', in C. Bianchi and C. Vassallo (2015), 181-205.
Dyer, R. (2009) 'The Wind in Fellini', *https://vimeo.com/8425475*.
Dyer, R. (2020) *La Dolce Vita* (London).
Fellini, F. (1967) *La mia Rimini* (Bologna).
Fellini, F. (1980/2015) *Making a Film* (New York: Torino 1980).
Flaiano, E. (1982) 'Una storia d'Italia in sogno', *Il Corriere della Sera*, 20.11: 13.
Gagetti, E. (2009) '*Satyricon* di Petronio e *Fellini-Satyricon*. Una comparazione', in R. De Berti, E. Gagetti, and F. Slavazzi (2009), 303-18.
Gargiulo, M. (2016) 'Il circo delle lingue', in Idem (ed.) *Lingue e linguaggi del cinema in Italia* (Rimini), 119-35.
Gianneri, M. (2017) 'Lo scorrere delle cose. Appunti sul palesarsi del vento al cinema', *https://ariarivista.org*.
Gianotti, G.F. (2012) 'Petronio e gli altri nel *Satyricon* di Federico Fellini', *Lexis*, 30: 565-83.

Grazzini, G. (1977) 'Satyricon (o Fellini-Satyricon)', in Idem, *Gli anni Sessanta in cento film* (Roma/Bari), 296-301.

Grazzini, G. (ed.) (1988) *Federico Fellini: Comments on Film* (Fresno, CA).

Greene, S. (2020) 'Racial Difference and the Postcolonial Imaginary in the Films of Federico Fellini', in F. Burke, M. Waller, and M. Gubareva (2020), 331-46.

Grisolia, R. (2006) 'L'"esprit de vin". Mythologie, transformation et aberration de l'image corporelle dans *Fellini-Satyricon* et *La grande bouffe*', *Revue de Médiation et Information*, 23: 69-73.

Hodsdon, B. (2017) *The Elusive Auteur. The Question of Film Authorship throughout the Age of Cinema* (Jefferson).

Hough-Dugdale, A. (2020) 'The Liquid Hyperfilm: Fellini, Deleuze, and the Sea as Forza Generatrice', in F. Burke, M. Waller, and M. Gubareva (2020), 237-49.

Huxley, A. (1954) *The Doors of Perception* (London).

Kezich, T. (2002) *Federico. Fellini, la vita e i film* (Milano).

Liehm, M. (1984) *Passion and Defiance: Film in Italy from 1942 to the Present* (Berkeley).

Longoni, A. and Rüesch, D. (eds.) (1995) *Soltanto le parole. Lettere di e a Ennio Flaiano (1933-1972)* (Milano).

Lothe, J. (2000) *see above, sect. 1.*

Marcus, M. (2002) 'Fellini's *Ginger and Fred*: Postmodern Simulation Meets Hollywood Romance', in F. Burke and M. Waller (2002), 169-87.

McCay, W. (1905-1927) *Little Nemo in Slumberland,* in A. Braun (ed.) (2016) *The Complete Little Nemo*, I-II (Köln).

McNally, D. (2003) *Desolate Angel: Jack Kerouac, the Beat Generation and America* (New York).

Mollica, V. (ed.) (2006) *Federico Fellini - Disegni* (Vicenza).

Moravia, A. (1971) *Io e lui* (Milano).

Moravia, A. (1978) 'Dreaming up Petronius's, in P. Bondanella (1978), 161-68.

Morelli, G. (2001) 'Mackie? Messer? Nino Rota e la quarta persona singolare del soggetto lirico', in Idem, (ed.) *Storia del candore. Studi in memoria di Nino Rota nel ventesimo della scomparsa* (Firenze), 355-429.

Pacchioni, F. (2014) *Inspiring Fellini. Literary Collaborations behind the Scenes* (Toronto).

Pacchioni, F. (2020) 'Fellini and Esotericism: An Ambiguous Adherence', in F. Burke, M. Waller, and M. Gubareva (2020), 95-108.

Pace, N. (2009a) 'La doppia lente. Petronio attraverso Fellini, ovvero Fellini attraverso Petronio', in R. De Berti, E. Gagetti, and F. Slavazzi (2009), 17-41.

Pace, N. (2009b) 'Colloquio con Luca Canali su *Fellini-Satyricon*', in R. De Berti, E. Gagetti, and F. Slavazzi (2009), 43-58.

Paul, J. (2009) '*Fellini-Satyricon*. Petronius and Film', in J. Prag and I. Repath (2009), 198-217.

Perruccio, A. (1991) 'Frammenti inediti di un carteggio fra Ennio Flaiano e Federico Fellini', *Nuova Antologia*, 2177: 378-93.

Pesando, F. (2010) 'Suggestioni per un archeologo: in margine a *Fellini-Satyricon. L'immaginario dell'antico*', *Lanx*, 5: 194-207.

Petrucci, A. (1985) *Potere, spazi urbani, scritture esposte* (Roma).

Podgorski, D. (2016) 'The Flawless, Eery use of the Protagonist Narrator in Billy Wilder's Sunset Boulevard', *The Gemsbok*, May 12.

Pravadelli, V. (2017) 'Italian 1960s Auteur Cinema (and beyond): Classic, Modern, Postmodern', in F. Burke (ed.), *The Blackwell Companion to Italian Cinema*, Hoboken (NJ) (2017), 228-48.

Preziosi, D. (ed.) (2009) *The Art of Art History. A critical Anthology* (Oxford).

Rigoletto, S. (2014) *Masculinity and Italian Cinema. Sexual Politics, Social Conflict and Male Crisis in the 1970s* (Edinburgh).

Ruozzi, G. (2016) *Ennio Flaiano, una verità personale* (Roma).

Sala, E. (2009) '*Qualcosa di arcaico e di modernissimo al tempo stesso.* Primi appunti sulle musiche di Nino Rota per il *Fellini-Satyricon*', in R. De Berti, E. Gagetti, and F. Slavazzi (2009), 93-107.

Sala, E. (2018) 'An Ethno-electronic Soundscape: Nino Rota's Music for *Fellini's Satyricon* (1969)', *Music and the Moving Image*, 11: 3-21.

Secchiaroli, T. (2001) *Satyricon Redivivum: Centum Imaginum Catalogus, Totus Lingua Latina* (Paris).

Segal, E. (1971) 'Arbitrary *Satyricon*: Petronius & Fellini', *Diacritics*, 1: 54-7.

Sharrett, C. (2002) '*Toby Dammit*, 'Intertext', and the End of Humanism', in F. Burke and M. Waller (2002), 121-36.

Sisto, A. (2020) 'Sounding Out Fellini: An Aural Continuum of Voices, Musics, Noises', in F. Burke, M. Waller, and M. Gubareva (2020), 251-65.

Slavazzi, F. (2009) 'L'immagine dell'antico nel *Fellini-Satyricon*', in R. De Berti, E. Gagetti, and F. Slavazzi (2009), 59-92.

Snyder, S. (1978) 'Color, Growth, and Evolution in *Fellini Satyricon*', in P. Bondanella (1978), 168-87.

Stubbs, J.C. (2006) *Federico Fellini as Auteur. Seven Aspects of his Films* (Carbondale).

Suderburg, E. (2020) 'In Bed with Fellini: Jung, Ernst Bernhard, Night Work, and *Il libro dei sogni*', in F. Burke, M. Waller, and M. Gubareva (2020), 79-92.

Sullivan, J.P. (1991/2001) *see above, sect. 1.*

Surliuga, V. (2020) 'Masina and Mastroianni: Reconfiguring C.G. Jung's *Animus* and *Anima*', in F. Burke, M. Waller, and M. Gubareva (2020), 191-204.

Sütterlin, A. (1996): *see above, sect. 1.*

Taddei, N. (2000) *Tuttofellini. Materiali di studio (Metodologia Taddei)* (Roma).

Toffetti, S. (ed.) (2020) *Federico Fellini. Il libro dei sogni* (Milano).

Vanelli, M. (2020a) '*Io non me ne intendo*: Fellini e il linguaggio cinematografico', *Cabiria*, 194-195, 5-80.

Vanelli, M. (2020b) '*Io non me ne intendo*: Fellini's Relationship to Film Language', in F. Burke, M. Waller, and M. Gubareva (2020), 207-21.

Van Watson, W. (2002) 'Fellini and Lacan: The Hollow Phallus, the Male Womb, and the Retying of the Umbilical', in F. Burke and M. Waller (2002), 65-91.

Villa, C. (2020) 'Fellini-Satyricon', in F. Burke, M. Waller, and M. Gubareva (2020), 483-85.

Waller, M. (2002) 'Whose *Dolce vita* Is This, Anyway? The Language of Fellini's Cinema', in F. Burke and M. Waller (2002), 108-20.

Waller, M. (2020) '*Il Maestro* Dismantles the Master's House: Fellini's Undoing of Gender and Sexuality', in F. Burke, M. Waller, and M. Gubareva (2020), 311-28.

Watson, S. (1998) *The Birth of the Beat Generation: Visionaries, Rebels, and Hipsters:1944-1960* (New York).
White, C.B. (2015) 'Introduction. Federico Fellini: Cartoonist, Screenwriter, Director', in F. Fellini (1980/2015), ii-xiv.
Winkler, M.M. (1997) *see above, sect. 1.*
Winkler, M.M. (2001) *see above, sect. 1.*
Zanchetti, G. (2009) '... *Vitrea fracta et somniorum interpretamenta*? Fellini-Satyricon e l'arte contemporanea, tra originario, fantascienza e beat', in R. De Berti, E. Gagetti, and F. Slavazzi (2009), 133-61.
Zanelli, D. (ed.) (1969) *'Fellini-Satyricon' di Federico Fellini* (Bologna).

FELLINI'S FILMOGRAPHY[1]

1950 *Luci del varietà* (*Variety Lights*)
1952 *Lo sceicco bianco* (*The White Sheik*)
1953 *I vitelloni*
1953 *Un'agenzia matrimoniale* (*Marriage Agency*), episode in *Amore in città* (*Love in the City*)
1954 *La strada*
1955 *Il bidone* (*The Swindle*)
1956 *Le notti di Cabiria* (*Nights of Cabiria*)
1960 *La dolce vita*
1962 *Le tentazioni del dottor Antonio* (*The Temptation of Dr Antonio*), episode in *Boccaccio '70*
1963 *Otto e mezzo* (*8 ½*)
1965 *Giulietta degli spiriti* (*Juliet of the Spirits*)
[1966 Planning of *Il viaggio di G. Mastorna* (*The Voyage of G. Mastorna*), a never implemented project: original typescript at 'Diogenes Verlag AG', Zürich]
1968 *Toby Dammit*, episode in *Histoires extraordinaires*, also called *Tre passi nel delirio*, and *Spirits of the Dead* (from Edgar Allan Poe's *'Never Bet The Devil Your Head'*)
1969 *Block-Notes di un regista* (*Fellini: A Director's Notebook*)
1969 *Fellini-Satyricon*

[1] See Bondanella, 1992, 335-44; Burke-Waller, 2002, 233-6 (both of which include Fellini's major screenplay contributions as co-scriptwriter).

1970	*I Clowns* (*The Clowns*)
1972	*Roma*
1973	*Amarcord*
1976	*Il Casanova di Federico Fellini* (*Fellini's Casanova*)
1979	*Prova d'orchestra* (*Orchestra Rehearsal*)
1980	*La città delle donne (City of Women)*
1983	*E la nave va* (*And the Ship Sails On*)
1985	*Ginger e Fred* (*Ginger and Fred*)
1987	*Intervista* (*Interview*)
1990	*La voce della luna* (*The Voice of the Moon*)

FELLINI-SATYRICON (1969): PRINCIPAL CREDITS[2]

Free Adaptation from Petronius Arbiter's *Satyrica*

Director	Federico Fellini
Story and screenplay	Federico Fellini, Bernardino Zapponi
Script supervisor	Norma Giacchero
Director of Photography	Giuseppe Rotunno
Editor	Ruggero Mastroianni
Supervising Editor	Enzo Ocone
Set Design and Costumes	Danilo Donati
Set Design Sketches	Federico Fellini
Architect Set Designer	Luigi Scaccianoce
Assistant Architect s.d.	Dante Ferretti
Pictorial Supervisor	Italo Tomassi
Visual Advisor	Antonio Scordia
Music	Nino Rota, Tod Dockstader, Ihan Mimaroğlu, Henri Pousseur, Andrew Rudin - original score supplied by: Unesco, Ocora, Cellograf, Philips, Ly-

[2] Cf. IMDb: *Fellini-Satyricon* (1969) - 'Full Cast & Crew'. See Zanelli, 1969, 301-3; Betti, 1970, 56-60; Taddei, 2000, 298-302; Bondanella, 2002, 191; De Berti-Gagetti-Slavazzi, 2009, 541-2.

	ricord, Nonesuch, Argo, Le Chant du Monde, Bam
Production Companies	PEA = Produzioni Europee Associate
Producer	Alberto Grimaldi
Production Manager	Roberto Cocco
First Assistant Director	Maurizio Mein
Second Assistant Directors	Liliana Betti, Lia Consalvo
Camera Operator	Giuseppe Maccari
Latin Language Consultant	Luca Canali
Creative Consultant	Ettore Paratore
Cast	Martin Potter (*Encolpio*), Hiram Keller (*Ascilto*), Max Born (*Gitone*), Salvo Randone (*Eumolpo*), Mario Romagnoli (*Trimalcione*), Magali Noël (*Fortunata*), Fanfulla (*Vernacchio*), Gordon Mitchell (*il predone*), Alain Cuny (*Lica*), Capucine (*Trifena*), Tanya Lopert (*il giovane Cesare*), Joseph Wheeler (*il suicida*), Lucia Bosé (*la matrona*), Donyale Luna (*Enotea*), Hylette Adolphe (*la schiavetta*), Pasquale Baldassarre (*Ermafrodito*), Luigi Montefiori (*Minotauro*), Gennaro Sabatino (*il traghettatore*), Marcello Bifolco (*il proconsole*), Tanya Lopert (*l'imperatore*), Danika La Loggia (*Scintilla*), Giuseppe San Vitale (*Abinna*), Eugenio Mastropietro (*Ermerote*), Elisa Mainardi (*Arianna*), Antonia Pietrosi (*la matrona di Efeso*), Carlo Giordana (*il capitano della nave*), *others*
Voice Dubbing	Antonio Casagrande, Carlo Croccolo, Giacomo Furia, Corrado Gaipa, Aldo Giuffrè, Gianni Giuliano, Oreste Lionello, Benita Martini, Rita Savagnone, Vinicio Sofia, Renato Turi

Filming Locations	(Lazio, Italy) Cinecittà Studios, Fiumicino, Fregene, Latina, Ponza Island, Rome, Tyrrhenian Sea
Filming Dates	9 November 1968 - 23 May 1969
Release Details	Italy 3 Sept. 1969 (4 Sept. 1969 Venice Film Festival); France 19 Dec. 1969; USA 11 March 1970; UK 10 Sept. 1970; Spain 21 Oct. 1976; Japan 2 April 1994

Technical Specifications[3]

Runtime	129 min
Sound Mix	mono
Color	Color DeLuxe
Aspect Ratio	2.35 : 1
Laboratory	Technicolor
Film Length	3.710 m
Negative Format	35 mm
Cinematographic Process	Panavision (anamorphic)
Printed Film Format	35 mm

[3] Cf. IMDb: *Fellini-Satyricon* (1969) - 'Technical Specifications'.

INDEX OF PETRONIAN PASSAGES

Petronius Arbiter - Petronian Narrative

Satyrica

INDEX OF MODERN AUTHORS

Numbers in ***bold italics*** refer to extended or more substantial discussions.

INDEX OF FILMS, FILM-DIRECTORS AND OTHERS

About the Author

Andrea Perruccio began as a Lecturer in Italian Language in Finland (Jyväskylä University) and spent the rest of his career as a high school teacher in Prato and Florence. Residing in Florence, he presently works as an independent scholar on Greek and Latin literature, and on the history of cinema. In his many publications, he skillfully combines the Classics with twentieth-century Italian cinema, specifically on Pasolini and Fellini. His latest publications include: "La ricezione del poeta satirico Lucilio nell'Africa romana" (*Rheinisches Museum*, forthcoming); and "Pasolini traduttore dell'Agamennone di Eschilo" (*Cabiria. Studi di Cinema*).

www.ingramcontent.com/pod-product-compliance
Lightning Source LLC
LaVergne TN
LVHW091144080826
845145LV00008B/2255

* 9 7 8 1 5 9 9 5 4 2 0 9 6 *